A LIFE IN THE BALANCE

The Billy Wayne Sinclair Story

A Journey from Murder to Redemption
Inside America's Worst Prison System

BILLY WAYNE SINCLAIR
and
JODIE SINCLAIR

with an introduction by
Richard Hand

Arcade Publishing • New York

364.15

FIRST EDITION

Library of Congress Cataloging-in-Publication Data
Sinclair, Billy Wayne, 1945–
   A life in the balance : the Billy Wayne Sinclair story / Billy Wayne Sinclair and Jodie Sinclair.
      p. cm.
   ISBN 1-55970-555-8
      1. Sinclair, Billy Wayne, 1945– 2. Prisoners—Louisiana—Biography.
3. Prison reformers—Louisiana—Biography. 4. Prisons—Louisiana.
I. Sinclair, Jodie, 1938– II. Title.

HV9468.S57 A3 2000
364.15'23'09763—dc   00–60589

Published in the United States by Arcade Publishing, Inc., New York
Distributed by Time Warner Trade Publishing

Visit our Web site at www.arcadepub.com

10 9 8 7 6 5 4 3 2 1

Designed by API

EB

PRINTED IN THE UNITED STATES OF AMERICA

This book is dedicated to Richard Clark Hand who, as a friend, was there every time he was needed and who, as an attorney, represents the very best that the legal profession has to offer.

This book is written with deep appreciation to Ross Maggio, Jr., who represents the very best the corrections industry has to offer.

Preface

This book fulfills a journalist's obligation to put the story on the record.

It was written under difficult circumstances. They include facing moral and ethical dilemmas that could have destroyed our integrity. We reveal these challenges in the text along with opinions we have developed over the years that might influence the story.

My personal involvement in the story is openly and frankly reported. My coauthor recounts his crimes and failings in detail. (They make a valuable guide for anyone studying the causes of crime.) But we maintained our allegiance to the record throughout, ignoring my desire for privacy and fears of ostracism and his feelings of shame.

I am a firm believer that stories pick reporters. This one certainly picked me. I went to the Louisiana State Penitentiary at Angola in 1981 to begin shooting a television series on the death penalty. What I found changed my life. Ultimately, I became part of the story.

Some would say this involvement made me less a journalist and more a protagonist. Is my reporting flawed as a result? If I had returned from Mars after marrying a Martian, would my account of the experience be less valid?

Journalists are not entirely unbiased. Their reporting is shaped by their backgrounds and points of view; the truth comes from the synthesis of their voices as each strives for objectivity in his or her reporting. With this book, my husband and I have added our voices to that mix. We write from both knowledge of the facts and experience.

I am a reporter by nature as well as by training. Curiosity and a sense of outrage are two of the inborn traits that propelled me toward a career in journalism. Certainly, I have been outraged by what I found in Louisiana's prison system.

My coauthor is also a journalist. He came to reporting by accident. But his credits include some of journalism's top honors — the George Polk Award, the Sidney Hillman Award, the American Bar Association's Silver Gavel and Certificate of Merit, and a Robert F. Kennedy Journalism Award. This book is the story of his life. It is a compelling account of thirty-five years behind bars after a murder conviction.

Sometimes, as I sit holding his hand in the cell block on visiting days, I find myself thinking about the question that people always ask when they learn about us. How could I marry a man convicted of murder?

The answer goes beyond journalism. It is found in scripture and liturgy and the aphorisms I learned as a child in Catholic schools. But it serves journalism well because it permits me to see beyond stereotypes. It is a simple creed.

I believe in redemption.

My husband is not the man who pulled the trigger in 1965. That Billy Sinclair was shucked off, molted like an old, dirty skin, long before I met the Billy Sinclair I married. But he understands, just as I do, that he is responsible for the crime that put him behind bars.

I believe in forgiveness.

Murder carries a high price. But equity begs for an impartial standard, fairly applied. One person should not be held to a stricter rule than others. Freedom should not be forfeit to politics. In that, I ask no more of the State of Louisiana than others have who have received its mercy.

And I believe in love.

Eighteen years ago, I pledged my life to Billy Sinclair. I have never been tempted to leave him. Love and loyalty are opposite sides of the same coin.

Our marriage has brought me suffering. And I expect more. The criminal justice system in Louisiana is seriously flawed. It is a throwback to the Dark Ages, the Spanish Inquisition, or the witch trials of the seventeenth century.

One day, history will lay bare the distortions of fact and public hysteria that gave rise to a merciless view of people like me and Billy Sinclair. Until then, it is a journalist's job to question a society obsessed beyond all Christian measure with revenge.

Jodie Sinclair
August 6, 2000
Houston, Texas

Acknowledgments

Those whose words and deeds contributed to this book: Richard Hand, Peggi Gresham, Eddie Boeker, Wilbert Rideau, Raphael Goyeneche, Jack Martzell, Ralph Stassi, Veronica Porteous Scheinuk, Keith Nordyke, Trudy Oppenheim, Carol and Mike Costello, Joe Whitmore, P. Raymond Lamonica, Charles Grey, Fred Kennedy, Riis Suire, Mary Sinderson, State Senator Tom Casey, Governor Charles "Buddy" Roemer, Yvonne Foreman Campbell, Gus Kinchen, Allen Abbott, Bill Archer, Evan Moore, and Ross Maggio, Jr.

Those whose love and support has sustained us through the years: Carol and Allen Abbott and family, Melanie Decker, Sam Decker, Katherine Archer, Mike and Ginnie Bell, Julie and Tom Margules, Hugh Bell, Noelie Romero Holtz, Mary and Tom Preston, Ann Schneider, Sylvia Perez, Scott Daniels, Kori Hoesel, Ellen Durckel Vestewig, Chris McDaniel, Sherry McDonnell, Scott James, Ida and Edward R. Baird, Toni Kinchen, Curtis and Gladys Earnest, Joyce Corrington, Richard Hand's wife, Jean, who patiently edited early chapters of this book twenty years ago, and Richard's law partner, Werner Zumbrunn, of Zumbrunn and Hand in Babylon, N.Y., who, without knowing us, selflessly agreed to the pro bono hours Richard devoted to this case.

Those whose dedication and vision made this book possible: our agent, William J. Birnes, of Shadow Lawn Press; our editor, Jeannette Seaver; and our publishers, Richard and Jeannette Seaver of Arcade Publishing, Inc.

Introduction

I REMEMBER READING parts of this book twenty years ago and encouraging Billy to stick with the writing, all the while wondering how anyone could survive for long in the Angola he describes. At least a record of that time and place — the way it really was — would endure, I recall thinking. Perhaps his would not be just another life lived on society's outer fringes, encountering people and places that gave me nightmares and chilled me to the bone. Most of all, I remember thinking that he would probably end up in Angola's graveyard for paupers, nameless and forgotten.

It is the year 2000 now and, much to my surprise, Billy Sinclair is still alive. Chapters have been added to the manuscript as he has lived out his life in confinement. These have shifted in tone and direction, moving from the daily walk with death in the Angola of the 1970s and the 1980s to themes of prison journalism, pardons-for-pay schemes, other forms of official corruption in places high and low, and the resulting court battles brought to stem that corruption's ugly, constant tide. They include the story of an unlikely marriage that somehow has survived eighteen years of hard and unforgiving challenges.

I suppose I am the person most qualified to introduce this book by dint of having witnessed so much of Billy Sinclair's journey. My goal here is to relate, from an ordinary man's perspective, what I recall of Angola so others will understand why, springing in mystery and miracle from deep inside the walls of a southern prison, this book somehow manages to strike like thunder at so many important aspects of our shared human experience in the free world.

I worked as a lawyer in Baton Rouge for a scant eighteen months, from September 1970 to March 1972. It was a short stay, but an awful lot happened in that brief, distant time span. Its events remain with me in unnaturally sharp focus. Chief among those was my appointment by a federal judge to represent Sinclair and other prisoners confined on Angola's death row in a lawsuit challenging the conditions of their confinement. Surprisingly, my relationship with Sinclair has managed to outlive that case by some thirty-odd years. The same age, we have grown old together, I in the free world, he behind bars.

I had come to Baton Rouge from New Orleans, where I had been working as a VISTA attorney at the Desire public housing project. Our central office in New Orleans had taken on a case that challenged Angola's longstanding use of the "inmate guard" system in which some of its most dangerous prisoners were armed with shotguns and instructed to "guard" their fellow prisoners. The system saved the state money. But too often the inmate guards, in their zeal to fulfill their responsibilities, mistook the word "guard" for the word "shoot." These unfortunate misinterpretations were likely to occur during the autumn's sugarcane-cutting season, when a line of prisoners, stretched out over distances of three miles or more, hacked away at the stalks of cane under the shotguns of their fellow prisoners. A lone free man rode the line on horseback armed only with a holstered pistol. He was but a distant dot when viewed from most points on the line. Accidents happened.

We were aware that the inmate guard system was under attack in Mississippi. Preliminary court rulings there hinted at its unconstitutionality. When the chance came to go to Baton Rouge on a legal fellowship and take the inmate guard case with me, I jumped at it. Soon the federal court in Mississippi ruled against that state's inmate guard system. Then the Louisiana defendants settled our case, eventually passing legislation that earmarked funds to hire sufficient free world guards. The inmate guard system, barbarous and insane, was all about cash. It was abandoned not because it was barbarous and insane, but because the state had no choice.

So it was and so it is that, when reduced to its essentials, the criminal justice system in this country, racially and socially skewed in its application, sings to a familiar, underlying melody: politics and cash, cash and politics. It is the constant current that flows through the particulars of this book. And Billy Sinclair's life experiences show us that the criminal justice system in Louisiana routinely wrongs even guilty men and women at both the trial and punishment stages. The uneven playing field inherent in an inept, underfunded trial defense and a style of captivity that is destructive to the basic decency and humanity of captive and captor alike are shown to be part and parcel of that system.

Sinclair's trial and conviction illustrate just how uneven that playing field can be. He killed a man, but it wasn't a capital case. Intent to kill was lacking and the armed robbery attempt was over when the shooting occurred. The state's prosecutor, rapacious and bent upon a capital conviction, failed to turn over to the defense eyewitness statements that established both elements. Worse, on the eve of trial, Sinclair's principal attorney left Baton Rouge to attend a family funeral, leaving behind a seventy-year-old substitute to conduct the trial. Old Mr. English, forced to try the case despite his protestations that he was unprepared, did his best; but he was no match for the wrath of this prosecutor. Sinclair, without resources and having killed a favored southern son, had his fate sealed before he ever set foot in a courtroom.

But even had the case come out as it should have, at most a murder II conviction, Sinclair would still have landed in Angola, but not have been confined on death row. I remember so well the death row he describes. The oppressive heat, the smell and dirt of it; the yelling commotion and violent, spit-out curses and street epithets that rattled back and forth off bare concrete walls like unsheathed sabers. The blaring radios. But mostly I can picture the caged, condemned men, stalking their space, forever stalking and fidgeting. Waiting for the sparks to fly.

Life in prison is compressed, oddly energized, so that even the most innocuous act, the smallest thing, can explode into consequences that are totally out of proportion and wholly unforeseeable. And one can't just do the time and stand apart from the madness, refuse to encounter the routine unpredictability. You don't survive very long that way. I remember a client from a prison in Virginia. John M. was a black man, big in stature, but he was in for a white-collar crime and in no way street connected. He was on his own in prison and tried to describe for me what daily life was like:

> Hey, I got only eighteen months to do; I just want to do my time, man, and get out of here alive. Do my own time; mind my own business. You see the yard, middle of summer, dudes with long fatigue coats on in all of that heat. They ain't hiding packets of sugar, man. There's some heavy-duty shit out on that yard. Every day I got to get up from my bunk, go to mess, go to work, maybe spend some time in the dayroom, go on back to my bunk, and I got to stare straight ahead. Can't chance to look left or right, can't stop to bullshit. 'Cause if I happen to see something go down, or if a dude even thinks I saw something go down, then I'm in it, man, like it or not, I'm in it. And some kind of nasty shit is always going down in here, brother, believe that.

I believe it. John M. never made it out of prison alive, and that same summer two other clients, young black men caught up in the drug trade so prevalent at the prison, also had their sentences reduced. Permanently.

The wonder of the Sinclairs' book is how a tale with its roots in tragedy — the death of an innocent young man in an act of murder — can have redeeming value. But it is the story of a resolute journey toward change. After recounting his crime, seemingly fated, as such events often are, by a childhood of hard abuse, Sinclair pulls us through a dark tunnel into the collectively depraved psyche of Angola's death row in the late 1960s and early 1970s. Then, from worse to worse yet, the book takes us into the prison's "Big Yard," the hub of Angola, a place where death comes lightning quick, unforeseen and brutal. Such violence spun unchecked in the midst of a "profit center" with drug "wars" and bitter racial divides that were encouraged by prison officials as a means of lining their own pockets and controlling the prison population.

The story begins to chronicle changes in Sinclair, at first those that were the result of an awakening intellect: his gained expertise as a jailhouse lawyer, a status of important currency in the prison world; his writing partnership with a black inmate on *The Angolite* where the two spun out a brand of prison journalism that, in topic and content, pricked at its prison sponsors and astounded free world critics; and his adept ability, a key to his prison survival, to move with credibility among and about the various prison cliques and power brokers, a talent that would place him in the middle of the integration of the prison.

It becomes clear, though, that other changes were afoot in Sinclair, changes having more to do with heart than head. For seven years his own death stalked him, grinning over his shoulder in his death row cage, eagerly waiting to watch while they toasted him up brown and served him with his own boiled blood to quench the public thirst. But we find it was actual death that was more transforming: his brother's in Vietnam; old Emmitt's, by prison neglect and plain uncaring; Bobby's, stuck through the heart in a dispute over a stick of butter; White's, an angry, spiteful suicide by Sinclair's best friend; and Breaux's, murdered good and dead while trying to play the hero.

And because much of that death took place in the context of institutional systems forced to deal with it, and because of the unhappy, grossly uneven manner of that dealing, I believe anger, time hardened into resolve, also changed him. For throughout much of this story, the Sinclairs focus a harsh light on the not-so-hidden failings of our criminal justice system. They simply confirm, through a southern prism, what we already know: that our system of establishing guilt and handing out punishment is riddled, from start to finish, with ineptitude, neglect, corruption, and unequal access to resources. We read about it daily from the O. J. Simpson trial to the flawed Illinois convictions and that state's moratorium on executions which has revived the national debate over the death penalty.

I remember reading a book in the early 1970s, *Struggle for Justice*, in which the criminal justice system is likened to a funnel. At the top are bunched all of those who have committed crimes. At the bottom are those who actually end up in prison, a kind of college of crime. Those who commit crimes, but aren't caught, shake out. Those who are caught but aren't prosecuted, for whatever reason, don't graduate. Those who are prosecuted but work a plea often avoid it. Only a chosen few actually complete the journey. But — and here's the hitch — many of those graduates share common characteristics which markedly enhance their chances of joining what seems at first like a random pool of candidates. They are the poor, the uneducated, the offspring of abusive parents, or the products of broken families. A great number are minorities.

This aspect, let's call it the "social selectivity" of crime and punishment in America (sounds Darwinian, doesn't it; as though certain people are fated to be locked away), represents only a piece of the larger puzzle. Another essential piece is the caprice of the local and national body politic. It is a world fueled by quick reaction to shifting consensus, where many politicians are driven not by principle or personal conviction but by the compulsion to take hard stands on issues that will get them into office and keep them there. So when times are good economically and federal and state coffers are flush, politicians beat the crime drum to an audience squirmy with fear.

The result? Plea bargains decrease. Releases on probation or parole drop. Harsh punitive sentencing laws are enacted and prison construction goes up. The mouth of the funnel widens and the business of criminal justice flourishes for reasons not even remotely connected to solutions for the root causes of crime. As the Sinclairs demonstrate in this book, Louisiana's political system not only follows that pattern, it is a star in the firmament of political opportunism, ingrained corruptibility, and the quick fix; of government gone awry.

In 1972, I took a position in the District of Columbia and left the prisons of Louisiana behind. In a sense, Sinclair did too. He gradually had been pulling away from the criminal culture that surrounded him. But that process was completed when he met and later married the coauthor of this book, Jodie Sinclair. Improbably, Sinclair met a woman who fell deeply in love with him and, despite all that had gone on in his life, he discovered it was a love he was able to return in kind. Even from the distance of a cage.

For years, my wife and I have been involved in marriage preparation through our local church. One of the things we always emphasize is that married love involves a decision to love; that a commitment based upon feelings that come and go is no commitment at all but is simply convenience. The Sinclairs' marriage of eighteen years has been nothing if not inconvenient. Physical separation; retributive transfers; six hundred miles of weekend driving, year after year, to gain the chance at restricted, observed visitation; hopes raised, hopes dashed — if there are marriages made in heaven, this one has been lived out in hell. And maybe that's what they should have expected, but against such expectation their love has endured.

I have a picture in my office of Sinclair and me, taken on a summer day in 1971. It's here in this book, the only picture of the two of us that I know of. I had some medical experts flown in from New Orleans to examine the death row prisoners. We had landed a donated Cherokee Piper Cub in a field right next to the cell block, the crude landing strip marked out by an orange windsock tacked atop a wooden post. Funny the things you remember. We were taking pictures of the Row for evidence of the conditions there and someone must have snapped this one. I have saved it all these years, I'm not sure why.

I'm looking at the picture as I write this. I am struck by how young I look. And I am struck by something else. You cannot see Sinclair. He is not visible in the picture, blocked from view by the steel bars of his death row cage. 1971. It was the year of the Attica riot. In its aftermath, so much was written about the "hidden" prisons of America and the need to bring the way in which we punish people out into the open. To examine, with a bit more discernment, our motive, manner, and means of punishment. National study commissions were empaneled, reports and books were written, and various recommendations for "reform" poured forth.

As I look at myself peering into the bars of the death row cell thirty years ago, I can still picture from that time the face of prisons in America. I can see it in my mind in the form of a ghostly montage of all of the clients in all of the various prisons, some of whom really belonged there, and some who really didn't. Sinclair was one who really belonged there; and, I believe, he is also one of those who really no longer belongs there.

But this book is about so much more than that. It transcends one man's journey and gives us a rare glimpse of what it's like to be locked up in an American prison. It's a journey worth taking. And who knows? Maybe the face staring back at me in the picture will change somewhat as a result of this book, will recapture some of its lost youth and promise, left so long ago, somewhere way down South in a delta prison.

Richard Hand

A LIFE IN THE BALANCE

1

It was December 5, 1965.

Only five months earlier I had been released from a federal prison in Terre Haute, Indiana, where I had served a stint for stealing a car and taking it across a state line.

Now I was sitting in a stolen car, casing a Pak-A-Sak convenience grocery in Baton Rouge, Louisiana. A steady drizzle of cold rain occasionally lashed about by the wind could be seen falling under a nearby street light. I shuddered, taking another swig from the bottle of Jack Daniel's sitting between my legs. I needed courage, something to pump up the balls. I was about to pull my first armed robbery.

I reached over and removed the .22 caliber pistol from the glove compartment. It had a short chrome barrel and a white plastic handle. Despite its small size, the gun scared me. It represented raw, uncompromising power — a finger squeeze and it could snuff out a life. I opened the cylinder and counted five bullets. Shutting it, I left the firing chamber empty as a precaution.

I was a punk who wanted to take the money and run. I had no intention of hurting anyone. I figured the gun would scare the store clerk the way it scared me. I shivered, telling myself it was the wind, and lit a cigarette, only to see my hands shake. A life of crime was not what it had been cracked up to be in the joint. I slammed my palm against the steering wheel, muttering, "Fuck it."

A survival instinct warned me to drive away. It was like an ominous, foreboding voice telling me to go. I chalked it up to fear of taking the store down alone. With each small biting swig of whiskey, it became essential for me to walk through the door and pull the pistol. Destiny beckoned. I could not resist the force telling me to enter the store.

Two months earlier an ex-convict friend named John Alexander had come to New Orleans where I was working as a stock clerk in an office supply company. He told me he had escaped from a Texas jail and needed my help. It was natural that I help him. While in prison I had embraced a criminal values system, known as the "convict code," according to which an ex-con should always lend a helping hand to a con "on the run."

Alexander also dangled the lure of a "big score" at a small bank in his hometown in East Texas. It would bring sixty to one hundred thousand dollars, he said. The prospect of that much money — and the fast cars, nice clothes, and easy women it would buy — made me walk away from a steady job to chase the fool's gold of a petty thief. I had been brainwashed in prison with embellished stories about "scores and whores," and I wanted a piece of the action.

But there had been no escape. And there was no big score. Alexander was lying. We ended up on a petty crime spree: stealing two cars in Beaumont and Birmingham; and robbing three convenience stores in Biloxi, Shreveport, and Baton Rouge, and a hotel in Miami. I was the lookout. We only had one gun — a .380 automatic — and Alexander always carried it.

I didn't get a gun until November when Alexander bought me the .22 caliber pistol in a Dallas pawnshop. He had suggested a larger caliber weapon.

"You want something that will knock his dick in the dirt."

But I opted for a smaller weapon.

"No, I just want something that will make him give up the money."

Our criminal partnership didn't last long. We split up in Dallas in early December following an argument and near fight when he threw down on me. I headed back to Louisiana with a few hundred bucks in my pocket, driving a stolen car. I wanted one more score to get enough money to catch a merchant ship out of Mobile to South America in hopes the heat would blow over.

I turned the key, giving life to the little green Chevy II. I wheeled it into the parking lot of the store. I got out of the car, glancing toward a young store clerk sweeping the pavement.

With a tentative gait, I walked into the store and looked around. The clerk behind the counter, a large man named J. C. Bodden, was waiting on an elderly lady. I turned to my right, walking down an aisle. I picked up a can of shoe polish and a box of cereal, leaving my fingerprints on both items. I waited until the lady left before approaching the counter.

Bodden had sensed trouble the moment I walked through the door. He watched every move I made, priming himself for a confrontation. He slammed the cash register shut just as I walked up to the counter. He was committed to resisting the robbery.

"Put all the money in a sack," I said, pulling the small pistol from my waistband.

Bodden was not afraid.

"I don't have a key to the register — Ray has it," he said, pointing to the clerk sweeping outside. Bodden stepped away from the register, placing himself in a position visible to the outside. I tried to take control of the situation.

"Open the register," I demanded. "You just had it open for that lady."

Bodden backed toward the end of the counter as he whistled to the clerk outside.

"Ray has the keys."

An elderly couple named Katherine and Grundy Sampite drove up and parked directly in front of the store. Mr. Sampite got out of the car and entered the store. He picked up a newspaper from a rack near the door and walked toward the counter.

3

"Stay put," I said, as he turned to walk parallel to the counter. "This is a holdup — back away from the window."

Sampite complied, but Bodden used the old man's entry to move outside the counter. He now stood at the end of it, sandwiching me between himself and Sampite.

"Get back behind the counter and open that register," I shouted.

"Get out of here," Bodden replied, taking a couple of steps toward me.

A second customer walked into the store. He froze when he realized a robbery was under way.

"Back down that aisle," I ordered.

"Stay where you are, everybody stay put," Bodden shouted over my instructions.

I pointed the gun at the floor and glanced back toward the door. Ray Neyland, the clerk outside, had stopped sweeping and was easing toward it.

"C'mon in here!" I yelled.

Moving toward me, Bodden gestured with his hands for everyone to stay put. I pulled the trigger. The "click" of the hammer hitting an empty chamber was unusually loud in the quiet store.

"He's shooting paper wads," Bodden yelled. "He's firing blanks."

That mistaken belief propelled Bodden forward. I gave ground, backing up toward Sampite.

"Stay back, man," I pleaded. "I don't want to hurt anyone."

But Bodden had made his choice. He moved toward me, as though he were ready to make a tackle. I pointed the pistol at his leg and fired, hoping to stop his advance. I just wanted to get away. The muted explosion stunned everyone. Bodden froze, wavering on the edge of eternity. He looked down at his thigh. A patch of red blood was forming on his green pants. He still didn't believe, or care, that I was firing real bullets. He looked up at me. Our eyes locked, forever. Then he charged, screaming something I didn't understand. I turned and ran from the store. He picked up a broom as he chased me, lifting it over his head. I fired a shot as I ran out of the store across the parking lot. The errant bullet struck Bodden under the left armpit, traveled across his chest cavity, and nicked his aorta. He sat down on the pavement and bled to death in a matter of minutes.

I jumped into the little Chevy and backed up with tires squealing. I saw Bodden sitting on the pavement before I sped away. I still didn't realize he had been mortally wounded.

"Call the police, call the police!" he was screaming, pointing in my direction.

I sped away from the store, taking back streets and side roads to make my getaway. I knew nothing about Baton Rouge so I drove on blind instinct.

"Bulletin, bulletin, bulletin," the voice on my car radio blared. "We just received a report that a store clerk was shot to death during an armed robbery on Greenwell Springs Road. The police have issued an all-points bulletin for Billy Wayne Sinclair in connection with the murder."

As I sat in the car behind a deserted barn, listening to the wail of sirens, I stared at the little pistol in my hand. I had just used it to kill a man. I dropped it on the seat. It looked so harmless lying there. I leaned forward, pressing my forehead hard against the steering wheel. The word "murder" seared an indelible imprint on my brain. I was no longer Billy Wayne Sinclair — I was a murderer. Sartre has written that "the act of murder changes the victim into a thing and, at the same time, the murderer into an object."

"God, please forgive me," I whispered.

I heard the squawk of a police radio before I realized a slow-moving car was coming down the gravel road. The sheriff's car stopped, shining a spotlight around the barn. Paralyzed with fear, I prayed the officer would not get out for a closer look. I knew he would kill me if he did. The seconds passed through a time warp. I was like a blindfolded man awaiting the impact of the firing squad's bullets. The police radio squawked again and the car sped away, its siren piercing the night.

I got out of the car and tried to suck as much of the night air as I could into my lungs. My legs trembled as a muscle spasm erupted in my back. I walked to a nearby puddle of rainwater. Kneeling, I soaked my handkerchief and wiped the fear-sweat from my face. I looked out across the night knowing that I would never be the same; that I had fallen through the center of the world into a doomed colony of outcasts.

For a moment I thought of suicide, but instead of putting the gun to my head and letting my body be found in the winter mud, I got back into the car and sped away. I didn't have the guts to pull the trigger.

2

MY CHILDHOOD WAS CRIME'S CRADLE. It fitted me for nothing else.

I came into the world hated and regretted. I paid a terrible price for the accident of my birth. There is not a single memory of hearing either one of my parents say, "I love you." The first human acceptance I found was in prison among the ranks of society's outcasts.

My father tried to drown me in a washtub when I was eighteen months old. We were living in the small northeast Louisiana town of Rayville. John managed to break my collarbone before my hysterical mother could pull him away. I was never told why he wanted to drown me. I know only that it was the first of many times he tried to kill me.

I was the second born of six children — five boys and one girl. The third boy, James, died shortly after birth. He was the lucky one. I survived to endure a life of incomprehensible physical abuse and unconscionable emotional neglect. John reserved a special hatred for me, taking particular pleasure in abusing me. Perhaps it was my mother's alleged infidelity or nothing more than a senseless destiny the Fates chose for me. Whatever the reason, I brought out the worst in his brutal personality — one that derived pleasure from imposing pain on others.

John almost always beat me following dinner after he read the daily newspaper. I ate slowly on those nights, fear penetrating my brain like a laser light. My snail's pace was the futile effort of a terrified child trying to hold back the hands of time. I prayed for divine intervention — prayers that went unheard.

"You know what I'm gonna do?" John taunted. "I'm gonna blister that little ass. I might even draw blood tonight. Feels good to bleed, don't it, boy?"

I nodded my head in agreement as he jerked and twisted my ear, too paralyzed with fear to even scream. I was more afraid of John than any horror a child's mind might conceive. I flinched instinctively at any sudden movement he made.

"Please, Daddy, don't whip me," I finally managed to plead. "I'll behave — I promise I won't do it again."

He laughed, freeing my ear as he picked up another section of the newspaper. I was the prisoner of his power to abuse. He made me sit at the foot of his recliner as part of the ritual of terror. My brothers watched television while I sat with my back to the set. I leaned against John's leg, seeking mercy or some feeling of love. He pushed me away roughly as he would a stray cur. All I ever wanted was John's love. All I ever got was a kick in the gut or a fist in the side of the head — as often for doing the right thing as for doing the wrong thing.

"Your mother tells me you were in that old tree house again today," he said. Not waiting for my reply, he casually reached down and grabbed me by the hair. He dragged me to the bathroom — his private torture chamber.

"You just won't learn, you little bastard," he said as he slung me through the bathroom door.

Hollering at my mother to turn up the volume on the television set, John made me take off my pants while he turned on the bathtub water full force. He grabbed both my arms at the wrists and began beating me on the back and buttocks with his belt. I

8

screamed as loud as I could. He began slapping me about the head and face. When that didn't stop my screaming, he threw his belt down in rage and began beating me with his fists. I tried to crawl away, to escape the bruising blows. He kicked me into a corner under the sink, stomping at my feet and legs with the heels of his shoes.

When it was over, John made me go to bed alone. He told my brothers not to talk to me. But Pat, the youngest, always defied his wrath. He would slip into the bedroom, quietly easing into the bed. Curled up next to me, he would say, "I love you, Billy." John never beat any of the other children the way he beat me. He would often roughhouse with Pat, punching him in the stomach with a balled fist that sent the bow-legged kid sprawling across the floor. Laughing, Pat would wade back in for more, always ready for a fight.

As for my sister, John worshiped her. He bought her the best clothes and dolls. Mary was a beautiful child with long, blonde hair — the joy of John's life. Loving her was probably the only decent thing he ever did in his life.

But John directed a methodical and calculated cruelty at me, oblivious to the pain and suffering he caused. When we lived in a small apartment in New Orleans in the early '50s, he couldn't beat me as hard as he had in rural Richland Parish because my screams could be heard through the thin wall. The neighbors complained several times, saying, "He's gonna kill that kid one day." He got around that minor obstacle by loading the family into a smoking '48 Ford and driving us to the city dump. There he beat me with discarded boards or tree limbs. No one could hear my screams in the foul-smelling night. On the way home John always stopped at a drive-in where he bought each of us an ice cream cone. He laughed, talking as though nothing had happened. As swelling developed around my bloody wounds, I choked off the tears of pain rolling down my cheeks. I gave Pat the bottom half of my ice cream cone because he loved it so much.

"Why is Daddy so mean?" the child whispered.

"He hates me," I answered, not knowing why.

That hatred was unleashed in all its blind fury one night when John flew into a sadistic rage after I told Mother that he was with another woman. She confronted him with the allegation and he denied it. He became an enraged grizzly, mauling and slinging me all over the living room. I scurried behind chairs and the sofa trying to escape his vicious kicks and flailing belt. I cried out to Mother for help. She stood by, clutching the Bible.

"You shouldn't lie, son," she murmured.

Frustrated, John yanked the television cord from the electrical outlet and ripped it out of the back of the Muntz television set. He turned the sofa over and dragged me, screaming and pleading, into the bathroom. He tore off my clothes and forced my head into the commode, slamming the seat on my shoulders. He placed his knee on top of the seat to keep my head in the commode. He lashed me with the telephone cord until the blood ran down my buttocks and legs, forming a puddle on the tile floor. He kept yelling at me to tell mother I had lied. Under the influence of pain, truth becomes a lie and a lie the truth, depending upon what the tormentor wants. Many idealistic rebels around the world have learned this brutal lesson in cold, dank torture chambers.

"I lied, Momma, I lied," I screamed. "Please make him stop, Momma — please make him stop." Mother said nothing. She simply stood in the bathroom door clutching the Bible.

John then beat me for "lying." He kept punching me in the head with his fist. At some point I fell to the floor, nearly unconscious, and curled up into a fetal position under the sink. He kept kicking my battered body until my mother finally pulled him away. I locked my arms around the silver drainpipe. Mother stooped over and pried my hands loose, carrying me to the bedroom. The television cord had cut deep into my flesh, leaving ugly wounds.

"It's alright, son," she whispered, trying to soothe me. "Don't lie — just don't lie, son."

"I didn't lie, Momma," I sobbed.

I couldn't stop whimpering. John suddenly appeared at the door like a ghoul from the Dark Side.

"You little sonuvabitch," he cursed. "If you don't shut up that damn whining, I'll kill you. I should've done it a long time ago."

Recoiling at the threat, I shivered at the thought of more abuse. Still, I couldn't stop crying. The pain kept coming, like pounding surf. John stormed back into the bedroom and dragged me into the bathroom. He beat me again with the television cord —

for crying. I screamed and screamed until I lost my voice. I kept trying to scream but no sound came out. Through the blurred haze of pain, I heard my mother's voice, pleading: "Stop it, John — you're gonna kill him. For God's sake, please stop it."

Then they were gone. I was alone in the bathroom. Trying to form a sound, I stared at the blood splattered all over the tile walls and the mirror of the medicine cabinet. I thought I was dying. I managed to crawl to the door. Blood ran freely down my face from a deep cut in my forehead. I spat out its sweet taste.

I saw them on the couch before I heard them. The sound of their grunting passion penetrated my wall of pain. I crawled down the hallway toward the bedroom. The sounds tore at my heart. I learned at a young age that life revolves around sex and violence.

I don't know what spawned John's hatred and rage. His parents were North Louisiana sharecroppers, good people who were always willing to take us into their modest country home and treat us with love. But Grandpa Sinclair was afraid of his son John. Grandpa tried never to anger him. Once I saw John punch the old man in the face because he could not learn to drive a car.

John's explosions of rage were all the more terrifying because they were unpredictable. But there was one situation that always ended in violence — family drives on Sunday afternoons in our '48 Ford. Then John's rage would surface at its ugliest. He loved to chase sirens, especially ambulances on their way to wrecks. A body-and-fender man by trade, John would speed to wreck scenes where he would prowl through the damage. He found a perverse pleasure in the damaged vehicles and mangled bodies, lingering until the wrecked cars and injured people were hauled away. One Sunday, John was speeding after an ambulance when a car driven by a black man suddenly pulled in front of him, forcing John to slow down. The speeding ambulance pulled away. John exploded, pounding the steering wheel with the palm of his hand as he spewed out racial slurs. He finally managed to pull even with the driver. John and the black man began to exchange threats and curses. Both men gestured for the other to pull over and stop. Mother was hysterical, begging John not to stop the car.

The black man pulled over. John pulled up behind him. The man motioned for John to get out. John reached under the front seat where he kept an assortment of tools that could be used as weapons. He pulled out a ball-peen hammer — a standard body-and-fender tool. But this one had a sharpened four-inch point.

"You stay in the goddamn car," he told Mother as he got out.

John walked toward the black man. He kept the hammer concealed behind his leg.

"Oh God, no," Mother moaned. "John, no, no."

All of a sudden, John rushed the black man, cursing as he approached. He swung the hammer full force from behind his leg, burying the sharpened point in the black man's skull. The man fell to his knees and tried to grab the hammer out of his head. His mouth was open. No words came out as he toppled over. John walked back to the car and drove away.

"Don't open your mouth, bitch," he said, reaching over to slap Mother full across the face.

He double-clutched the car, ramming the floor shift into second gear in a futile attempt to catch the long-gone ambulance. I sat in the backseat with my brothers, Johnny and Dan, too afraid to cry.

3

AFTER ELUDING THE MASSIVE police dragnet in Baton Rouge, I journeyed across the plains of Oklahoma, through El Reno on Route 66, on through the snow-covered mountains of Arizona to be with John, who lived in National City, California. I don't know why I turned to John. I had no reason to believe he would help me. Perhaps, deep down, I wanted to be caught.

John called the FBI as soon as he hung up the phone with me, telling them I was on my way to see him. Several agents arrested me at the Jeep dealership where he worked. I was leaning against a car talking to him when I felt the barrel of a pistol in the small of my back.

"Don't move."

The agents quickly handcuffed and escorted me out of the building.

As the FBI led me away, I heard the last words John would ever speak to me: "I hope they put you in the electric chair."

That was Saturday, December 11, 1965 — my last day as a free man.

On Monday morning I appeared before a federal magistrate in downtown San Diego on a "flight to avoid prosecution" charge. I was surprised to see television cameras and reporters there to cover the event. I felt important for the first time in my life. I waived extradition back to Louisiana.

On Saturday, December 18, two high-ranking members of the East Baton Rouge Parish Sheriff's Department flew to California in a small jet to return me to Louisiana. I sensed their hostility. They did not attempt to interrogate me — an unusual sign that raised an internal alarm.

The plane made a stopover in Dallas in the rain. Once we got to the airport lobby, one officer went to get some coffee. I sat down as the other officer walked around. Then he disappeared too. I was sitting alone, handcuffed, in the middle of a large airport lobby.

The thought of escape crossed my mind. Looking around, I eased up from the lounge chair and made my way to the double glass doors leading out of the lobby. I was primed to burst through the door and make a run for it until I saw the reflection of one of the cops in the glass. His gun was drawn. He was waiting to kill me.

I turned and walked back to my seat. My legs were ready to buckle. The Baton Rouge deputies had been sent to California with a secret agenda.

Both officers returned at the same time. They carried no coffee. Nothing was said as they led me outside the lobby and into the plane. Once off the ground and high in the air, one of the detectives turned to look at me.

"At least you're not stupid, Sinclair," he said.

Nothing else was said during the rest of the flight to Baton Rouge. It was after midnight when the plane landed at the small city airport. A television reporter, along with a group of print reporters, covered my arrival. I was a front-page story.

The detectives quickly escorted me past the media and into a waiting car. It sped away to the parish jail where they placed me in a dirty solitary cell, a "drunk tank" used to sober up winos. The mattress stank of urine. The one dirty blanket was crusted with vomit. The jailers had installed a large light bulb in the ceiling light fixture. It was controlled by a light switch outside the cell. The jailers kept it on twenty-four hours a day. There was no escaping its blinding glare.

For the first few days, the jailers brought people to the cell at all hours to peer at me. Some were in police uniforms, others in civilian clothes. They cursed, threatened, and even spat at me through the food slot situated in the middle of the solid steel door. I cursed back, staring defiantly at the hate-filled faces.

I didn't understand the harsh treatment, especially since the state's most notorious killer occupied the cell next to mine. Wilbert Rideau was a black man who slit the throat of a white woman and tried to kill two other white people — the worst crime that could be committed in the South in the 1960s. Rideau and I could talk through the vents located at the bottom of the cell doors. He was being held in "close-security" because he was under the death sentence. But he was allowed the same privileges as other inmates — clean clothes, a daily shower, canteen privileges, reading material, and a radio. I was given nothing.

Rideau smuggled a few cigarettes and a pint of milk to me through a black jail trusty (a convict considered trustworthy and given privileges) who brought meals to the cells. The trusty then told the jailers, who warned Rideau not to give me anything else — he would lose his privileges if he helped me.

Two days after my return to Baton Rouge I made my first court appearance. The courtroom was packed with spectators, reporters, and members of the Bodden family. The jailers sneaked me into the courtroom through the judge's chambers.

"It's for your own safety," one deputy said. "A lot of people want you dead, but we're not gonna let that happen. Your ass is gonna burn in the electric chair."

Ossie Brown, a well-known criminal defense attorney, was appointed to represent me. Gasps of dismay and expressions of anger were heard throughout the courtroom when the appointment was announced. Brown visited me in the jail the next day. He was a glib, fast-talking lawyer who would later become one of Louisiana's most powerful district attorneys.

"I'm gonna lay the cards on the table, Sinclair," he said. "I can't represent you. I've received a dozen messages from your victim's father telling me not to take your case. I have to live in this community with these people — I will hold political office here one day. There's no mileage in your case — none whatsoever. Frankly, the court will be hard pressed to find a good attorney who will defend you."

I said nothing. I was a hostile, suspicious twenty-year-old in wrinkled denims facing a well-dressed criminal defense attorney. Brown stood to leave.

"Let me give you a piece of advice," he continued. "First, don't say anything to the police. Second, when you get an attorney, tell him to plead you insane. If he can get you sent to the nut house for a year, he might be able to work a deal. This is not a capital murder case. J. C. Bodden was killed outside that store after the robbery attempt was over. He was not killed inside during the robbery attempt. That's not felony murder."

Ossie Brown did not waste his insight and legal expertise on me. Citing his close ties to the Bodden family, he filed a motion to withdraw as counsel. The court granted the request. Ossie was a political animal. In the 1960s, he was an avowed segregationist, reflecting the views of southern voting majorities. On the campaign trail, he told voters that "having been born and reared in Louisiana, I firmly believe in segregation. If elected district attorney, I will do everything in my power to maintain segregation without compromise and without any bias or prejudice."

He represented a group of Ku Klux Klansmen in Bogalusa, Louisiana, that the Justice Department wanted enjoined from intimidating and threatening civil rights advocates, businessmen, and Bogalusa city officials. He also represented another Klansman suspected in the nighttime killing of Washington Parish's first black deputy sheriff, although the case was never prosecuted.

The Boddens lived in an all-white enclave in North Baton Rouge known as "Little Dixie." Blacks feared the neighborhood. Klan sympathizers were said to live there. Little Dixie's demographics fitted Brown's natural constituency. Its residents had left Mississippi to seek jobs in Baton Rouge in the 1940s.

J. C. Bodden attended Little Dixie's Istrouma High School and played football on the popular 1953 team. Its coach, "Fuzzy" Brown, became a legend in high school athletics, producing eight state championships for the Indians.

By 1965, many of Istrouma's players and supporters had risen to the middle echelons of city, parish, and state government and other positions of prominence. Fuzzy Brown was on his way to becoming president of the influential Louisiana High School Football Association. Others moved up in the East Baton Rouge Parish school system and the police and sheriff's department. The most prominent member of the 1953 Istrouma football team was Billy Cannon. In 1959, Cannon made LSU football history when he returned a punt eighty-nine yards on Halloween night to win the game for LSU against Ole Miss as the clock ran out. Later that year, the football great won the Heisman Trophy. Cannon's prowess on the gridiron led to a professional football career. He signed a one-hundred-thousand-dollar-a-year contract with the Houston Oilers and eventually retired from the Kansas City Chiefs after an eleven-year career in pro ball. It was said that the road to political office in Baton Rouge traveled through Billy Cannon. He was a political kingmaker until federal agents dug up $2 million worth of bogus hundred-dollar bills in two Igloo coolers on Cannon's property in 1983 and charged him with running a counterfeiting ring. But Cannon's conviction and his five-year sentence to a federal penitentiary did not spell the end of his popularity in Baton Rouge. Every Halloween weekend, local television news departments replay video of his famous punt return in Tiger Stadium as he led LSU to victory over arch rival Ole Miss in the last minutes of the game.

Several weeks after Ossie Brown withdrew from the case, I was returned to court to have another attorney appointed. Once again members of the Bodden family and the Istrouma football fraternity attended the hearing. Robert "Buck" Kleinpeter and Kenneth Scullin were appointed to represent me. Kleinpeter was a highly respected criminal defense attorney from a prominent, wealthy Baton Rouge family. He had never lost a capital case. Scullin, on the other hand, was fresh out of law school.

"Do you have any money?" Kleinpeter asked during our first and only interview.

"No."

"Does anyone in your family have money?"

"No."

"Well, Sinclair, there's not a lot I can do for you," he said. "A good defense in a case like this would start at fifty thousand dollars. You don't have a nickel. You might get lucky, though — the court might appoint you a lawyer who wants to cut his teeth on a hard case."

Kleinpeter and Scullin filed a joint motion to withdraw. The court granted the motion.

A lynch mob mentality infected the Baton Rouge judicial system. A politically powerful football fraternity had decided I would die. While I did not know their names or recognize their faces, I was determined to fight them. I saved the brown paper that my daily bologna sandwiches came wrapped in, and with a smuggled pencil, I wrote a letter to a local federal judge listing a litany of civil rights abuses — lockdown in the filthy, roach-infested cell; denial of basic hygiene, family correspondence, and visitation; threats of physical harm and verbal abuse; and the psychological torture of the twenty-four-hour light.

The letter never reached federal court. It was intercepted and given to the warden of the jail. He had me brought to his office where he assured me he knew nothing about the "abuses." Clearly nervous, he said I would be removed from the cell and placed on a tier with other inmates, provided I didn't mail the letter. I agreed. I walked out of the warden's office with the knowledge that I had a source of power after all.

I was placed in a cell block called the "short tier" because it had ten four-man cells while the other jail tiers had twenty such cells. It was the jail's maximum-security tier. It housed hardcore inmates — murderers, rapists, armed robbers, and repeat offenders. Each tier in the jail (black or white) was controlled by an inmate "line judge." He occupied the first cell on the tier. He told the inmates when to clean up, when to shower, when to make "store," and when to use the telephone. Inmates who gave the line judge money got special treatment when it came to receiving these privileges.

It was a system of extortion, sanctioned and protected by the jailers. Since there was no on-tier supervision, the jailers relied upon the line judge to maintain order and discipline, irrespective of the means. The jailers picked the biggest and toughest inmates for line judges, giving them carte blanche to use fear and brute force to enforce their "rules." In exchange, the line judge was given a carpeted cell, extra food and coffee, unrestricted telephone privileges, and unsupervised "special visits."

The line judge on the short tier was a former Angola convict named David Ellis. He had three flunkies in his cell. They had the inmates on the tier buffaloed. At 6:00 A.M. the inmates had to leave their cells and remain in the bull pen until 8:00 P.M. The bull pen was located at the front of the tier. It was nothing more than a large cell. It had four metal dining tables and benches bolted to a steel wall. A shower and commode were located at the back. Inmates sat at the tables reading and playing cards or lying on the concrete floor trying to sleep. On visiting day, every Wednesday afternoon, inmates had to peer through hard, clear plastic windows at their visitors and speak through the small holes just below them.

Ellis and his flunkies, on the other hand, were allowed to move freely about the tier. He could go anywhere in the jail, in fact. He had claimed the first table in the bull pen as the "line judge table." He forbade anyone to sit there. The table was complete with tablecloth, salt and pepper shakers, toothpick dispenser, and napkins. It was served first by the trusties running the food cart. Ellis could take as much as he wanted from the cart. He often took "extras" — little tokens he gave to some of the inmates later at night, like a king taking care of the servants who pleased him most.

A list of "Line Judge Rules" was posted on the bull pen wall. Inmates were conditioned to accept the rules when they were put on the tier. Those who questioned or resisted the rules were made to comply by brute force. Ellis and his flunkies beat them into submission.

One of their rules required prisoners who received money from home to put a "reasonable amount" in the tobacco-and-coffee kitty. The kitty was supposed to be set up to buy those commodities for inmates who didn't have money. In reality, the money was used to buy cigarettes and luxuries ("zoo-zoo," as inmates called them) for the line judge cell.

I had been on the tier a couple of days when a quiet burglar named Wally Reed approached me. I was leaning against the bars staring at the free world four floors below.

"Let me give you some advice, Sinclair," he said. "Watch Ellis. His cousin works for the sheriff's department. He's been told to fuck you up. He'll create a situation and crowd you with his boys."

I had spoken to no one on the tier but I had observed Reed. He didn't mingle with the others. He always sat alone, generally reading a book.

"Why are you concerned about me?" I asked.

"I'm not. They crowded me when I was put in here because I wouldn't pay Ellis the dollar 'toll' to use the phone. I put up enough of a scuffle that they leave me alone now."

Paranoia rustled like a quiet April breeze in my brain.

"You still haven't answered my question."

"I don't like Ellis or the line judge system. I caught part of a conversation the other day when I went out to see my lawyer. Ellis's cousin and another deputy were talking. I picked up enough to know that Ellis is supposed to fuck you up. Do what you want with the information; I'm just passing it along."

Ellis made his move a couple of days later. I had just received ten dollars in the mail from my family. He knew the letter contained money. The jailers opened all incoming mail, providing the line judges with a list of inmates who got money.

Flanked by his three flunkies, Ellis walked up to me as I lay on the bull pen floor reading *Hondo*.

"Sinclair, you're new on the tier," he said, standing over me, "so you probably don't know about the tobacco-and-coffee kitty. When you get money, you're expected to put something in that kitty. The kitty is there to help inmates who ain't got nothing. We all take care of each other. Now, you just got some bread in the mail . . ."

"I don't smoke or drink coffee," I lied, putting the book down and easing up from the floor.

"That don't matter, dude. Everybody puts his issue in the kitty when he gets money. That's a line judge rule."

"Okay, I'll go get my issue."

An ancient bagpipe started playing in the back of my head —

the plaintive music of my Scottish ancestors. I walked across the bull pen to a shoe box where I kept writing paper. I had collected a dozen discarded radio batteries and had put them in a sock, tying off the sock at the toe to make a solid weapon. I was ready to fight. It was an inevitable confrontation. Ellis was the kingpin on the tier and the media had painted me as a hardened, cold-blooded killer. My presence on the tier posed a threat to Ellis's power. In his eyes, I was a coup waiting to happen.

With the sock wrapped around my right hand, I walked to the front of the bull pen where Ellis was leaning against the wall whispering to one of his flunkies. Reed stood up. With all my strength, I swung the battery-filled sock. The blow landed on the side of Ellis's head, stunning him. I didn't let him recover. I beat him about the head and upper body until he sank to his knees. Blood flowed freely down his semiconscious face.

Reed decked one of the flunkies with a vicious right hook to the jaw. The other two ran into the hallway outside the bull pen. They began "rappin' the walls" — a signal that there was an emergency on the tier. A slew of jailers charged onto the tier just as I was dragging Ellis to the door.

"Get this piece of shit out of here," I said, dropping Ellis at the door of the tier.

The jailers carted Ellis away. I turned to the two dozen inmates who had gathered around. "We're not going have a line judge run this tier," I said. "No one is going to sell you state food or charge you to use the phone or force you to buy his coffee. That's over on this tier."

Reed stepped forward. "Sinclair's right," he said. "We don't need a line judge."

Like Bolivian citizens, the inmates cheered the change of order. They expected dictators to be deposed and replaced. I brought an end to the line judge system on the short tier and eventually throughout the entire jail, but not without paying a near fatal price.

An hour after my attack on Ellis, several jailers escorted me to a solitary cell located in the back of the jail. The cell had an iron bunk without a mattress and a stainless steel sink and commode. There was no window. The food slot in the solid steel door was the cell's only opening. I could see no one and no one could see me

unless the slot was opened. Twice a day food was shoved through —
a half-rationed lunch and a bologna sandwich for supper.

I was kept in the cell for sixty-three days without being allowed
to shower, shave, or brush my teeth. It was mid-January. The jailers
turned on the air-conditioning full force, pumping refrigerated air
into the cell through a vent located above the toilet. The cold was
unbearable. I wore short-sleeved white coveralls. I had only a thin
blanket for cover. I could not lie or remain seated in one spot very
long because of the cold. I paced back and forth across the floor
wrapped in the blanket, shivering, until exhaustion allowed me to
sleep.

I could cope with the isolation, rationed food, and unsanitary
conditions, but the cold nearly broke me. A thousand times I
wanted to scream out for mercy, begging for warmth. Instead, I
paced and paced, knowing that my keepers had set out to break my
will. But an ingrained Scotch-Irish stubbornness served me well. I
refused to break.

Several weeks after I was placed in isolation, Rideau was transferred to a cell near mine. At night we climbed on our commodes
and talked through the vents. Because I had to stand on my tiptoes,
I could only talk for short periods of time. Besides the jailers who
fed me, Rideau was the only human contact I had. He became a
source of strength, always offering encouragement when my will
seemed to waver.

I had been in the cell approximately six weeks when a quasi-
official attempt to kill me was put in motion. An inmate opened my
food slot at supper and handed me the bologna sandwich. I had
never seen him before.

"I'm here to help you, Sinclair," he whispered. "Reed and some
of your friends want to help you. The jail's fire escape runs down
the building in the back of your cell. There's a steel door at the end
of this hallway and it leads to the fire escape. All you have to do is
get the key to that door and go down the fire escape to freedom."

Huddled with the blanket wrapped tightly around me, I tried
to look down the hallway in front of my cell. But I could see only a
few feet through the slot.

"How do I get the key?"

"The old jailer who feeds you has the key on a ring he carries.

All you have to do is take it from him. I'll get you something to use to take it. You can get him to open this door by putting a roll of toilet paper in your commode and stopping it up."

The inmate looked furtively down the hallway before turning back to me, saying: "I've got to split. The old man let me feed you tonight because I told him some of the fellas wanted to send you some candy bars. But he only let me have the key to the food slot. He keeps all other keys on his key ring."

The inmate left. I paced the floor thinking about the escape plan. It was too easy — there had to be something wrong. But the more I paced and shivered, the more convinced I became that the old deputy had the key to the fire escape door. I had been beaten down by the cold, the hunger, and the isolation. I was often disoriented, unable to distinguish night from day because I had forgotten which meal I had eaten last. I risked discussing the escape plan with Rideau. His cell had a barred window covered by a thick screen. He could see the fire escape. He was receptive to the plan, saying I could hurry around to his cell once I was out of mine and let him out.

"It won't take you two minutes to come around here and open my door," he said. "I've got the death sentence and you're gonna get one. You've got to give me a play, too."

Two days later the inmate returned. He handed me a bologna sandwich.

"Be careful when you bite into it," he said. "There's a switchblade in it. Just stop up your commode and throw down on the old man when he opens the door. He won't put up a scuffle when he sees the knife. He's afraid of you anyway. Just leave him locked in the cell. The sarge at the desk won't miss him for fifteen minutes or so — and you should be long gone by then."

The inmate slammed the food slot closed and left. I unwrapped the sandwich and found a new switchblade knife in it.

"I've got the knife," I told Rideau later that night. "I'm gonna make the play tomorrow night."

I went back to my pacing routine. But this time I clutched the knife in my pocket. While I couldn't shake my suspicions that the plan was too easy, I managed to shove them aside, attributing them to paranoia.

Rideau interrupted the pacing by calling my name.

"What's up?" I asked, stretching to reach the vent.

"Something ain't right, man," he replied. "I can see a car parked across the street. It's been there most of the night. Somebody's in it because I saw them light a cigarette a few minutes ago. I think it's a police car; they've got the back of the jail staked out."

"It's a setup," I said, my mind snapping into clear focus at last. I remembered the airport lobby. "They want to take me out when I come down the fire escape. That's what this thing is about — they put me in here to kill me."

I climbed down from the vent and slung the knife across the cell. The isolation, hunger, and freezing temperatures had been part of the setup, designed to wear me down, to make me receptive to the lure of freedom. Had I been killed going down the fire escape, it would have been a legal murder.

I waited, knowing a shakedown was coming once the jailers realized that I wasn't going to take the bait. Two days later a couple of road deputies (not assigned to the jail) came to my cell and quickly found the knife. They didn't utter a word to me. Through the partially open door, I saw the arm of a man standing down the hall. I could only see a gray suit sleeve. The man had come with the deputies. An hour later a regular jailer came to my cell and took my coveralls and blanket.

I stayed in my underwear in the brutalizing cold for two weeks until one night I hollered at Rideau:

"They're trying to freeze me to death."

The next morning he smuggled a message to the short tier telling Reed I needed help. Rideau said he would start rappin' the walls at a certain time and urged the short tier to join in. When the jailers responded to the "rapdown," Rideau asked to see the warden.

Warden A. B. Cutrer went to Rideau's cell.

"What's the problem?"

"It's Sinclair," Rideau said. "They're trying to freeze him to death back there."

Accompanied by a deputy, Cutrer opened the cell door and found me crouched on my heels in a corner, shivering uncontrollably.

"Damn it, who ordered this crap?" he said, throwing the door open. "Get this man some clothes and turn that goddamn air conditioner off."

As the jailer scurried away, Cutrer turned back to me.

"Sinclair, I didn't have anything to do with this," he said, "and I'll have the head of every shift supervisor who did. How long has this been going on?"

I told Cutrer about the two-month ordeal, including the escape plan initiated by the unknown inmate.

"There's someone I want you to talk to," he said. "I want you to tell him everything you've told me."

After Cutrer left, the shift supervisor let me shower and gave me a clean set of clothes. I stayed under the steaming water for at least half an hour. Then a deputy escorted me to the jail's kitchen where I was given coffee and a hot meal. When I had finished, I was taken to Cutrer's office where he and William "Hawk" Daniels were waiting.

"Hawk is an investigator with the district attorney's office," Cutrer said by way of introduction. "Tell him what you told me."

I began with the fight with Ellis, the reason for it, the extended lockdown, and the escape setup. He listened intently until I finished.

"There's nothing I can do about what's been done," he said. "You did attack Ellis and you accepted the knife with a mind to escape. I believe both incidents were setups but you reacted to them in the wrong way. You made it easy for those behind the setups to say you were wrong."

"What was I supposed to do? Pay extortion to Ellis?"

Daniels was an intelligent man. Intelligence, it could be said, was his profession. He had a distinguished record in military intelligence.

"Let me give you some advice, Sinclair," he said. "The deck is stacked against you. There are people who want you dead, and I don't know to what lengths they will go to see you in a grave. You must measure your response to each situation. Don't be your own worst enemy."

But that die was cast on December 5, 1965, when I shot J. C. Bodden. His friends packed funeral services for him at the Istrouma

Methodist Church in Baton Rouge. Four ministers presided. In addition to the six pallbearers, there were honorary pallbearers — the entire Istrouma High School football teams of 1951, '52, and '53 and their coaches.

While I was searching for a way out of Baton Rouge the night Bodden died, his widow was standing in the emergency room of Baton Rouge General Hospital waiting to see his body. She never got over his murder. Sadie Bodden DeLee told a Louisiana pardon board in 1988: "I would have killed Billy Sinclair myself that night if I could have found him. I don't think anything he has ever done can make up for the pain he caused."

Her words were the mantra for a generation of his Little Dixie friends. The bullet that killed J. C. Bodden created an army of avengers. Their names would appear on sign-in sheets at my pardon and parole hearings for years. By rights I should have felt remorse for what I did. But remorse got lost for a long time in the avalanche of their hatred and a nightmare of prison brutality.

4

In MARCH 1966, the court appointed J. St. Clair Favrot and Harris M. English to defend me. Favrot was the lead counsel. He had a reputation as an effective, honest lawyer who had been the district attorney in Baton Rouge for sixteen years. Favrot had also been president of district attorneys' associations at the state and national level. English was a good man in his seventies, but a speech impediment and Parkinson's disease prevented him from being an effective courtroom advocate.

"An attorney cannot divorce himself from his personal feelings," Favrot told me during our first interview. "I don't like being assigned to this case; I don't like what you did. But I'm going to give you the best defense I can. You're entitled to it and I have a professional obligation to provide it. I will protect every due process right you have."

A balding, diminutive man, Favrot made up with the force of his personality what he lacked in size. There was an aura of professional dignity about him. He commanded respect, especially in the courtroom.

"Let's not have any misunderstanding," he continued. "I'm not doing this for you. I'm doing it because I have an ethical responsibility to do it. The other attorneys appointed to this case opted for the easy way out. The legal profession has too many of their kind. They don't want their reputations or their political ambitions hindered by handling a 'hot potato' case like yours."

Favrot launched a standard investigation into the facts of the case. He was surprised at the political opposition he encountered with law enforcement and prosecution officials.

"I don't understand it," Favrot confided to me one night. "No one on the inside is talking about your case. No one! I can't get any information, and I have some good sources in the DA's office and sheriff's department. But they won't let me in on this one. They say it's too hot. In all my years as a practicing attorney, I've never seen a case with so much power and politics involved. There's more to it, and I can't get at who's pulling the strings. It frustrates the hell out of me."

My trial was set for June 1966. There would be no continuances. District Attorney Sargent Pitcher, up for reelection in August, stated he would seek the death penalty. It was the first time in decades a white man had faced the death penalty in East Baton Rouge Parish.

"Ralph Roy will prosecute your case," Favrot told me prior to trial. "He's the best prosecutor in the district attorney's office. He's ruthless. He will do whatever it takes to get the death penalty. That's the political objective in this case."

At age twenty-one, I could not comprehend the death penalty or the years I would spend in a solitary cell before being strapped in the electric chair.

"What are my chances?"

Favrot looked up from his legal documents, staring hard at me.

"Not good," he said. "The DA's office has convinced the media you're a cold-blooded killer, and the media has portrayed you as such. You haven't helped your own situation much with some of your exploits in jail. Hell, you're almost a legend among the 'courthouse gang.' There's more talk about you than the upcoming election. All we can hope for is one juror who will hold out against the death penalty. That's my job — to select a juror who will vote his principles, not his emotions."

The district attorney had elected to prosecute me under Louisiana's "felony-murder doctrine." Under that doctrine, the prosecutor did not have to prove I had a "specific intent" to kill Bodden. He had only to prove Bodden was killed during the commission or attempted commission of a felony.

"What about the witnesses who saw Bodden chase me outside the store?" I asked. "They know it wasn't a cold-blooded murder. Even Ossie Brown said it wasn't a felony murder because Bodden was shot outside the store after the robbery attempt was over."

"I've tried to find out who those witnesses are, or if they even exist," Favrot said, putting his papers back in his briefcase. "The prosecution is not saying anything. I can't even talk to their witnesses. All I have about the witnesses is what you tell me; but if they exist, I will find out who they are at trial by forcing the prosecution's witnesses to identify them or commit perjury."

I stood up.

"I didn't mean to kill J. C. Bodden, Mr. Favrot."

"I believe you, son. You're not a killer. You play the badass role, and if I were in your situation, I'd probably do the same thing. You're a screwed-up young man who threw his life away."

He peered up at me through glasses that always sat perched on the edge of his nose.

"You still don't understand what you've gotten yourself into," he said, a sympathetic sparkle in his eye. "Baton Rouge is the worst place you could be. It's a city ruled by power and politics — a Mafia town. I don't know who they are, but some powerful people are involved in your case. Sarge Pitcher is not one of them but he is susceptible to their influence. These people want you in the electric chair."

On the first day of the trial, Monday, June 6, 1966, Favrot filed a motion to have the case removed from state to federal court. He argued that the systematic exclusion of women from jury duty in capital cases violated my constitutional rights. The unusual, last-minute legal maneuver angered Ralph Roy and my trial judge, Fred LeBlanc. They were caught by surprise. It proved Favrot was going to be a tough adversary.

Visibly angry at having to hold one hundred prospective jurors in limbo while Favrot got the removal petition ready to file in federal court, Judge LeBlanc said, "We've held the court up for some fifty-five minutes. I think some apology to the court is in order."

"I'm not here, nor is Mr. English, because we want to be," Favrot replied. "However, I intend to give my client the best defense I can up to the point of being discourteous to the court. I've been around the track with this case."

Scowling and obviously disgusted with the defense maneuver, Ralph Roy stood to oppose the motion. "Your Honor, we're ready for trial. We have witnesses subpoenaed here, some who have come from as far away as California. This eleventh-hour tactic is taking unfair advantage of the state and the court."

The case was transferred to federal district court for a hearing on removal petition. During the hearings, Favrot received a message that his mother-in-law had died in North Louisiana. "My mother-in-law just passed away," he told me during a break in the federal hearing. "I must go to my wife to be with her in her bereavement."

The federal court denied the removal motion, ordering the case sent back to state court. Judge LeBlanc made it clear that the trial would commence the next morning. Favrot came to see me late that afternoon. "I've just spoken with Judge LeBlanc," he said. "The judge has reluctantly agreed to grant a continuance for at least seventy-two hours. I will return to Baton Rouge as soon as the funeral is over. Harris English will file a written motion for continuance in the morning. I am sorry to have to leave you like this, but my wife needs me. I will be back for the start of the trial. You have my word."

On Tuesday morning, June 7, English assured me the trial would be continued. Judge LeBlanc, however, made it clear at the outset of the hearing that he was not about to grant a continuance. English was stunned. He pressed forward.

"Your Honor," he argued, "the court appointed Mr. Favrot as lead counsel and he has been acting in that regard, preparing the defense in this case. He had a death in his family and left the city, as he informed Your Honor. Before he left, he joined me in a motion for continuance on the grounds of the death in the family and his having to leave the city. I would add that I am unprepared to proceed with this trial under any circumstances. Considering my age and the service I've given to this honorable court, I don't think I should be forced to go through this trial alone."

A tall man with distinguished silver hair and hawkish features, Roy rose immediately to oppose the motion for a continuance. "Your Honor," he countered aggressively, "I haven't seen the written motion he's filing, but the state unequivocally opposes any continuance. The state and the defendant are entitled to a speedy trial. You appointed two attorneys in this case, and it's a terrible indictment for Mr. English to stand before the bar and tell Your Honor that he is not prepared to go to trial."

Unlike the professional presence cast by Roy, English was a large man with an obvious stoop in his back. He was a slouchy dresser who continuously scribbled illegible notes and stuffed them into various pockets.

"But I am not prepared to give this man an adequate defense," he said. "Now he's certainly entitled to that under the Constitution."

The judge was not impressed. He denied the motion for a continuance.

A total of forty-nine prospective jurors were examined. Twenty-one were excused because they had conscientious scruples against the death penalty. Twenty prospective jurors had heard of, read about, or discussed the case. Another twenty-six were not asked if they were familiar with it.

The first prospective juror examined during voir dire worked in the circulation department of the local newspaper. "It was the best news at the time to sell newspapers and that's what I am in the business for," he said.

Eight of the twelve jurors chosen had read about it. Three of the remaining four were not asked. Only one juror said he had not read or heard anything about the case.

In selecting the twelve-man jury, English exhausted his twelve peremptory challenges. The last two jurors chosen were close personal friends of the district attorney and the warden of the parish jail. One juror lived only eight blocks from the store where J. C. Bodden was killed, and two others lived in Bodden's neighborhood.

It was a jury primed to convict. One of the last prospective jurors realized as much. Roby Bearden, a chemist at a local plant, told the court he did not have any scruples against the death penalty. "But in this case I do have a reservation against it," he said. "It is, I suppose, an opinion formed from what I've heard sitting here in court for the past two days. It is hard for me to believe that asking for the death penalty in this case would be exactly fair. I will put it that way." Judge LeBlanc excused Bearden without giving him a chance to explain his feelings.

Ralph Roy's opening statement made it clear that the death penalty was his objective, and he engineered his case to get it. He suppressed mitigating evidence and used perjured testimony. According to his prosecutorial theme, I walked into the store, demanded money, shot Bodden through the heart when he refused to open the register, and calmly walked to my getaway car. To bolster his theme of methodical, cold-blooded murder, Roy introduced evidence that Alexander and I had been on a "cross-country crime spree," stealing cars and robbing convenience stores. It took the jury less than an hour to convict me of capital murder.

Sixteen years later, I discovered a suppressed police report containing the statements of four witnesses who told the police that Bodden chased me out of the store, waving a broom over his head, and was shot in the parking lot outside. Roy not only suppressed these witnesses, he allowed a close friend of Bodden's to commit perjury. Larry Sullivan changed his testimony to fit Roy's prosecutorial theme. According to the police report, Bodden died at 8:06 P.M. When questioned by the police the night of the crime, Sullivan said I was in his restaurant between 7:50 and 8:20 P.M. When questioned by the prosecutor during the trial, Sullivan said I was in his restaurant thirty minutes before that "looking like somone trying to find a place to rob."

"The state proved the accused was five minutes away from where Bodden was killed thirty minutes before this unfortunate thing happened," Roy told the jury. "I think Larry Sullivan made one of the best witnesses it has been my experience to see on the witness stand."

In 1981, after discovering through the Louisiana Public Records Law the police report that was buried in my pardon board file, I learned that the evidence file in the clerk of court's office, the investigation files in the sheriff's department and city police department, and the coroner's file, including the autopsy report, had disappeared. The disappearance conveniently covered up the conspiracy to send me to the electric chair.

"I give you one promise, Sinclair," Favrot told me after the conviction. "You will never see the electric chair. I'll blow the lid off this thing if they try to execute you."

Favrot's assurance had a hollow ring. I was convinced that he had abandoned the case like the other attorneys. He could have returned from North Louisiana before the trial ended. Instead he allowed Judge LeBlanc to relieve him of his appointment. The death of his mother-in-law provided an easy way for him to step aside and maintain his professional dignity.

I hatched a plan to escape. I wasn't going to the chair without a fight. Three months after my conviction I spent $150 to post bond for a burglary suspect named Noel Hines. Two nights after his release from jail, Hines walked up to the courthouse building where I was incarcerated in the jail on the fourth floor and tied a packet of hacksaw blades to a string that I lowered through a hall window. I pulled the blades up. Hines was arrested on another burglary charge a week later.

Hines joined Reed and me in our futile attempts to cut through the case-hardened steel bars. We eventually gave up trying to saw our way out of the jail. But a few days later, as the three of us sat in the bull pen discussing ways to smuggle industrial hacksaw blades into the jail, I focused on an air vent in the ceiling.

"What are you looking at, Sinclair?" Hines asked.

"There must be a way to remove that vent," I answered.

"It's made of the same case-hardened steel as the bars," Reed said.

Hines leaped to his feet, examining the rivets holding the heavy barred vent in place.

"You can't cut the steel but you can cut the rivets," he said excitedly.

He was right. It took less than thirty minutes to cut through the two dozen rivets and lower the heavy vent to the floor. We concealed it in the shower. There was no time to waste. We went to our cells, made crude dummies, covered them with blankets, and tore our sheets into strips that we tied together. Every inmate on the tier knew we were about to escape but no one said a word. They wanted me to get away.

Reed and I lifted Hines up through the vent opening. He reached down to pull me up. Reed pushed me from behind. We both pulled Reed up. We crawled around the attic of the jail until we found a large air duct connected to the jail's air-conditioning system. It was a tight squeeze, but we managed to squirm through the duct onto the jail's roof.

The three of us crawled out on a narrow ledge encircling the top floor of the building and slowly began edging our way around to the dark side. We clung to small concrete railings four floors up as we inched along the ledge. Several police cars pulled in and out of the parking lot below. None of the officers looked up.

The "women's tank" was located in a corner of the building. It had been added to the structure. To get to the dark side of the building, we had to pass a barred window in the women's tank. It looked directly out onto the ledge. When we got to the window, two lesbians were trying to iron out a lover's spat. We were forced to crouch in a squat on the ledge for half an hour before they left. My left arm, locked around the concrete railing, went numb, as did one of my legs, while I waited.

When we finally reached the dark side of the building, we lowered the rope fashioned from strips of jail-issued sheets. We split up and went in different directions after we climbed down the rope. I found a pickup truck with the keys in the ignition and drove the 250 miles to Monroe, Louisiana, in six hours. I contacted an old girlfriend there who gave me a place to stay. She bought me clothes and a .22 caliber pistol — all before deputies in Baton Rouge discovered the jailbreak.

The escape was front-page news. It allowed Sheriff Bryan Clemmons and other public officials to demand and ultimately secure a new maximum-security jail. The sheriff ordered an investigation into the jail's security system that resulted in the suspension of two deputies.

But my freedom was short-lived. Five days later, I attempted to rob a convenience store in Pine Bluff, Arkansas, because I was out of money. While I was careful not to fire the gun, I still bungled the robbery, fleeing the store in panic when a customer started screaming. I was arrested a few blocks from the scene. My girlfriend was taken into custody at a local motel where she was waiting for me. Sheriff Clemmons flew to Pine Bluff to escort me back to Baton Rouge. A bevy of reporters were on hand to record my return to Baton Rouge.

I was locked down in the same maximum-security cell where I had spent sixty-three days. This time there was no brutal mistreatment. I learned that my girlfriend had been charged in Monroe with aiding and abetting my escape. Feeling responsible for her predicament, I sent word through Cutrer to Assistant District Attorney Cheney Joseph that I wanted to "make a deal."

Sheriff Clemmons and the district attorney's office wanted me in Angola. But I could not be transferred because I was awaiting sentencing. The district attorney's office had an unrelated armed robbery charge pending against me. Alexander had already received a twenty-five-year sentence in the robbery.

I told Joseph I would plead guilty and consent to a transfer to Angola if the charge against my girlfriend was dropped. He contacted the authorities in Monroe who agreed to the deal. In a special late-night court session that pulled Judge LeBlanc out of bed, I entered a guilty plea to the robbery charge. He sentenced me to twenty-five years in Angola.

In the pre-dawn hours of November 4, 1966, I was led, shackled and manacled, from the parish jail and transferred under heavy guard to a maximum-security section at Angola known as CCR (Close Custody Restriction). I remained in CCR until March 2, 1967, when I was returned to court and formally sentenced to die in the electric chair.

5

SHACKLED AND MANACLED in the backseat of a police car, headed for my death, I stared without seeing at the landscape during the fifty-mile drive from Baton Rouge to Angola, where I was to be strapped into "Old Sparky," the state's electric chair. For the last twenty miles of the trip, the car rode the twists and curves and sudden drops of a narrow two-lane road, past the occasional hardscrabble shack, scruffy mobile home, or well-kept house.

And then it stopped. The road's dips and hairpin curves had come to an abrupt end. Before me loomed Angola's broad alluvial plain and the prison's Front Gate.

Sunshine lay across Angola's vast fields, stretching to the horizon as far as the eye could see — eighteen thousand acres of the continent's soil, silt the Mississippi River had deposited there for thousands of years.

Secret graves were said to lie on the dark green plain. From 1870 to 1901, as many as three thousand convicts — men, women, and children — died from overwork, exposure, brutality, and murder, as Louisiana contracted out its inmate labor force to greedy overseers focused on profits. Prisoners still tilled Angola's fields, herded under mounted guards from cell and dormitory to stoop-labor servitude in the fertile dirt.

In the distance, groups of low buildings hugged the land. Green guard towers rose above them. The road into the prison slanted down from the surrounding hills. Their woods were the last trees for miles. To the right of the Front Gate, hard up against the hills, stood a separate building — death row. Hunkered down against the hillside like a prophecy of doom, its bunker-like concrete hulk was covered with flaking green paint. Beds of rose bushes incongruously dotted the lawn inside its fenced enclosure.

The building's grimy appearance struck fear and suspicion in the minds of all incoming inmates. I was no exception as I stared at the structure where madness and isolation awaited me. An inmate trusty working in the flowerbed in front of the building glanced up furtively at me, as though peering at a freak.

The two deputies who had driven me to the prison escorted me to the Security Office in the building's Reception Center. A red-faced prison guard greeted them. His eyes were mean and hateful.

"Well, what have we got here," he mocked, flashing a tobacco-stained smile at the deputies.

"This here is Billy Wayne Sinclair," one of the deputies replied.

"Oh yeah, I heard about you, boy," the guard said. "We been expecting you."

"The name's Sinclair."

The guard tried to conceal his rage at my insolent reply.

"That's alright, boy," he mocked, spitting tobacco juice in a trash can. "Get smart all you like. We can't treat you death row fellas like we do other convicts. The federal courts won't allow that shit no more."

Grinning, the deputies turned and walked out of the office, waving as they left.

"He's all yours," one shouted, snickering and slapping his partner on the back as they walked out of the building.

The guard began searching through the paper bag containing my personal belongings. He cut loose a childlike hurrah at the discovery of a *Playboy* magazine.

I turned to a large bulletin board hanging on the wall behind his desk. Several rows of mug shots were tacked to it. Above the scarred board, in huge black letters, were the stark words: DEATH ROW. The faces of the men posted on the board all looked alike. Each wore a look of dark despair and weary resignation. I felt instant kinship with the faces. Death row was our final dwelling place — the end of the line.

"Your mug shot will be up there tomorrow," the guard said. "Your number will be C-43, that means you're the forty-third man to come to death row. Don't take much to get up on that board, does it, boy?" An evil grin spread across his face.

"I remember when they burned that Ferguson boy. I helped go get him and let me tell you, that goddamn nigger fought like a treed coon. That's the last one they burnt. The federal courts done stopped all that now."

"When did they execute Ferguson?" I asked, touched by morbid curiosity.

The guard pushed a grease-stained straw hat back on his head, revealing a mop of curly red hair. He seemed almost friendly as he tried to recall.

"I don't remember exactly," he replied. "Back in '61, I think. Damn sure was. It was '61 'cause Jimmie Davis was governor — and Governor Davis didn't mess around none, especially with niggers like Ferguson. Ain't no way he was going to let one rape a white woman and get away with it. He was a good man. He sang that song, 'You Are My Sunshine.' Yes, sir, he was a damn good governor — and a religious man, too."

Ferguson's victim was black. The guard's mistake was a natural outgrowth of the racism that was still rampant in the South in the 1960s. Blacks never got the death penalty for raping blacks. Ferguson had to murder his black rape victim to join the condemned on the Row. Jessie James Ferguson went to the electric chair on June 9, 1961, for the rape and murder of Joyce Marie Thibodeaux, an eleven-year-old girl from Opelousas. Ferguson was the nineteenth man Jimmie Davis sent to the chair during his two four-year terms as Louisiana's governor.

"Fuck Jimmie Davis," I said.

The guard's face turned a dark shade of red as he choked down a primitive fury. He wanted to hit me, curse me — anything to satisfy the need for violence rooted in his backwoods southern soul. Angola was his natural habitat. It was a prison jungle where "goon squads" entered cells at midnight to catch inmates asleep and then beat them senseless. It was the necessary mind-set for service in a southern prison.

"Sam, get in here," the guard shouted at a black convict guard sitting in an adjoining room.

"Yes, suh, boss," Sam said as he scurried into the Security Office. Inmates called convict guards "khaki-backs" because they wore khakis.

The system of using inmates as guards was established in 1917 after Warden Henry L. Fugua fired most of the prison guards and replaced them with the most "trusted" inmates. The convict guards, however, ultimately proved to be as brutal and murderous as the whip-toting free guards they replaced.

Sam was the epitome of a convict guard. Without hesitation, he would beat, maim, or even kill another inmate if told to do so.

"Go tell Mr. Jewell to come get Sinclair," the guard said, gesturing toward me with obvious contempt.

Jewell walked into the office a few minutes later. He was death row's main guard. A short, stolid, fat man, Jewell's life was an unending chronicle of trouble and sorrow. He hated Yankees, liberals, and Russians; and loved butter beans, mustard greens, and cornbread. He alternately cajoled and threatened death row inmates in a tireless effort to gain respect for his authority. He was famous among the condemned for his haranguing speeches, shameless ass-scratching, and fits of Prince Albert coughing. We were his wayward children and he our pathetic patriarch. He listened to our litany of complaints and demands, waiting only for the first opening to launch into his latest encounter with sorrow and suffering.

As keeper of the condemned, Jewell's life was continuously menaced by the black horror of death. The "Row" nonetheless made him feel at home. He was at peace among its condemned denizens.

"Mr. Jewell, take this smart-ass sonuvabitch and stick him in one of those cages," the guard said.

Jewell didn't respond to the sarcasm. He simply touched my elbow, escorting me out of the office.

"Sinclair, I hope I'm here when they burn your sorry ass," the guard yelled out behind me.

Jewell led me down a long hallway through two sets of barred doors. Inmates lounging in the hallway lowered their voices as we passed.

"Another one for the Row," one whispered.

They spoke about death row as though it were a secret, hidden world within the prison. The Row held as much mystery for them as the earth's core.

Jewell motioned me through a solid steel door into a small lobby overlooking two fifteen-cell tiers. He and Sam watched over the condemned from the lobby. Jewell opened the barred door to A-Tier. The crescendo of noise staggered me. Radios and television sets blared at full volume while inmates engaged in shouted conversation over the maddening opera of noise.

The loud clang of the tier door stifled the din, creating an eerie silence. Hands holding pieces of mirrors glued to strips of cardboard, known as "jiggers," were thrust through the bars of most of the cells so the inmates could see out. A stranger was entering their midst.

"Who's dat, man?" a guttural voice whispered.

"Some white boy," another replied.

I was placed in a dirty gray-and-white cell, the first on the tier. It was considered "jinxed." Ferguson had occupied it. A yellow index card with my name, crime, and date of sentence hung above the door. No one knew why or when the practice of putting the cards above the doors began. It was one of the Row's myriad mysteries.

I stared at the solid concrete cell. It had a worn, depressed look of finality about it. A steel table and bench were bolted to the left wall facing the back of the cell. A steel bunk, with a dirty, lumpy cotton mattress, was bolted to the right wall. A white commode stood in the left rear corner. Rust had stained its bowl a harsh brown. A sink was located in the middle of the back wall with a push button for cold water. The cell was six feet wide, eight feet deep, and ten feet high. The bottom half was painted a dull gray; the top half, white.

Death row cells were infested with rats and roaches. After

heavy rains, rats often crawled into the pipes and came up through the commodes. They emerged into toilets while condemned inmates were using them. Some were so afraid of the rats they refused to sit down on the toilets, opting instead to squat over the edges when nature called.

I stepped through the door. It slammed shut on outside experiences. I was alone, suspended somewhere between heaven and hell. A brutal feeling of helplessness came over me. The thick walls closed in on me. I gripped the cell bars and stared out across the prison yard at the dense trees rooted in the hillside; a scene that became a fixture in my brain. For six years it was my only view into reality from the madhouse to which I had been consigned.

"Say, man, what's your name?" a voice called out.

"Sinclair," I said after a few moments, irritated at the intrusion.

"Oh, yeah," a voice exclaimed. "That's the white dude who killed that man in Baton Rouge."

Someone whistled.

"Hell, who was that dude anyhow," someone said. "The way those papers played your case up it was like you killed the mayor. He must have been more than a store clerk."

"Leave the man alone, Shiphead," another voice interjected. "The man's got to get his shit straightened out down there, you noisy fucker. You got about as much respect as a fart."

"That's alright, Daryl," Shiphead hollered above the tier laughter. "My momma ain't never slept with no gorilla."

Every man who came to the Row had to grapple with that first terrible day. It was a day that reduced him to utter and absolute insignificance.

6

M Y MIND REBELLED AT THE HORROR of being caged
in a death row cell waiting to make the trip to the electric chair. I
reached for a ready source of relief: state-dispensed narcotics. I had
never taken drugs before. An occasional beer or drink of hard
liquor, as long as it resembled a lemonade (like a Tom Collins), were
the only mind-altering substances I had ever consumed. Drugs
were not part of the rural southern culture in the '50s and early '60s.
While our honky-tonks and pool halls had their share of drunks,
narcotics were major league vices confined to the big cities.

The Row introduced me to drugs. As a means of pacifying condemned inmates, prison officials allowed us to order pills from the
dispensary as casually as ordering coffee at a truck stop. I took a
dozen to two dozen downers a day — redbirds, yellowjackets, Mil-
towns, Darvons, and phenobarbitals. I got two redbirds, two Darvons,
and four phenobarbitals every day from the dispensary and hustled
the others from inmates who didn't want their "issue." I swallowed
everything I could to escape the madness of my caged existence.

I lived in a stupor, emerging only to take more pills. Under their influence, I could avoid thoughts of spending years in a cell and an eventual trip to the chair. I swallowed a steady diet of pills for months, feeling threatened only when their effects wore off. Then I took more pills until I drifted into welcome oblivion. I only thought about my death sentence while I waited for the pills to take effect.

The pills allowed me to face my death sentence in stages. They let me adjust gradually to the idea of my own execution. Given time, the human mind can accept almost any horror. Uninterrupted thoughts of my fate (and there was no way I could think of anything else) might have driven me insane.

The pills were the only humane aspect of the Row. But they were not provided for the good of death row inmates. They were simply a cost-effective means of pacification. We were easier to manage on a daily basis if we were drugged.

The pills nurtured our illusions. We were a meager and wretched lot suckling unrealistic hopes and expectations: a "new trial" was always coming next month; a sentence would be overturned; a new lawyer would present a better case; the "real" culprit would confess.

Our pasts were scarred by child abuse, incest, alcoholism, and poverty. For most of us, crime was a natural social response. We created elaborate justifications for our wrongs, often transforming them into perverse forms of self-righteousness. Our only dignity, if we had any, lay with the moralists crusading against the death penalty. We depended on them for even that slice of humanity.

The nature of the Row forced me to direct an eye inward to escape its perversity. I seldom spoke to anyone. A brooding silence possessed me like an ancient ghost. I went six months without uttering a single word. I just stuck my hand through the bars and pills were passed down the line to me. Everyone knew the drugs were feeding madness but no one dared defy the only mutual pact we had on the Row — each man had a right to go to hell in his own way. While the pills insulated me from the noise and the cell madness, the cost was high. My sanity hung in the balance.

Early one summer evening in 1968, the cord of self-destruction snapped. I had been living in a drug-induced stupor for nearly eighteen months. That morning, I had taken more pills than usual. I woke up, bent over my toilet, repeatedly pressing the flush button, the sound of the spinning water enticing me into the vortex.

I lurched to my feet and stumbled to the bars of my cell. An observer would have seen a freakish sight. My hair hung in long greasy streaks, matted with body oil. My eyes were sunk deep in their sockets, glazed by an emotional vacancy. I was skin and bones: less than 130 pounds of flesh hung slackly on my six-foot frame. I gripped the bars until my hands turned white. I knew I was at the end of my rope. Mustering all my mental energy, I telegraphed a prayer for salvation out across the night. My entire being focused on it. Somewhere out there, somehow, there had to be a reason for living.

The prayer broke the hold of madness on my brain. I didn't count it as a religious experience. By then, I had been an agnostic for years. But I was desperate. I realized the pills were killing me. A need to return to reality seized me. I was tired of fleeing, tired of trying to escape the inevitable.

My thoughts began to take focus. The disparate pieces and elements floating in my brain gradually coalesced into a whole. I was able to see what I had become. The glimpses of self, seen through a drug stupor over the previous months, rose up to disgust me.

I resolved to take no more pills. Swede, one of the few intellectuals on the Row, noticed almost immediately.

"Welcome back," he said one day, commenting on my sobriety.

He gave me a large box of books to occupy my mind. It contained works on philosophy and psychology and a Great Books series. I had never read a book except for comics and classroom texts. Before being expelled from school in the tenth grade, I had been on the honor roll in my freshman year. But I lost interest in school after a series of upsets at home. By then, Mother and John had been divorced for six years. At fifteen, I had just broken up with a teenage girlfriend. She was my first love. I would grieve over the breakup for the next ten years.

It was 1960. John Kennedy was still our prophet of hope, a symbol of social awakening. My girlfriend, Glenda, came from an upper-class family — her father was a downtown executive; her mother, a member of the bridge club; and her older sister, a beauty queen. They lived in a beautiful home several blocks from our apartment complex. I met Glenda one afternoon when a friend invited me to play badminton at his house.

Within weeks Glenda and I were going steady. Her parents accepted me despite the difference in our social backgrounds. They often invited me to their home for dinner.

"You should take up the piano, young man," Glenda's father told me one evening at the dinner table. "You have the fingers of a pianist — or a gambler. But don't ever gamble, son. There are too many safe bets in the world."

"I wanna play in the major leagues," I said. "I wanna play for the New York Yankees — the greatest team in baseball."

"It's good that you have dreams," he said. "They will keep you alive when nothing else will."

But there was a hitch in my dreams. Glenda hated Ouachita High School, the working-class school I attended as a freshman. She wanted me to enroll in Neville High School, a middle- and upper-class school. I resisted the suggestion. We argued. She jumped up, threw my ring on the ground, and stormed off. We never spoke another word.

Anger soon turned to heartache. I sat for hours staring at the phone, longing to call Glenda. I was too proud to pick up the receiver. Many times I have wondered what I might have become if I had enrolled at Neville. A lawyer? A doctor? A baseball player?

I sorted through the books Swede gave me, reading passages here and there. As I rummaged through the box, I picked one out to read. It was an experiment that gave way to a passion.

The book was Thoreau's *Walden Pond.* I went on to devour all of Swede's books: works by Plato, Aristotle, Kierkegaard, Camus, Sartre, Malraux, Freud, Fromm, Adler, Skinner, and Tolstoy. Often, the words were long, with many syllables. I tried to sound them out in my head before looking them up in the dictionary. Sometimes, I had to look up every word in a sentence before I could string them together and reconstruct the thought.

I developed a scattergun intellect as pieces of information and enlightened thinking filled in the holes of my underdeveloped world. I bought a 1922 Underwood typewriter for a carton of cigarettes and taught myself to type. The Texas Society to Abolish Capital Punishment donated a set of Wharton's Criminal Evidence law books to me. Doggedly, I schooled myself in law.

I established a schedule for my studies and stuck to it without fail. It was the first attempt I had ever made to control my life. I developed an almost superstitious belief that strict adherence to my routine was the secret to survival.

Experience had taught me that a lack of self-control produced dire consequences. Before the Row, I had lived aimlessly, without goals or ambition. It ruined my life. My first year on the Row was no different. Drugs were my escape. I conquered that habit through determination and a plan and the rigid schedule that I established. At that point in my life, I was like a laboratory flatworm learning a simple behavior to avoid a painful stimulus. I embraced self-discipline for the first time and became a fanatic devotee.

Intellectual activity born of self-discipline, I found, held the key to coping with the psychological brutality of a death cage. While the pills had been a destructive way out, books proved to be the best escape. I could forget the past and reach beyond the moment. I could go anywhere in my mind, or be anyone I chose. A man who has nothing assumes the right to everything. I would stand at the bars of my cell at night, utterly focused on my dreams.

The power to dream helped me through the worst of my prison years, on death row and after. I learned to lock my mind on living, to believe that I had a future. There was nothing about my past I wanted to remember. Without a future, there would have been no purpose to living.

The Row taught me patience. It burned away my habit of recklessness when I grew frustrated in the pursuit of a goal. I learned that dreams can be realized through self-discipline, fueled by a desire to reach beyond the moment. The trick lay in believing that I could actually reach my goals. I made believe that obstacles were temporary, dreams permanent. They became an integral part of my survival. While pragmatism now rules my life, it has never overruled my dreams. In the end, my dreams proved to be stronger than the realities of death row.

7

I HAD NEVER THOUGHT MUCH about the electric chair until I was sentenced to death. After that, white terror imagining it frequently seized my brain. I endeavored to learn as much about the chair and its sordid history as I could while I awaited its fatal embrace.

I imagined it poised like a cobra in the death chamber, utterly lethal. There was something innately evil about the worn leather restraining straps that choked off the last struggling efforts to live. The beast of death was fed by a generator that sent powerful surges of electricity through the body of a condemned man, often bringing his blood to a boil. An exhaust fan sucked out the stench of burnt flesh triggered by an executioner who remained hidden, masked by official secrecy.

All instruments of death strike terror in the minds of the condemned. The level of my fear increased as I read the history of the electric chair. Experts say that death in the chair is painless, that the condemned man never knows what hit him. But the history of the chair says otherwise.

The first condemned man to be electrocuted was William Francis Kemmler. He was executed on August 6, 1890, at the Auburn State Prison in New York for the hatchet murder of his girlfriend. New York was the first state to adopt electrocution as a means of carrying out the death penalty. It came about after a group of lawmakers witnessed a fat man's head ripped off at a public hanging.

New York officials, however, questioned whether the electric chair would work. Prior to strapping Kemmler in the chair, prison officials executed a cat, dog, horse, and finally an orangutan (the size of a small human) before they became convinced that the chair would kill a human being.

These precautions notwithstanding, the Kemmler execution was ghastly. The chair began to rock when the first surge of electricity hit Kemmler, causing his body to lurch against the straps. Smoke rose from the condemned man's burning body as it turned brilliant red when an extra large voltage of electricity was administered. An autopsy revealed that the four minutes Kemmler spent in the chair baked his brain "hard" and turned his blood "to charcoal."

One of the most bizarre executions in history involved Louisiana's electric chair. The malfunctioning device had to be used twice to kill an eighteen-year-old black man named Willie Francis. Francis was sentenced to die for the 1944 murder of a popular white druggist in New Iberia, Louisiana. The chair was transported around the state in the back of a prison truck when needed for an execution after the Louisiana legislature had changed the state's method of execution from hanging to electrocution in 1940. It would later be moved permanently to Angola, where it was installed in a shack next to the Red Hats, the prison's most infamous cell block.

In his well-researched book *Death and the Supreme Court*, Barrett Prettyman said Willie's trial lasted three days. Since there were no witnesses to the crime and the FBI had lost the murder weapon, the state's case was based on Willie's two confessions. No motion for change of venue was filed, no transcript of the trial was kept, and no appeal of the conviction was taken. In less than a week, Willie was convicted and sentenced to death. Five months later Governor Jimmie Davis signed Willie's death warrant, setting the date of execution for Friday, May 3, 1946, between the hours of noon and 3:00 P.M.

On the morning of the execution, the heavy chair and its large panel of wires and switches were unloaded from the prison truck. It was taken inside the courthouse and placed in the middle of a room. It was so heavy it didn't have to be screwed to the floor. The prison electrician attached the wires of the chair to the panel and then attached wires from the panel to the truck's generator. He set the voltage at twenty-five hundred volts and ran the generator for about five minutes to make sure it was working properly.

At high noon the sheriff and his deputies opened Willie's cell and told him it was time to go, ending his visit with a local Catholic priest. Willie rose slowly to his feet, gazing at the priest, and walked hesitantly to the death chamber. A dozen men were present to witness his execution when Willie entered the death chamber accompanied by the priest.

Hypnotically, Willie stared at the chair, ignoring the witnesses. Two deputies quickly led him to the chair, strapping him firmly in it. A prison captain placed a piece of gauze dripping in salt water around Willie's head to help conduct the electrical current. The initial charge always dried the gauze and burned the condemned man's head. Electrodes were attached to Willie's left leg and to his head.

The prison captain then walked to the window and told the inmate electrician he was ready. The generator was running and the gauges checked out okay so he nodded approvingly. The priest stepped back as the sheriff placed a black hood over Willie's head. While it covered his eyes, Willie's mouth was free to breathe through a slit cut in the cloth. The sheriff gave the signal of death to the captain, who checked his instrument panel one last time and whispered in a quiet voice, "Goodbye, Willie."

With a quick downward motion, the guard threw the switch. Prettyman describes what happened next:

> But even those who were witnessing their first execution knew something was wrong. Willie's body, though arched, was obviously not at the point of death. Captain Foster, all in one motion, frantically threw the switch off and then on again. Those closest to Willie heard him strain out the

49

words, "Let me breathe." Captain Foster yelled out the window at Venezia to give him more juice. The startled Venezia yelled back that he was supplying all the electricity he had. His gauge showed that it was being generated and he could not understand what the difficulty was.

Only a few seconds had passed, and yet the horrified spectators inside the jail felt as if they had stood transfixed for minutes. As they stared at Willie they saw his lips puff and swell like those of a pilot undergoing the stress of supersonic speeds. His body tensed and stretched in such catatonic movements that the chair, which had not been anchored to the floor, suddenly shifted, sliding a fraction of an inch along the floor.

"Take it off. Let me breathe."

The agonizing words spewed out from between the puffed lips. They roused Sheriff Resweber into action. He signaled to Captain Foster, who by now knew that his apparatus would not kill Willie Francis. He threw the switch back into an upright position. All in all, about two minutes had now passed since the switch had been thrown, and some of those present realized they had hardly breathed during the entire procedure.

During a post-execution examination, Willie said only that the electricity had "tickled" him. Governor Davis decided to give Willie a reprieve from an immediate second electrocution attempt. The case captured the nation's imagination. Willie's story appeared in newspapers across the country. Letters poured into the governor's office asking that Willie's life be spared. The case was appealed all the way to the United States Supreme Court, only to have the court rule that putting a man in the electric chair twice was not cruel and unusual punishment.

A new date, Friday, May 9, 1947, was set for the second execution attempt. All last-minute appeals to the governor and the courts proved futile. Willie was walked through the entire death ritual a second time. The second switch was thrown one year and six days after the first. This time the gauze on Willie's head dried up and the burns appeared where they should have the first time. This time, the coffin was used and the morbid crowd outside the courthouse was not disappointed. This time the chair killed Willie Francis.

Death awaits everyone. Execution is a fate reserved for a select few. Most people contemplate death in the abstract, hoping only that it will come painlessly and quickly. But it is quite another matter to think about your own death being carried out in a specific manner on an exact day at a precise hour. The thought made each of us on death row conjure up countless Kemmler/Francis terrors about what it would be like.

Men, of course, react differently to being put to death by the state. In his book *Sentenced to Die*, Stephen Gettingher described one Texas condemned inmate who walked down the hallway to the death chamber with his eyes closed singing "Swing Low, Sweet Chariot." He kept singing as he was strapped into the chair, as the hood was lowered over his face, and until the first surge of electricity tore through the song in mid-verse. Some men fight to the bitter end, kicking and screaming all the way to their deaths. That was the case with Aaron Mitchell, who was dragged, babbling and moaning, into California's gas chamber in 1967. He was still crying when the cyanide pellets were dropped into the acid beneath him. Then there was the Florida inmate who reportedly rushed up to the electric chair and kissed it before sitting in it.

When an execution drew near on Louisiana's death row, the condemned man was transferred to the infamous maximum-security cell block known as the Red Hats. The Red Hats was a "super punishment" cell block built in 1933. It was a one-story building at Camp E with thirty cells. Each one was six feet long and three feet wide with a solid-sheet steel door. Inmates had one twelve-inch square window for ventilation. They wore felt hats dipped in red enamel. Each cell had a steel bunk with no mattress and a bucket for a toilet. Red Hat inmates worked the fields and ate leftovers from other prisoners. The food was dumped in buckets and taken to the cell block in wheelbarrows.

The long rectangular building in which the Red Hats was located sat alone in a sugarcane field near the prison's sugar mill. This was Angola's torture chamber in the 1940s and '50s. The state's most notorious gangster, a killer named Charlie Fraizer, was welded into a Red Hats cell for seven years after killing a warden during an escape in 1933. It was the end of the line for unruly, rebellious prisoners. Inmates sent to the Red Hats were brutally beaten by convict guards going in, beaten on a daily basis, and beaten coming out. They were fed bread and water twice a day. Some inmates were broken; others died from abuse and neglect. Some sent to the Red Hats during that era simply disappeared, never to be seen or heard from again.

It was fitting that Angola's electric chair, Old Sparky, sat in a small building adjacent to the Red Hats. The chair had claimed the lives of sixty-six men and one woman by the time I reached death row. The inmates being hauled to work in tractor-pulled trailers looked upon the Red Hats and the raggedy shack sitting next to it with awe and terror. Every Angola inmate knew a Red Hats or Old Sparky story. Most were embellished, but virtually all were based on fact.

A Red Hats holding cell was the condemned man's final dwelling place. As he felt its walls closing in on him, he could hear an inmate electrician testing the electric chair, letting its powerful generator hum for hours before the actual electrocution. It was not easy for the condemned man to imagine that a filthy cell was the last thing he would know. When he walked out of the cell, he left life behind.

Each man had to decide how he would go — fighting to the bitter end or walking on his own to the chair. The warden would ask him how it was going to be. Most realized they were going to be put in the chair one way or another. The condemned man was helpless. When death is imposed by strict command, everything is beyond the condemned man's control. In those final moments of life, "the woe of his life washed up on him at all he had not done, and all that he would never do, and he wept the harsh tears of a full-grown man," as Ford Madox Ford once said.

In the final analysis, it didn't matter how those sixty-seven condemned people chose to die. Die they would. Prison officials made sure of it, even if they had to hold the condemned man down while they packed cotton in his rectum and nose. It was part of the ritual — a nightmare of waste and loss. It was a perverse process that forced a man to cooperate in his own demise as part of what Gettingher called the "etiquette of dying."

For six years I waited to feel the chair's leather straps cut into my flesh and my heart explode as the powerful current of electricity ripped through it. The chair's dark menace became my cell mate, shadowing my thoughts and invading my dreams. Those thoughts became a cruelty far worse than the reality facing me in the chair.

8

MOST HUMAN BEINGS crave contact with others. Each of us, no matter how deranged, had that need. Our social interactions, though pathetic substitutes for normal human contact, were all we had, except for an occasional visit from a family member or attorney.

Life on the Row was episodic. It lurched from one insane event to the next. They might be connected in time or separated by days. Whenever they occurred, they were proof of the insanity that death row fostered in its residents. But they provided the only relief from its stultifying monotony.

Caged in social isolation in eight-by-ten-foot cubicles for years, we were tortured by feelings of utter insignificance. A starvation far worse than physical hunger gnawed at our souls. Our attempts to assuage it were met with tragic consequences.

With the pill madness gone from my brain, and my studies well under way, I became curious about those on the Row with me. Like a man whose eyes have become accustomed to the dark, I began to perceive the outlines of the personalities locked up around me. Over time, I knew some well. Others have slipped from memory.

I remember Swede, Brodie, Crook, Eddie, Bobby, and Emmitt the best. Eddie and Crook went insane. Brodie, I remember for his stumbling ignorance; Swede for his intellect; and Emmitt and Bobby because they were murdered on the Row. Each touched my life, changing it irrevocably. Some were my friends, others not, although friendship had a different meaning on the Row. Life was too fragile to get close to anyone.

Swede was gifted with a genius IQ. He stood six foot four and weighed more than three hundred pounds. He had the death sentence for killing a fellow inmate with a knife in 1965. The prisoner was the second he had murdered in ten years behind bars. For the most part, Swede was a loner. He rarely displayed love, hate, happiness, or sadness.

Swede was also known as the "naked man" of the Row. Because we had to wash our own clothing in toilets or the shower, Swede never wore clothes. He shocked the newly appointed director of corrections, David Wade, who had a disciplined military background, during the director's first tour of the Row. Passing the huge man's cell, Wade saw Swede naked inside. He ordered him to get dressed. Swede nonchalantly said he would wear clothes only when the director provided regular laundry service.

"Until then," Swede said, "you can kiss my naked ass."

The director never came to the Row again.

Brodie, on the other hand, was a gap-toothed bumpkin sentenced to death for the 1958 murder of an old man during a twenty-dollar robbery. He was one of the first men placed on death row after it was established at the state penitentiary. A decade of cell confinement and two trips to the mental institution with electroshock therapy (and mind-altering drugs) caused him to move with a dull, confused gait. His Neanderthal features made him a prime example of Cesare Becarria's "criminal man."

He once avoided a date with the electric chair by talking to and petting a dog that he claimed accompanied the psychiatrist sent to examine him to make sure he was fit to be executed. The doctor was convinced that Brodie saw the dog.

Crook was living proof that every corner of the world has its lowest wretch. He was pressed out of a prostitute's womb in one of New York's worst rat-infested alleys. By some sardonic quirk of fate, he survived — perhaps because a unique role in Louisiana's capital punishment history awaited him. He was the only white man on the Row convicted of rape. To achieve that historic distinction, he had to viciously beat his white victim beyond recognition and tear open her rectum while sodomizing her.

Crook was first introduced to rape at the age of eight when his uncle threw him on a dirty floor in a Bronx housing project and brutally raped him. That kind of childhood violence made death row an inevitable consequence. He became an addict of sexual abuse. But none of the death row inmates wanted to sexually abuse him. There were no monsters willing to feed his insatiable need to be abused. The tolerance, even acceptance, he found on the Row drove him mad.

One day he charged out of the shower and ran naked up and down the hallway, screaming in a language only he understood. The usual volume of noise on the tier shut down like a blaring radio suddenly unplugged from the wall. No one said anything as Crook ran babbling past our cells.

"I can't take it anymore," he screamed. "Please deliver me from this hell. I need a dick, oh merciful God. Please give me a dick."

Jewell walked up to the tier door.

"What's gotten into you, Crook?" he whined. "You gone crazy, boy? You better get back in that cell, and I mean right now."

Crook ignored Jewell as he continued to run up and down the hall screaming for a dick, occasionally skipping in the air like Tiny Tim.

"C'mon, Crook," Jewell pleaded, "get your ass back in that cell . . . I ain't never done you nothing, boy. Why you gonna pull this shit off on my shift?"

"I once made it with a whole tank of men," Crook screamed. "Sucked every dick in that fucking jail."

Jewell slammed his keys against the tier door.

"Goddamnit, Crook, I'm not gonna tell you again to cut this crazy shit out and get back in that cell. I'm gonna get the goon squad and put your ass in that hole upstairs. You better get some sense in that crazy queer head."

Suddenly Crook stopped running. He walked slowly to his cell. He fumbled with a razor and removed a double-edged blade. He backed against the wall in front of his cell where we could see him, staring at the razor blade in his hand. A half-smile played on his lips. One could almost sense the perverse joy of self-destruction working in his scrambled brain.

"Don't do it, Crook," a voice said, breaking the strange silence.

"Hell, let him do it," said another.

"Let's see some blood," Brodie muttered, waking up in the middle of the human tragedy.

Crook acted as though he didn't hear us. Our eyes focused on him like the eyes of a circus crowd on the man on the trapeze wire. An insane little pervert had become the center of our attention. We anticipated the moment the little bastard would slip and fall. With brutal swiftness, he began slashing himself with the razor blade. His bony body was soon covered with blood. He sank to the floor, staring vacantly at his mutilated body.

The sound of the tier door being kicked opened shattered the death-like stillness. The goon squad charged down the tier toward him.

"Goddamn, what have you done, Crook?" Jewell whined. "Why didn't you wait to do this dumb shit on the other shift? I never done you nothing, you crazy faggot."

Crook was carted off the tier like a sack of garbage. Sam punched him in the face as he was hauled away. He was transferred to the state's mental hospital. He would later die of a heart attack.

Eddie was another that the Row pushed over the edge. He was the one man on the Row whom I believe was innocent. I came to that conclusion after long conversations with him about his case. He was one of the dozen black men on the Row convicted of raping white women. Between 1930 and 1968, 455 men were executed in America for rape — 405 of them were blacks and most were put to death in southern death chambers.

Eddie was arrested in a rural North Louisiana parish after being chased to the ground by baying bloodhounds. He learned more about physical pain and psychological torture over the next three days than he ever imagined possible. The sheriff wanted a confession, the key to a capital conviction prior to Miranda. But Eddie would not give him one. Late one night the sheriff went to his cell.

"I'm gonna talk straight to you, nigger," he said, leaning against the cell door. He pulled a .357 magnum with a dark-stained handle from his hand-tooled holster.

"I ain't done nothing, Sheriff, I swear to Jesus I ain't done nothing," Eddie pleaded.

"I know you ain't, boy," he said. "That white bitch let you fuck her, I know the woman. She's been sleeping with local coloreds for years. But that ain't what we're dealing with here, boy. You got caught with her, and that's what we're dealing with. You should've kept that black snake in your pants. I have to uphold the law, and the law in this parish says that when a nigger fucks a white woman, it's rape. That's the law."

Eddie stared at his broken left hand. He understood the law — the white man in the police uniform had the power to arrest, abuse, and even kill him without good cause.

"But I ain't done nothing, Sheriff."

The sheriff was visibly angry.

"Goddamnit, nigger, what do I have to do to make you understand. It doesn't make any difference that you ain't done nothing. Now, I've been easy on you. You ain't got nothing but a good ass-whipping. I could've let Boss Honeycutt and his boys have you. But I don't want those federal people in my parish. So I expect some consideration."

The sheriff reached into his shirt pocket and handed the typed confession to Eddie.

"Now, nigger," he said, pointing the .357 directly at Eddie's face, "you gonna sign that goddamn paper or I'm gonna blow your fucking brains all over that wall."

Eddie looked directly into the sheriff's eyes. He had not the slightest doubt that the sheriff would pull the trigger.

"I need a pencil," he said wearily.

Two months later Eddie was sitting on the Row. The swiftness of southern justice stunned him. He had known hoboes, drunks, and vagrants in county jails but he had never been around murderers and rapists. He could not bear to think of being locked in a death cell, labeled a rapist, for the indiscretion of having sex with a white woman.

Ten years passed before Eddie realized they were forever gone. His eyes lost that wanderer's sparkle and the muscled frame he had developed through hard work shrank from neglect. A man who could once pick four hundred pounds of cotton a day had disintegrated into a shrunken shell. He nurtured a brutal shame and self-hatred for what he had become. He constantly cursed black pride and masculinity, growing trends in the late 1960s.

"You gotta razor blade, Ronald?" Eddie asked his next-cell neighbor one night after television had signed off the air.

"Yeah, man. You shaving this time of night?"

"Yeah, I wanna shave."

Ronald passed Eddie a razor blade. A few minutes passed.

"Call for the Man, Ronald," Eddie called out in a choked voice. "I just cut off my dick."

"You did what!"

Ronald stuck his jigger through the bars so he could see into Eddie's cell.

"Jesus Christ," he screamed. "Look at the blood. This crazy nigger cut off his dick. I mean off."

Eddie was sent to a free world hospital where doctors managed to save part of his penis. He was later transferred to the same mental hospital with Crook. The following day, the warden sent a psychiatrist to the Row to interview any inmate who had a problem. Only a few agreed to talk to him.

Crook and Eddie ceased to be items of conversation the moment they left us. We returned to our monotonous routine as soon as they were gone. New voices soon replaced Crook and Eddie in their cells down the hall. But I can still hear them. They were the first men I knew who went insane.

9

EMMITT HENDERSON WAS AN OLD MAN who died because the prison system didn't care about him. His death had a lasting impact on me. It spawned a fervent desire within me to challenge the prison system. Theories of justice and equality had sprouted in my mind as a result of the reading and legal studies I was doing on the Row. But they were mere intellectual concepts. Emmitt's death gave them life. It put me on a collision course with the system, sending me down a road that would transform me into one of the most controversial and notorious inmate leaders at Angola.

Prior to his death, Emmitt Henderson precipitated a gradual change in my racial views. I had always accepted the southern tradition that blacks belonged in the back of the bus; that integration was a "communist conspiracy" designed to undermine the democratic values of white America. But I did not hate blacks the way I hated my father, John. I simply did not understand a language and customs that were different from mine. Understanding them had never been important. I knew how to fight "niggers." Louisiana's prison system taught me that.

Emmitt was the first black man I came to know as a human being. A twelve-year veteran of death row, Emmitt was its senior citizen — he was sixty years old when he died. A classic Uncle Tom, Emmitt's face always wore a mask of fear and docility. The mere presence of white authority evoked a broad, white-toothed grin. While that slavery-inherited behavior had never bothered me before, it infuriated me to know that a social system made it as natural to him as a bowel movement.

Emmitt was barely able to take care of his daily hygienic needs. He showered once a week, always wearing the same ragged tennis shoes and tattered underwear. He received one piece of mail each year — a Christmas card from a court-appointed attorney who remembered his name but did little about his appeal.

Though most of the black inmates found Emmitt's Step-'n-Fetchit behavior irritating when he came, hat in hand, to borrow the makings for a cup of coffee or a pack of tobacco, they always accorded him respect. Everyone on the Row liked him. We respected his age and the depth of his suffering. We knew that he had committed only one crime in his life. He raped the wife of a white farmer who employed him. He had spent a lifetime looking at white women through veiled eyes, and for reasons only understood by him, he reached a point where he could not endure it anymore. Perhaps, as Eldridge Cleaver suggested in *Soul on Ice*, the rape of a white woman was the only rebellion rooted in his soul.

Two months before Emmitt's death, I embarked upon a personal crusade to teach him how to read and write. I gave up one of my fifteen-minute shower periods each week to sit in front of his cell teaching him how to read. I began with the alphabet and turned to words familiar to our environment: cell, bars, soap, comb, pencil, etc. I made him spell the words over and over, having him write each new word twenty-five times on a piece of paper for the next session. He not only began to understand but he developed a desire to learn. I found him each lesson day sitting on the floor, pencil and paper in hand, waiting to begin. He would spend most of his own shower period sitting in front of my cell asking me to go over difficult words with him. He would occasionally send me a piece of paper with new words written on it. I would grade the paper, always giving him an A. He kept those papers in a neat folder, protecting them as a lawyer would important documents.

Emmitt told me about his daughter who was kicked in the head by an ornery plow mule when she was twelve years old. Holding the girl in his arms, he ran to a nearby sharecropper's house to borrow a truck. The white farmer was in the fields. His wife refused to let Emmitt use the truck. Their teenage son forced him off their property with a shotgun. Emmitt walked the five miles to town, knowing his daughter would die in his arms before he reached the doctor's office.

"Why didn't you fight?" I asked.

A mixture of fear and amazement flickered in his eyes.

"A nigger can't fight a white man."

"Why not?"

"Do you fight that man with the keys?"

Death began stalking Emmitt early one Friday morning. He called Jewell to his cell, complaining of persistent stomach cramps.

"Mr. Jewell," he said in his usual servile tone, "I need to go to the hospital. I got cramps in my stomach."

Jewell removed a finger from his nose and wiped it across his pants leg.

"I don't know what to tell you, Emmitt," he replied. "We ain't got a patrol van to take you. So you'll just have to wait till Monday."

The cramps became more frequent and severe. It was obvious that Emmitt was seriously ill. He tried unsuccessfully throughout the night to get a guard to take him to the hospital. He was given the same excuses — there was no patrol van to drive him the two miles to the prison hospital.

By Saturday morning, Emmitt was coughing up blood. We began shaking our cell doors to get Jewell's attention.

"What's wrong with you, old thing," Jewell said as he sauntered up to Emmitt's cell.

Barely able to speak, Emmitt whispered his complaint to Jewell.

"Godammit, Emmitt, I told you that you gotta wait till Monday," Jewell said as he rolled a Prince Albert cigarette. "There's nothing I can do. They just don't have a patrol van on weekends.

The bastards tore them up. The state spends good money for those trucks and khaki-backs tear them up as fast as they get them."

"Shut the fuck up, Jewell," a voice called out. "Nobody wants to hear your country-ass shit. The man's sick."

"That's all right. I try to treat you all right, but the hell with you. I ain't doing nothing for none of you."

Jewell stormed off the tier in a self-righteous huff. Despite our repeated calls for assistance, he sat at his desk reading a newspaper and watching Sam shell butter beans. When the next shift came on duty, the guard called the hospital for medical assistance. The hospital sent an untrained inmate nurse who gave Emmitt a laxative.

Sunday morning was one of our three weekly shower periods. When my turn for a shower came, I went directly to Emmitt's cell. He was dying. I could sense it. A man develops a nose for death in prison. Emmitt lay in his own dried waste, body partially covered with filthy, bloodstained sheets, his eyes half-opened. He didn't even recognize me. I walked to the front of the tier. I would not let him die without a fight.

"Jewell, come here!" I shouted.

Jewell slowly sauntered up to the barred door.

"What you want, Sinclair?"

"Emmitt's dying," I said, unable to conceal my disrespect.

"So what you want to do?"

"Send the man to the hospital."

"Can't — we ain't got a patrol." Jewell removed a toothpick from his mouth. "Besides, you all got smart with me yesterday. I don't care what happens to any of you."

"Jewell, so help me God, if that old man dies, I'll sue you in every fucking court I can drag you through."

Fear registered in his eyes. My reputation as a jailhouse lawyer was just beginning to take hold and Jewell was a coward. He didn't want to be named in a lawsuit; it would mean questions and explanations. He liked to keep things simple.

"Well, I'll see what I can do," he said. "But you all better not curse me anymore."

I walked back to Emmitt's cell. His eyes stared with the vacancy of death. I stared back, relishing the fight against authority

63

that I knew was coming. In threatening Jewell, I was questioning the awesome power of prison guards to kill through neglect and indifference. I was genuinely incensed at the incredible inhumanity that Jewell had shown toward Emmitt. It was a by-product of his racism. Being black, Emmitt was as insignificant as the dried blood he lay in.

He was transferred to the prison hospital that Sunday morning and died a few hours later. We learned of his death when Sam removed his few shabby belongings from his cell. He was buried at Point Lookout, the prison's pauper cemetery.

"Emmitt's dead, Sinclair," Sam whispered as he passed my cell.

The news enraged me. I was determined to get revenge. Although I had threatened Jewell, I had never launched a legal broadside on the system that the guards represented. I drew a line in the sand. I wrote a letter to the local district attorney requesting a grand jury investigation of the circumstances surrounding Emmitt's death, particularly Jewell's negligence. Nothing was done about the request, but Jewell was removed from the Row. Death row inmates hailed it as a major victory.

In retaliation, the guards labeled me a troublemaker. They launched a campaign of harassment against me. My mail was censored, lost, or destroyed. Sam was warned not to smuggle me any more supplies for my legal work. (I had been buying them at outrageous black-market prices.) My visitors were strip-searched and my visiting time reduced. The campaign against me finally escalated beyond harassment.

A guard attacked me one day when I stepped out of my cell for a shower. As the cell door slid open, I stuck my head into the opening and reached back for the plastic "laundry bucket" filled with my sheets, which I had been soaking in bleach and water. The guard suddenly slammed the door shut on my head. The bucket absorbed most of the impact, preventing it from crushing my skull.

I screamed curses of pain at the guard, who kept working the door's controls, trying to jam it tighter on my head. Sam shoved the guard aside and released the controls. I fell face forward into the hallway, blood flowing from a deep cut on the side of my head. I was rushed to the prison hospital where I suffered for several days from blurred vision and partial hearing loss. The guard maintained it was an accident; he claimed he didn't know my head was caught in the door when he tried to jam it shut. Sam told me later that it had been a deliberate attempt to kill me.

Challenging the status quo in prison is the most threatening act a prisoner can commit. It quickly incurs official (and unofficial) wrath. For years, Angola's guards and inmates had carefully preserved a system of mutual cooperation through a quasi-official arrangement designed to share the prison's wealth and power. It was the basis for homosexual slavery and the drug trade that flourished throughout the prison. Guards and inmates would immediately turn against anyone who threatened it. An inmate who challenged the system would be cited for a disciplinary infraction. Inmate witnesses against him were not hard to find. Such is the perverse, criminal nature of prison.

Thus, prisoners who reported guards for murdering other prisoners were "lying." Those who reported inmates for raping weaker prisoners were "interfering." I would have been a "good" inmate had I let Emmitt's death go unchallenged. Questioning the authority that allowed it put me at odds with the system. And the system brooked no challenges.

10

I HAD COME TO ACCEPT that my cell on the Row would be my last stop in life. Powerful people wanted me dead. I knew them only as "they" — the word conjured up a thousand paranoid terrors. I reached for books and newspapers to keep the demons at bay. As long as I was reading — stuffing my mind with ideas and information — I could hold the level of terror down.

My cell held little else to distract me. I had few belongings. A radio sat on a shelf that I had made and glued to the wall with Elmer's Glue. A small black-and-white television set sat on a heavy cardboard box covered with a flowered towel. My trusty old Underwood typewriter, dictionary snug against it, sat on a small iron table bolted into the solid concrete wall. My clothes and books were neatly stored in cardboard boxes under my bunk. Everything had its place. A man who spends years in a cell learns to use efficiently every inch of the precious space allotted to him.

Keeping things clean was a never-ending task on the Row. I

washed my sheets, jeans, and shirts in the shower, always letting them soak in a bucket of soap-and-bleach water the night before. I strung a clothesline across my cell and dried these heavy items with an oscillating fan. I washed my underwear in the cell, either in the commode or the face bowl, depending on the water pressure. In the face bowl it was often reduced to a bare trickle.

I was transfixed by a newspaper headline one day. "Justice has been done," it read. It was a story about Billy Ray White, who had just been acquitted of a double murder by a jury in New Mexico, a crime that had earned him a spot on the FBI's Ten Most Wanted List prior to his capture. Billy Ray was the only real friend I had in the prison system. I first met him in a federal prison in 1964.

I had started doing time for the Feds earlier that year at a reformatory in El Reno, Oklahoma, for a Dyer Act conviction (taking a stolen car across state lines). Located about thirty miles from Oklahoma City on Route 66, then the nation's busiest cross-country highway, the reformatory housed eighteen- to twenty-five-year-old Chicano, Indian, black, and white inmates. They all formed racial cliques that were subdivided into "home boy" cliques.

Chicano inmates were divided into two major cliques — San Antonio and Houston. Indians were divided into a litany of cliques along tribe and reservation lines. Black divisions were simple — north and south cliques. White inmates had three cliques — Dallas, Houston, and Arkansas-Louisiana-Mississippi inmates.

While "home boy" cliques disliked each other, they quickly banded together when there was racial conflict. That was frequently the case in the federal prison system, especially at El Reno where race riots were frequent. Whites generally allied themselves with Chicanos. Indians and blacks fought together when "war" broke out.

I met Alexander in El Reno. He ran with the Dallas clique. He was a smooth-talking con who was a car salesman on the outside. Alexander was four years older than I was. He was serving a six-year term for a Dyer Act conviction. At nineteen, I was impressed with his tales of criminal exploits. He spoke of pimping whores from Kansas City to Oklahoma City and pulling armed robberies from Odessa to Mobile. He glorified the easy money and fast living of a thief's world. We became instant buddies — he was the fast talker and I the naive listener.

Being from the South, Alexander and I formed a natural bond. We belonged to a clique of "white boys" who had not come to terms with racial integration. We didn't talk to blacks or Indians. We only socialized with Mexicans on occasion. In El Reno, all ethnic groups had their own turf. Whites had the weight pile; blacks, the basketball court; Mexicans, the handball court; and Indians, the baseball diamonds.

El Reno had several serious racial brawls during the summer of 1964. Our clique was involved each time. One day, a member of our group was attacked by a group of blacks. Retaliation was not only expected, it was required. We armed ourselves with pipes and baseball bats and attacked a large group of blacks congregated on the basketball court. Guards broke up the melee with nightsticks and tear gas, but not before dozens of black and white inmates were seriously injured.

Racial strife and violence were woven into the fabric of the federal prison system in the mid-'60s. Every black/white altercation in El Reno resulted in violence. I became a clique leader because I was not afraid of the blacks or the guards. Prison authorities labeled me a ringleader.

As a matter of policy, the Federal Bureau of Prisons transferred problem inmates to institutions with a higher grade of security. Alexander and I were transferred to a prison in Terre Haute, Indiana. It had solid-door cells on double tiers. There was one trusty dorm. It housed organized crime figures. Everyone else, including the guards, was scared of them except for the few "white boys" from the South and the Mexicans from Texas.

I had been in Terre Haute just three days before I got into a fight with a black inmate. I cut him across the stomach with a shank. It was a superficial wound but it served a message. I was "not to be fucked with." The incident established my name and earned me a thirty-day stint in isolation.

I met Billy Ray White when I was put back in general population. Alexander and I were sitting at a table in the prison dining room. Billy Ray was standing in the chow line with about fifty other inmates. His intense eyes flicked back and forth like a cobra's tongue as he looked out across the dining room where several hundred inmates were already eating.

By choice, blacks sat on one side of the large dining room and whites on the other. I noticed a large black dude striding across the mess hall. I nudged Alexander's knee under the table. A confrontation was imminent. The cause was a recent fatal stabbing. Then I caught sight of Billy Ray with his back against the wall. He was directly across from our table. When I saw him clench his right hand into a fist, I knew the impending battle was his. As the black inmate moved closer, the two men's eyes locked in a riveting stare of mutual hatred. I had never seen a man's eyes so intense, so unwavering, as Billy Ray's. He clearly relished the approaching threat.

"White, you took Cookie out," the black inmate said as he cut in front of Billy Ray, "but one of the brothers will get Garcia. That fucking spic friend of yours will never leave this joint alive."

The sound of metal spoons clanging against metal trays gradually slacked off. The perpetual hum of vulgar conversation eased like a dying fan motor. Every inmate in the mess hall was watching the confrontation. The challenge had been laid down. Prison is a world of narrow choices. Billy Ray had never walked away from a challenge in his life.

"Get the fuck out of my face, nigger," he said evenly, not the slightest trace of fear in his demeanor.

I saw the black inmate's hand move to his back. I reached for a heavy glass sugar container on the table. The black inmate pulled a crude shank from his waistband. I pitched the sugar container to Billy Ray who, in the same motion, caught it with his right hand and smashed it across the bridge of the black inmate's nose. Blood and sugar splattered everywhere. As the black inmate's hands rose to clear sugar from his eyes, Billy drove the toe of his shoe into the wounded man's groin. A choked cry spewed from his mouth.

The sound of whistles and running guards broke the silence surrounding the bloody hand-to-hand combat. With hundreds of inmates standing, a few pushing and shoving for better positions, the guards led the two inmates away.

"Right on, Brother," a chorus of black voices shouted. "We'll get the honky motherfucker."

Several white inmates stood together.

"Billy Ray, Billy Ray, Billy Ray," they slowly chanted.

Other white inmates stood up, joining in the chant. I rose with them. Then every white inmate was on his feet. The chant became a crescendo of white solidarity: "Billy Ray, Billy Ray."

A low hum of threats and curses spread among the black inmates. They were not intimidated. The tension was deadly. The slightest spark would have triggered a violent explosion. A special unit of guards dressed in riot gear spread out and patrolled around the tables. They spat warnings to both black and white inmates.

"Cool it!"

An uneasy calm gradually settled over the dining room. Fragile coexistence returned.

I learned later that Billy Ray had killed a black inmate named Cookie. The "grapevine" said Cookie had snitched on Pete Garcia, a popular Mexican drug dealer. Garcia was suspected of killing a Muslim leader. The Muslim had warned Garcia not to sell drugs to black inmates. The Muslim was found in the machine shop with a large screwdriver through his heart.

Guards put Garcia in maximum-security lockdown. They beat him regularly in an effort to break his will and make him confess to killing the Muslim. Garcia sent word to Billy Ray, his close personal friend, to "take care of Cookie." Cookie was found hanging in his cell several days later. Everyone knew that Billy Ray had killed him. Billy Ray was a "solid convict" who always honored the convict code.

After his release from "the hole," Billy Ray sought me out. He walked up as Alexander and I sat together in the dining room during an evening meal. He sat down at our table uninvited. Billy Ray never asked permission to do anything. He did as he pleased, always prepared to accept the consequences.

"My name's Billy Ray White," he said, extending his hand across the table. "I owe you for the other day. The nigger knew he had me short. I'd just got out of the hole. That's why the coward made his play. I would've stuck that shank up his black ass — but you made it easy for me. I appreciate it."

"It was no big deal," I replied, in awe of his presence. "I just did it."

Billy Ray's intense blue eyes looked straight through me.

"I've heard about you, Billy Sinclair," he said. "You handled yourself well in El Reno. People respect you. How old are you anyway?"

"Twenty."

"You're much older than your years. You carry yourself better than most of these dudes in here who call themselves 'convicts.' You were not afraid to pick up that sugar container. You've got balls and intelligence — that's why we're namesakes."

I tried to conceal the blush of pride. Billy Ray White was one of the most feared and respected inmates in the federal prison system. I had heard of his exploits in El Reno. At twenty-one, he was already a legend in prison folklore, admired for his intense loyalty to friends and respected for his fanatical dedication to the convict code. He was a "convict's convict," and that was more important to him than life itself.

"You sure showed that nigger, Billy Ray," Alexander said. "I was hoping some of them coons would take up his beef — I wanted some nigger-ass."

Without the slightest change of expression, Billy Ray turned to Alexander.

"You wouldn't have done nothing, asshole — the best thing you can do is get out of my face before I rip your eyes out of their sockets."

A stunned silence engulfed the table. An expression of fear flickered across Alexander's face, betraying the indignation he tried to feign. Without a word, he pushed his chair back, picked up his tray, and walked away. I too was stunned. Alexander had a solid convict reputation. It was just the first of many times I would see Billy Ray strip strong men of their will to fight with a look.

"I'm sorry about the dude," he said, sensing my uneasiness. "Alexander's a jive-ass coward, an ex-whore from the Walls in Texas."

"But he's my friend," I stammered, trying to hold my ground. "We went through a lot together in El Reno. He stood by me in that fight with the blacks."

"I respect your loyalty," he replied. "But the dude is a user, a hanger-on. He stood with you because he had no choice. You and the other white boys in that fight were his balls — even a cowed cur will fight in a pack. Since he's your friend, I won't say anything else to him. But your loyalty in him is misplaced. I only hope I'm there to back your play when things go sour with him."

"Why would you back my play?"

Billy Ray laughed — a full, healthy, infectious laugh.

"You have a friend for life, Sinclair," he said. "You risked your life for me. You didn't know me, so you had nothing to gain. It was destiny. Perhaps you're my other side, the good side of me — the side I would like to be. Our paths crossed for a reason, and I don't need that slant-eyed motherfucker Confucius to tell me that. One day we will know the reason."

Following his release from Terre Haute in 1967, Billy Ray went to Kansas City, Missouri, where he set up a lucrative shoplifting ring and a small fencing operation. A skilled poker player, he was soon playing in high-stakes games throughout Missouri and Illinois.

Then came another call from Pete Garcia, who had ruthlessly taken over Albuquerque's growing heroin market after his release from federal custody. Billy Ray went to New Mexico where he killed three rival drug dealers for Garcia. While in New Mexico, Billy Ray ran across a small-time hood he had known in the federal prison system who set him up with a "score" in a nearby Albuquerque community: an elderly couple supposedly keeping a large cache of money at a trading post.

Billy Ray didn't count on the old man's western grit. With three elderly women in the store, he fought like a wounded grizzly to protect them. He wrestled Billy Ray on the floor in a vicious struggle for the gun before Billy Ray managed to free it for the split second needed to pull the trigger.

He slowly stood up over the old man's body, as it convulsed in death throes. The old man's wife went berserk, jumping on Billy Ray's back and clawing at his face. In a swift reflexive action, Billy Ray swung the pistol over his left shoulder and pulled the trigger. The force of the bullet tore her face away, killing her instantly.

One of the two remaining women hid in a storeroom. The other stood transfixed in shock. Covered with blood, Billy Ray was calm — violence and death did not rattle him. He searched briefly for the woman who had disappeared. Unable to locate her, he returned to the lady still standing in shock. She was muttering incoherently. He tied her hands, bound her feet, and taped her mouth. He put the pistol to her head as she lay helpless on the floor.

"But I couldn't kill her," he said later. "Every instinct in my body told me to pull the trigger. I just couldn't do it. She kept looking at me, her eyes pleading with mine. I turned and walked out of that place knowing I was leaving a witness behind who could identify me — and the bitch did."

It was nearly a year before the FBI captured Billy Ray in Illinois. The witness died of a heart attack before he could be brought to trial in New Mexico for the double murders, ending in the acquittal I'd read about.

"I live a charmed life," Billy Ray often said. "A cat's charm protects me — no man will ever kill me. I am the master of my own fate, the captain of my soul."

Death and violence were not always fixtures in Billy Ray's life. There was a time when he was just a kid walking down a worn path to an old oak tree in rural Alabama and sitting in the shade for hours looking down on the railroad tracks, hoping a freight train would pass. There he found peace, dreaming of one day being a writer or a poet. Hope beat like a wild drum in his heart — dusty cotton fields and slow-moving tractors seemed to fade from his mind.

But the dark side of life always tugged at his soul, and he could never resist its lusty temptations. He often slipped through the back alleys into the "niggertown." He had become familiar with the tough but good-natured sounds of this hidden community. He knew the horrible smell of thick sewage running through backyards, the howl of Lightnin' Hopkins blaring through paneless windows, and the sounds of garr-fish frying in cheap, sizzling grease.

Billy Ray would slip up alongside a rowdy honky-tonk known as the Wine Jug. With the beat of "gut-bucket blues" pounding in his ears, he would peer through the cracks at the blacks who cursed, laughed, and did bump-'n-grind dances that sexually enthralled him. Late one Saturday night, as he stared at the large stain of dried blood on the rickety saloon floor left from a razor fight the night before, the large hand of a huge black man snatched him off the ground.

"Wha'cha doin' out here, white boy?" the black man demanded.

Though startled by the unexpected jolt, Billy Ray was not afraid. Potential danger and threat of the unknown, such as the dark and ghost stories, had never frightened him.

"Nothing — just looking," Billy Ray said belligerently, looking hard at the black man.

"You about a brave little white boy, ain't you?"

The black man's laughter rolled above the window-rattling wail of a misery-inspired blues ballad. He half-led, half-dragged Billy Ray into a nearby shanty. It was a dilapidated two-room structure whose windows were covered with Carnation milk boxes and tin foil. A stolen railroad lantern sitting on an apple crate bathed the room in an eerie glow. The black man sat on a battered GMC truck seat converted into a sofa.

Then Billy Ray saw her — a "high yellow" sitting backwards in a straw-bottom chair. Long, sleek black hair hung to the middle of her back.

"This white boy here wants a nigger gal," said the black man as he passed the pint of Tiger wine to Billy Ray.

The woman stood up. Billy Ray took a gulp of the wine, fighting down the temptation to wipe his mouth because he was drinking after a black person.

The rhythm of the blues still filled the night as the high yellow began to slowly move about the small room — a slow gyration building in her firm body, easily visible beneath a white slip. She stopped before Billy Ray, turning her backside to him. She pulled her hair forward over her head and began to shake her hips. The sweat-soaked slip clung to her cheeks. She was so close Billy Ray could smell her sultry odors.

The high yellow turned to face Billy Ray, pulling her slip slowly up to her waist. Billy Ray took another deep swig of the wine as he stared, mouth agape, at a thick patch of black body hair. She began to move her lower body in a slow circular motion, gradually thrusting herself forward in a hard, grinding manner as though fucking an imaginary lover.

Billy Ray bolted and ran for the door. As he fled, he heard the black man's raunchy voice saying, "Come heah, bitch."

A wild exhilaration beat in Billy Ray's heart like a black stallion racing through the night. "It's the only time in my life I ever ran from pussy," he would later say.

After reading the article about Billy Ray, I jumped out of my bunk and moved to the front of my cell, close to the barred door where I could talk to Bobby, my next-door neighbor. Ashen-faced and prematurely gray, Bobby had been convicted in 1960, at age nineteen, of killing a service station attendant during a holdup attempt. He had become an intellectual pacifist who idolized Bertrand Russell. He was consumed with an idealistic concern about world hunger, political corruption, and the Vietnam War. He and I often spent long hours in discussion and debate as our budding intellects fashioned new social theories and philosophical beliefs.

"Read this article about Billy Ray White," I said, passing the newspaper through the bars. I had often talked about Billy Ray to Bobby.

"Is that something to be proud of?" Bobby asked as he passed the newspaper back to me.

"What do you mean?" I asked, my feelings pricked.

"C'mon, Billy, you know what I mean. Billy Ray is a dangerous, violent criminal. He always has been and he always will be. You knew him in a different time, a different setting. Do you really think he could accept you as you are today?"

The question struck a chord deep inside me. I was evolving into a completely different person from the young hoodlum who met Billy Ray in Terre Haute. But I believed that friendship transcended philosophical beliefs.

"Yes, he would," I replied instinctively. "Bobby, I do not have to be like Billy Ray for him to be my friend. He will accept me as I am, just as I accept him for what he is."

Bobby ground out a cigarette in a sardine can that he used for an ashtray.

"I can't accept that," he said. "What we believe, what we are, determines the kind of people we will stand with or against in this life. I could not call a man like Billy Ray White my friend. I want to undo the wrongs I've done to my fellow man. And I could not honestly do that by sharing loyalties and allegiances with men like Billy Ray. I don't believe there is honor among thieves."

"Life is more than book notions and intellectual beliefs, Bobby. You'll always find men of honor and courage in war, revolutions, poverty, and, yes, even prisons. The kernels of human suffering and misery shape these traits in the worst of us. Convicts have died protecting guards during prison riots just as soldiers have died protecting each other in battle."

"And I thought I was the idealist here," Bobby laughed.

11

I AWAKENED EARLY ONE OCTOBER MORNING on the Row in 1968 with a deep sense of foreboding. I made my bunk, brushed my teeth, and swept the floor, but I could not quiet the nagging feeling that something was wrong. I was on a second cup of coffee, staring at the dingy gray-and-white walls of my cell, when it hit me. Something had happened to Pat. I recoiled at the thought.

My baby brother had lied about his age to get into the marines so he could fight in Vietnam. I began to worry about him as his letters grew increasingly bitter. They no longer spoke of the enemy but of "kills." It was clear that at only seventeen, he had become proficient at killing. He hated the Vietnamese and their miserable country with its jungles, rice paddies, and monsoons. He only wanted to do his tour of duty honorably and get the hell out of a land whose fields had been fertilized with the blood of invading forces for centuries. He wrote that the "fat-assed politicians" would not let the generals fight to win because they were afraid of the "evening news." Politicians, he said, were sacrificing the pride of a nation and the blood of its fighting men to the "peace movement."

From his letters, I knew that the Vietnam War was hideously violent. Everyone was the enemy — men, women, and even children. The Vietnam War was the only conflict in America's history in which her fighting forces were the "bad guys." The war embittered my John Wayne–loving brother.

As I pulled my knees up to my chest, I recalled my last visit with Pat before he left for the Far East. It was a few days before Christmas in 1967. We sat on hard wooden benches talking through the thick screen that separated death row inmates from their visitors. He was clean-cut and wholesome in his full-dress marine uniform.

"I really had to talk to keep Mother from telling the corps that I lied about my age to join up," he said, a half-chuckle rolling out through a big grin. I slicked back strings of greasy hair that fell across my eyes, a desperate look on my face.

"Why are you doing this, Pat? You don't have to go. Go to college like Daniel."

An edge of fear tinged my words.

"But I do have to go," he replied. "As corny as it may sound, I believe in God, country, and the right of all people to be free. We followed different paths, Billy. It almost killed me when Mother told me you murdered a man; I cried myself to sleep for a week. You really tested my love. You broke Mother's heart and I can't begin to tell you the shame you brought the rest of us."

A long, somber silence passed between us. I clutched the wooden bench on my side of the mesh screen, tears of shame stinging my eyes.

"But I love you, Billy — I always have, and I always will, no matter what."

It was true. He was the only member of the family who had truly cared for me. Our eyes locked. He put his hand to the screen. I placed mine against it. Our fingers touched through the mesh. My heart ached with love and regret.

"If I don't come back," he whispered, "I want my death to give you life. Mother will be the beneficiary of ten thousand dollars in life insurance. I've told her to take the money and get a good lawyer to get you off death row."

"Don't talk like that, Pat. You'll make it through okay." A vise had seized my throat. I could hardly get the words out.

"This is different, Billy. I have this feeling that I'm not coming back. The test of a good marine is to go when he knows he's not coming back."

He stood to leave. His body was hard from the rigorous training at boot camp.

"Some of us have to die to make this thing right. I don't believe in the 'do it if it feels good' approach to life."

He turned and walked away without looking back.

Jewell suddenly interrupted my thoughts of Pat.

"You have a visit, Sinclair."

The moment I walked into the visiting room and saw Mother's face, I knew.

"Pat's dead," she said, bursting into tears.

My brother Daniel put his arms around her. He was crying too.

"How did it happen?"

It was all I could do to get the words out. Mother recounted the brief story that the corps told her. I filled in the details from the stacks of Pat's letters to me about the war.

It was September 6, 1968 — just another day in Vietnam. The men on patrol were grimy, dirty, and tired. They had hacked through deep underbrush most of the morning to make their way. Their lieutenant was a good leader who pushed his men, forcing each to go as hard as he could. Pat squatted on his heels, his dark brown eyes piercing through the sweat and mud streaking his face. He was still a boy, and the youngest man in the platoon, but the violence of war had already hardened him. That morning, a firefight with the Viet Cong had kept his platoon pinned down for several hours. It had felt good to finally encircle the black pajama–clad enemy and kill them. Pat was always awed by how small they were when he saw them lying face down in the mud.

Cruel and vicious things were done in Vietnam both to and by Americans. But the soldiers who fought the war should not be judged severely. The average age of an American soldier in Vietnam was nineteen. It was twenty-six in World War II. The Vietnam War was a "kids' war." Its young soldiers fought an enemy who didn't draw clear battle lines or claim specific territories. Attacks could come from anywhere.

American soldiers were under perpetual mental siege, driven by anger and frustration because the enemy would not come out and "fight like a man." It was a brutal war of psychological attrition. Marines had been trained to "kill, kill, kill," only to find that the enemy used stealth, darkness, and deception to cover his deadly intent. He fought by ambush and sniper attack, and always with the element of surprise.

Many marines, like Pat, became embittered and enraged. The more dead and wounded comrades they carried out of the rice paddies, the more intense their hatred of the enemy became. Pat developed a near-worship of the "kill." He talked about his own death as casually as he wrote of the deaths of others. He was no longer the baby brother who had marched off to war worshiping John Wayne.

"Alright men," the lieutenant called out, "it's time to move out. Who's gonna take point across the river?"

"I got it," Pat said.

Even when he was exhausted, Pat pushed his body hard on patrols that were all alike, where everything looked the same. The stream was swollen from recent heavy rains. It had a vicious undertow. But Pat's thoughts were not on the stream. He was thinking about the sniper he knew was concealed in the tree line on the other side; an enemy who would try to pick his comrades off as they crossed.

Pat had almost made it when he came under fire. He saw the bullets biting into the water a fraction of a second before hearing the crack of the automatic weapon. He closed his mind to the bullets slicing the air around him. I could see him doing it. Once when we were kids, he had severed his heel tendon on a piece of rusty tin while we were playing. As I ran for help, holding him in my arms with blood spurting everywhere, he didn't shed a tear. "I won't cry, Billy," he had promised after I had told him only sissies break down in tears.

Pat moved faster, cursing the sniper violently under his breath.

When his feet touched solid ground, he quickly moved into position to provide cover fire for the rest of the platoon. He held the sniper at bay while several other marines crossed the stream. One of the soldiers had nearly made it when the sniper's bullet struck him. The young man screamed as he fell into the turbulent water. Pat did not hesitate. He dove in after his friend. He reached his wounded buddy only to realize that the current was too strong. The rest of the platoon watched helplessly as the stream swallowed both of them up and swept them away. Pat's body was recovered five days later.

"The marines are going to award Pat a medal posthumously." Mother's voice penetrated my numb thoughts. "I will get the medal and flag, but they told me I can't look in the coffin. That kills me, Billy, I don't know if that's my Pat in there or not."

"Will you be allowed to attend the funeral?" Daniel asked.

"No."

I walked back to my cell and stretched out on my bunk with tears rolling down my face. I thought of Pat, the little mimic who followed me everywhere on childhood summer days; skimming rocks across the pond when I did, chewing grass when I did; Pat, the only one to comfort me after one of John's savage beatings, curling his fat, baby body up beside my battered one; Pat, the brother whose sudden laughter and easy smile could melt the hardest heart. Pat, the only one who really loved me.

It was so typical of him, the caring one, to reach out to a drowning friend; so typical of him to be willing to give up his life because it was the right thing to do. I was in agony as I thought of his final moments, the raging stream sucking him under, filling his lungs with water, choking out his life. And then I saw J. C., sitting on the concrete in front of the convenience grocery, choking to death on his blood. I thought of his family trying to comprehend its loss. And, for the first time, I understood the human dimensions of my crime.

12

CHRISTMAS BROUGHT POIGNANT LONELINESS and heart-breaking sadness to the Row. Our thoughts turned inward, relishing the memories of past Christmastimes. Memories of a brother's laughter, Grandma's sweet potato pie, the jingle of a beggar's cup, and the lights that turned downtown into Disneyland filled my brain. The volume on radios all over the Row cranked up every time we heard Charles Brown's "Please Come Home for Christmas."

I thought of the times I had roamed through large department stores, alone. The scurrying of the shoppers fascinated me: the healthy teenaged bobbie-sockers trying desperately to find the right gift for the key to their dream; the suave Mrs. Robinsons, with firm hips and lovely hosed legs, demanding service as they stood around sales counters in seductive, well-tailored clothes; or the harassed red-faced men trying to monitor their wives' spending or their children carelessly handling expensive toys.

But the holiday season also brought back memories of the

worst Christmas any child could ever know. Shame and humiliation blotted out joy. I was in the fifth grade. I had been selected to be in the school's annual Christmas play — a major accomplishment in my small world. Boys in the choir had to wear black pants, white shirts, and white jackets. I rushed home with the news, telling Mother what I would need to be in the play. She asked John to buy me the clothes. After making some derogatory remarks about the cost of my being in the "stupid play," John agreed.

I started doing odd jobs around the neighborhood to earn money to help pay for the suit. I pulled weeds out of the neighbors' flowerbeds long after dark until my hands were red and numb from the cold. I gave the change that I earned to Mother, hoping each day that John would take me to buy the clothes. I became more anxious as the play grew near, pleading with Mother to make John take me to the store.

The day of the play came. Every kid in the choir had on the special outfit except me. I promised my teacher that I would have mine in time for the play that night. But John had been drinking when he came home that evening. He and Mother argued. Inevitably, the argument turned to the suit he had neglected to buy.

"C'mon, you little bastard," John said. "I'm gonna get you that damn suit. I'm tired of hearing about the fucking thing."

John drove me to a used-clothing store in the worst part of New Orleans. True to his word, he bought me a pair of black pants, a white shirt, and white jacket. They were all men's sizes that were far too large for me. I refused to put them on. John hit me in the side of the head.

"You wanted a suit, well, you're gonna wear the damn thing," he said.

I put on the suit. I had to roll up the pant legs. John gave me an old necktie to use as a belt to keep the pants from falling off. The sleeves on both the shirt and jacket also had to be rolled up several times. I was a wretched sight. John dropped me off at the school auditorium, saying he would pick me up later. The auditorium was filled with parents and students waiting to see the play. I sneaked in the back door, too ashamed and humiliated to enter through the front.

"You poor child," the teacher in charge of the play said upon seeing me. "Where are your parents? They left you, didn't they?"

"Yes, ma'am," I nodded, unable to control the tears welling up in my eyes.

The teacher kept me out of sight by letting me open and close the curtains. I was grateful for her kindness. Another boy spoke the one line I had in the play, "The Lord is my shepherd." I stood alone behind the curtains. It seemed that I was destined to be a spectator in life, forever prevented from enjoying what is normal, healthy, and decent.

"Are you sleeping, Sinclair?" Bobby whispered through the bars.

I lay unmoving as I stared at the ceiling. A bitter sorrow squeezed my heart. The darkness of Christmas night was heavy with despair, as the Row strip-mined our bodies and laid waste to our souls.

"No," I said. "I'm just lying here wondering if this will ever be over."

"Me too. I can't get my mind off the free world. What do you think? Will we ever get out of this place alive?"

Our decomposing dreams filled the night air as time fed on us like a vulture.

"Yes, we will," I replied, a surge of anger and defiance rising within me. "We have to keep hoping. It's our salvation. We can hope as long as we're stronger than the cage we're in."

Earlier in the day, Bobby's mother had brought his son to see him. Bobby needed companionship to get through the night.

"Did you see my son today?"

Yes. He's a fine-looking boy. How old is he?"

"Almost ten, but you'd think he's fifteen by the way he talks. That kid is my life. He was just a baby when I got busted on this charge. It kills me to have him see me here. There's just no way to explain this place to a kid."

A cry of terror pierced the night. Brodie's recurring nightmares were a permanent fixture in our lives. He dreamed he had been cut in half by a huge blade. The bottom half of his body chased the top half, never able to catch up.

"God, I'm finished with this life if I ever get out of here," Bobby said, barely noticing Brodie's scream. "I thought it was cool to be on the thief's honor roll. I've heard these jailbirds knock the square-John's way of life but he's got more than we'll ever have. He doesn't have anyone telling him when to sleep or what to eat. He punches his eight hours with his lunch pail and goes home to a family. A convict does his eight hours and all he has is a plate of rotten food waiting for him at the end of the day."

"You will make it, Bobby. Just hold on to your dream. That boy is the pot of gold at the end of the rainbow; he'll get you through this."

"He's all I live for," Bobby said.

I looked at my watch. It was 4:00 A.M. We had made it through another Christmas. I adjusted my pillow and burrowed into it. The image of a man running, the pounding of my heart, and a child's scream in the dark drifted with me into sleep.

13

DEEP IN THE RECESSES OF THE PRISON, the Row was a lost world where every season was the enemy. Summer was the worst. It brought the funk of sweat, irritating gnats, bloodthirsty swamp mosquitoes, and pestering flies. The days were long and unbearably hot while the nights were sticky and stifling. I often prayed that the unending despair and agony of my caged world would explode, propelling my soul into oblivion. The heat seemed to accelerate cell madness, sinking us deeper into the extremes of absurdity. Our days seemed to drift on forever, our hours consumed by asinine arguments about soap operas and baseball.

"Man, the Astros done beat those jive-ass Giants six times this year," Daryl said, shouting down two other angry voices.

"Is you mad?" Shiphead screamed. "The Astros ain't beat the Giants but four times."

"Nigger, you're a stubble-footed, do-funny lie," Daryl shot back. "How you gonna sit there, talking out the side of your mouth, and say the Astros ain't beat the Giants but four times. Hell, I've won four packs of Bugler off you already with those Astros."

"I can settle that argument if y'all want me to," Ora Lee said, interrupting the dispute.

"Who the hell asked you, Jack," Shiphead spat. "Nobody pulled your chain over there. This is dead serious shit we're discussing."

"I'm just telling you that I know what y'all are talking about," Ora Lee replied, pleased with the hostile reaction he had provoked.

"Nigger," Shiphead said, anger rising, "you keep dipping off in my business and I'm gonna hang a foot in your snuff-dipping, country black-ass."

"You ain't gonna do nothing except jump out of the bushes and rape something," Ora Lee mocked.

I was four cells from the argument, the same one as the day before only with different players. I placed Wolfe's *Of Time and the River* on my homemade shelf. Yawning, I stretched sore, stiff muscles before rising from my bunk, not really wanting to stir about in the heat. I picked up a pack of Bugler, turned my fan away with my free hand, and expertly rolled a cigarette with the other, admiring the simple feat I had once thought impossible to perform.

Cigarette in mouth, I took three steps to my cracked, rust-stained toilet, where I urinated. The sounds of body-nature were so woven into the fabric of our existence that they were barely noticed. I wet a face cloth and slowly washed my perspiring body. The heat bore down with tropical intensity. Then a roar of laughter rang out. The argument would end on a peaceful note.

It was close to 5:30 P.M., almost time for the *CBS Evening News.* Watching the news was a religious ritual with me. I had learned to pronounce words that I only knew how to spell as I listened to Walter Cronkite and Eric Sevareid each afternoon. The news this day carried a segment about an act so inhumane that it skewered me, like a wooden stake in the heart.

"These eight men are to be executed today for the crimes of armed robbery," the reporter said. "Their executions are part of the Nigerian government's crackdown on the rampant increase in armed robberies which has plagued the country since the Biafran civil war. To make sure that the government's message is clear to the public, these men are going to be executed on this soccer field as part of the half-time ceremonies . . ."

"Hey, y'all, there's an execution on Channel 9," an excited voice called out.

As the channel selectors quickly turned with morbid anticipation, I lost contact with the reporter's voice. My attention was riveted to the scene being carried out on the small screen. Eight men, all dressed in tattered white uniforms, were led single file into the middle of the soccer field. Soldiers prodded them along with rifle butts. Two priests offered last-minute rites to the condemned men. Once in the middle of the field, the men were tied to stakes with barrels placed behind them to stop the bullets that would pierce their bodies.

I could sense an air of expectancy filling the stadium as the firing squad nonchalantly prepared itself. My eyes were drawn to two of the condemned men. One was obviously shouting his contempt at his executioners while the other simply let his head fall limp into his chest. The order to fire was given. Shots rang out. They were followed immediately by screams from the contorted mouths of the dying men. The firing squad reloaded. Once again, bullets tore through the bloody bodies of the eight men, some of whom were still desperately clinging to life. Finally, each of the eight bodies went limp as the camera panned to the reporter's face.

"Man, did y'all see that one dude smoking and jerking around," Shiphead said, laughing and clapping his hands.

"That's a shame," Bobby said disgustingly. "When is society going to learn that capital punishment is murder, pure and simple?"

"If a nigger killed my brother or raped my sister," Brodie chimed in, "I'd blow his ass away and that's all the due process he'd get."

"Shut up, you crazy old bastard," Ora Lee shouted above two or three other voices also cursing Brodie.

There were no executions while I was on the Row, although three dates were set. Each death date induced fear and apprehension. A mood of dark despair silenced the arguments, shouts, and laughter on the row. Hope of our eventual release dissolved as the reality of being locked up in death cages ate at testicle and heart.

One such date was set for Louis, who was seventeen years old when Governor John McKeithen signed his death warrant. He was fifteen years old when he and two other black youths were convicted of killing a popular grocery storeowner in St. Francisville. One day, the gaunt figure of Warden C. Murray Henderson showed up on the Row. He only came to the Row on one errand. Standing in front of Louis' cell, Henderson read the death warrant with terrible haste. Only silence remained after the sound of his departing steps faded away.

Louis sat down on his bunk to think about the piece of paper that said he had only three weeks to live. His execution date interrupted what passed for normal life on the Row. Some inmates resented Louis. He had suddenly brought the death penalty into sharp focus. The tribe of the condemned ostracized him like a sick, diseased old woman.

Several days after his death date had been set, Louis stopped in front of my cell. His eyes were restless and feverish. Rubbing his forearm as though he were cold, he squatted close to the cell bars.

"Feel like talking, Billy?"

"Sure." I rose from my bunk.

"Do you know anything about the chair?"

"Just what I read about it," I answered, knowing where his thoughts had been since the warden's visit.

"What's it like?" he asked, continuing to rub his forearm. "I mean, do you feel anything?"

"The surge of electricity probably kills the brain before pain has time to register on the body," I replied. "No one can say for sure — certainly not me."

"You've read a lot. How's a man supposed to die like this? How is he supposed to act? Them books tell you anything about that?"

"Fear is natural, Louis. It's nothing to be ashamed of. There are no rules about courage when they take you to the chair in the middle of the night. You simply put one foot in front of the other. You can feel or say anything you want. It's not going to mean anything when it's all over with. You just walk in, and die, and that's it."

"I hope I can hide my fear. I don't want to give the bastards the pleasure of seeing me afraid."

"Then be angry and defiant. Hate them as much as they hate you. It'll be the only honor you get out of the whole insane affair."

But Louis got a stay of execution. Noise and arguments returned to the Row. And summer faded into fall. Like weary soldiers after battle, we marched on.

14

By MARCH 1972, the years of waiting for my death had left me emotionally drained and a physical wreck. But my legal expertise paid off when I won a court case that vastly improved conditions on the Row. I had fought for three years to gain the right to outdoor exercise for condemned inmates and had finally prevailed. Victory came after the federal court assigned a young civil rights attorney named Richard Clark Hand to represent me.

Richard was a VISTA attorney assigned to the New Orleans Legal Assistance Corporation. From there, he went to the Baton Rouge Legal Aid Society on a poverty law fellowship. He was born in New York State. He came to Louisiana fresh out of the Georgetown University Law Center after graduating from the College of the Holy Cross in Worcester, Massachusetts. He and his wife, Jean Grover, were devout Catholics. He represented poor blacks in New Orleans' Desire housing project. We were the same age.

The appointment marked the beginning of a special attorney-client relationship that deepened into an abiding friendship of almost thirty years. When Richard left Louisiana to be a staff attorney with the District of Columbia's Public Defender Service, he did not abandon me. He flew back to Louisiana at his own expense to represent me free of charge when I needed him. His appointment marked a turning point in my suit to win exercise privileges for the Row. Attorney-client conferences found him sitting in front of my cell on the Row, enduring the same heat that left us almost too tired to breathe.

Prison officials had been interpreting a law requiring condemned inmates to be held in solitary confinement to mean that we could not be let out of our cells for more than fifteen minutes, three times a week. A federal district court said the practice amounted to cruel and unusual punishment. The court ordered prison officials to construct an exercise yard to allow us at least one hour of outdoor exercise.

Richard and I won the first prisoners' rights lawsuit in Louisiana. *Sinclair v. Henderson* also extended minimum due process rights to inmates facing disciplinary action at the state penitentiary. It began prison reform in Louisiana.

After months of official procrastination and two additional orders from the federal court, I felt the first rays of sunshine on my body in more than five years when prison authorities finally constructed three small exercise yards, one for each tier, separated by a wire fence.

We were handcuffed for the walk from our cells to the yard. The cuffs were removed once we reached the yard and replaced for the return trip to our cells. In addition to the hour on the yard, we were given an extra hour on the tier to shower.

The exercise yard brought us hope. It eased somewhat the feeling of being caged. But we were pathetic sights and the butt of ridicule from guards who watched our sorry attempts to exercise. Prolonged solitary confinement had devastating effects. We were afflicted with poor vision, atrophied muscles, decayed teeth, and infected body sores. But the psychological disintegration of years in small, bathroom-sized cells proved to be our worst affliction. Some of us had developed "cell madness." Inmates with cell madness were too emotionally dependent on their cells to venture out. They only felt secure inside the confines of a cell. The first day, just eleven of the forty-three men on death row exercised in the yard. While the number gradually increased over the next several weeks, ten never left their cells at all.

Those of us who dared to try the yard paid a physical price. We suffered from muscle cramps, nausea, dizziness, headaches, and disorientation. We could not judge distances or gauge space. We continuously fell into the fence or stumbled into each other as we tried to play football and basketball. Our cells had altered our sense of equilibrium. The dazzling amount of space on the yard left us reeling. Weeks passed before we regained a semblance of balance and coordination.

But the yard made us human again. It brought about perceptible changes in our personalities. We grew more confident. Once dull, passive eyes began to sparkle with energy and life. Slow, palsied gaits lengthened into strides. Our respect for one another grew. We were dealing with faces, not just voices down the hall.

But just as renewed life surged into us, we were again forced to face the ugly specter of death. The spring of 1972 found condemned inmates not only in Louisiana but across the nation awaiting a U.S. Supreme Court decision in *Furman v. Georgia*, a case that would decide whether we would live or die. Because I had no faith that the Court would declare the death penalty unconstitutional, I forced myself to confront a harsh political reality. There would be an immediate resumption of executions across the country, once the so-called moratorium was over. I would be among the first to be executed in Louisiana.

Edwin Edwards had just been elected governor in the closest election in Louisiana history. The state's black vote had given him the winning margin. He had said that if the court upheld the death penalty, he would commute some death sentences and let others be carried out. Of the forty-two inmates with me on death row, thirty-seven were black. The rest were white. I studied our crimes, the parishes of our convictions, the local politics in each case and concluded that Edwards would sign my death warrant and Wilbert Rideau's. To avoid any appearance of racial discrimination, I would die first because I was white and Rideau was black.

Like Louis, I wondered how I would face my death. When the time came, would I fight, forcing the guards to haul me out of the cell? Would I cry, making them drag me screaming down the hall? Or, would I passively walk to the fate reserved for me? I would be placed in the chair, one way or another. I knew that I was helpless in the scheme of things.

When an execution draws near, a condemned man thinks about the one thing he has spent a lifetime avoiding: his own death. The fear of dying grips his heart. His mind is riveted to the thought of being electrocuted in the chair.

As the day approaches, his thoughts turn to the death ritual. No matter how cold-blooded the crime of the condemned, it cannot match the methodical, calculated manner in which the state, in its monolithic power, snuffs out human life. Some of the people involved in the death ritual believe in capital punishment. They enjoy it or at least are able to watch with emotional detachment. For others, it is an unpleasant job that sickens them.

As I waited for the Court's decision, I cursed my luck. I was to pay the ultimate price for an unintended killing, indeed, one that I had taken precautions to avoid. I focused on the belief that electrocution is painless, as some experts in my studies of the chair claimed. But I felt no peace. Perhaps a man cannot prepare himself to die. Perhaps I was never close enough to death to feel the resignation said to come from knowing it is certain. I thought of the shame my execution would bring my relatives. They would quickly bury me in the Rayville dirt and erase my memory. The Bodden family would have nothing either, except the desire to dig me up and execute me all over again.

For four months I waited in acute agony. Finally, on June 29, 1972, the very last day of its term, the U.S. Supreme Court, in a sharply divided five to four decision, ruled that the death penalty, as it had been historically imposed, was unconstitutional. Its decision in *Furman v. Georgia* vacated the death sentences of more than six hundred inmates across the nation. Six in Louisiana were from East Baton Rouge Parish. The reversal of my death sentence was front-page news in the Baton Rouge paper. The other five cases were buried in a small article behind the classified section alongside one about a black inmate killing a white policeman, the sort of story that normally generated headlines in the South. But the local press gave me the play.

The *Furman* decision did not spell immediate release from the Row. It would be four months before the Louisiana Supreme Court ordered all condemned inmates resentenced to life in prison. Even that did not bring life on the Row to an end. Death row prisoners had to petition the court for action in each of their cases. Some inmates refused. They were the same group that preferred the security of their cells to the exercise yard. Ultimately, these victims of cell madness were legally "evicted" from the Row. But two more years elapsed before the Department of Corrections petitioned the court to have them resentenced and moved into other cell blocks or the prison's general population.

Life went on as usual as we waited for official action in our cases. One Saturday, in November 1972, Bobby and I stood talking through the fence during our exercise period. He had recently been transferred to another tier in a futile attempt to escape the noise. I missed our late-night conversations about politics, power, and life — intellectually stimulating exchanges that often pitted my pragmatist philosophy against his idealistic views.

Bobby had been locked up for nearly thirteen years, most of them on the Row. He had recently learned that the district attorney and his victim's family would not oppose his release. He was elated over the news. *Furman v. Georgia* had opened the door to his freedom. He was to go to court the following Monday for resentencing. He had every reason to be optimistic.

"I will be before the pardon board next month," he said. "The victim's family will tell the board I should be released. There's a good chance I will be home with my son in a couple of months. I never thought I'd live to see the day."

At thirty-one, Bobby showed the toll the Row had exacted. His hair had thinned and grayed during his decade in a death cell. He was going blind from glaucoma.

"You'll make it, Bobby," I replied. "It's been a long haul for you. But you will make it."

Bobby told me he was expecting a visit from his mother and sister later that morning. They were coming to pick up his personal belongings. He had everything packed in cardboard boxes.

"What are you going to do when you get out?" I asked.

"I've got a job lined up in Texas," he said, looking back over his shoulder. "I'm taking my boy with me. My mother's raised him while I've been down. He's fourteen now and he needs a father. I'm going to save everything I can for his education."

I detected nervousness in Bobby's demeanor. He kept looking over his shoulder at another inmate on the yard.

"What's happening, Bobby? You seem uptight."

He paused a few moments, staring at the rugged hillside that had become so familiar to each of us.

"I'm not sure, but I have a feeling Wing-Ding's got something on his mind."

Wing-Ding was a psychotic killer with a shriveled left arm who hated white people. His physical deformity made him lethal. He measured masculinity by the willingness to kill. He had received the death penalty for the murder of another black inmate. Wing-Ding had stabbed the prisoner to death as the defenseless man lay sleeping.

"Did you and Wing-Ding have a problem?" I asked.

Several days before, Bobby explained, Wing-Ding had asked to borrow a stick of butter. Bobby was a straightforward type. He didn't like Wing-Ding and had refused to give him the butter. Later, Wing-Ding saw Bobby give butter to a white inmate. It infuriated him. For his own warped reasons, he turned the proverbial molehill into a mountain.

"He made some broad statements about jive white boys sticking together," Bobby said. "I didn't think much about it. You know, Wing-Ding's always running off at the mouth. But all morning he's been saying some dude that thinks he's going home is in for a surprise. I think he's talking about me."

I looked across the yard at Wing-Ding, who was at the center of a small group of black inmates. He was lecturing them about the social value of hatred.

"Be careful with that one, Bobby," I said. "He's a coward. And that makes him dangerous. He'll sneak up on you like he did that old man. Don't turn your back on him."

Bobby was dead ten minutes later. When he and the other inmates returned to their tier, Bobby went straight to the washroom to do his laundry. He was washing his socks when Wing-Ding came up behind him and stabbed him with a homemade knife. Bobby spun around. The two struggled before Bobby took the knife away from Wing-Ding and threw it aside. Though mortally wounded, he pummeled Wing-Ding with his fists until he collapsed and died on the tier with a punctured lung. Bobby's mother and sister arrived to visit him an hour later only to be told that his body was in the prison morgue.

I heard the news in stunned disbelief. The one man on the Row for whom I had felt a kinship was gone so suddenly that it left me reeling. His murder was a portent of the violence facing me.

Two weeks later, I was returned to court and was formally sentenced to life in prison. I was to be transferred from death row to Angola's Main Prison. As I walked out of my cell, I turned back for a final look, knowing that luck had kept me alive. Little did I know how much more luck I would need to stay alive. The Main Prison would far eclipse any horror I had seen on the Row.

15

IN 1972, ANGOLA WAS KNOWN as "the bloodiest prison in the nation." Its inmates lived in a fierce dog-eat-dog world where the law of violence prevailed. Gangs, homosexual rapes, and drugs were prevalent. It was an era when everything was permissible, and almost anything possible. Stronger inmates routinely claimed weaker ones as their slaves. A new inmate, called a "fresh fish," had to pass a test of violence to determine if he would be a man or woman. The practice was woven into the fabric of the prison's sub-culture, sanctioned by the keeper and accepted by the kept.

Every Thursday, a patrol van brought the fresh fish from the Reception Center to the Main Prison complex. Four prisoners rode in the van with me on that December Thursday in 1972 when I was transferred from death row to the Main Prison complex. One was a fifteen-year veteran of the prison circuit. He had been in and out of the penitentiary seven times. Two others were young blacks from New Orleans. They said nothing during the two-mile trip to the

Main Prison and stared sullenly through the mesh screen that separated us from the driver.

The fourth inmate was a seventeen-year-old white kid named Jamie Parks. A member of a motorcycle gang, Parks was given a twenty-year sentence for his part in the gang rape of a fourteen-year-old girl. The gang, "The Galloping Gooses," had come from Texas to New Orleans for Mardi Gras. Parks didn't return with them.

"What was it like spending all that time on death row?" the kid asked, nervously looking at me.

I didn't want to talk, and certainly not about the Row. My thoughts were focused on what lay ahead on the Big Yard.

"It was hard."

"Did you ever think they would burn you?"

"No."

"I'll tell you one thing, if that had been me, they never would've put me in the chair. I'd have made them kill me first."

Parks needed a friend. He was afraid of the Big Yard, a community of sixteen sixty-man dormitories grouped in units of four. The units were named after trees: Oak, Pine, Walnut, and Hickory. The dorms were lined up in two rows, eight to a side, facing each other across a three-foot-high elevated walkway. Known simply as "the Walk," the walkway served as the main thoroughfare for the human traffic moving throughout the Main Prison complex.

"What do you think the Big Yard will be like?" Parks asked.

I didn't have time to answer.

"You're gonna find out, boy," the old con growled, "and the first thing you're gonna find out, is that you ask too many goddamn questions."

The color drained from Parks' face. He didn't have a prayer on the Big Yard.

"I was just trying, just trying to find out . . ." he stammered.

The old con leaned forward, placing a hand on the kid's knee.

"Listen to me, pretty boy," he lewdly whispered, "the best thing you can do is get a stud who will take care of you."

Parks' face was a study of terror. The old con had casually voiced his greatest fear — losing his manhood.

"Forget it, kid," the old con said, reading the kid's expression.

"You don't have the balls. You're gonna give up that pussy or they'll take it. It's too late to get scared. You should've thought about that before you raped that young girl. It's time to pay the fiddler."

The old con burst into laughter. It sounded like gravel being compressed.

The Big Yard was still segregated in 1972. White inmates were housed in the Oak dormitories. Blacks, who constituted seventy-five percent of the prison population, lived in the Pine, Walnut, and Hickory dorms. The division created two communities in one world. While the inmates ate together in the same mess hall, a wooden partition ran down the center of the huge building, separating the races. A mixture of racial, cultural, and geographic differences kept the races apart. Mainly, though, they did not mix because they didn't like each other, and they made no bones about it. Whites stayed in their part of the prison, blacks stayed in theirs.

The patrol van came to a screeching halt at the prison's Sally Port. A tower guard pushed a button, slowly opening a large fence gate to let the van in. The van pulled up next to a guard shack. The gate closed behind it. A guard stepped out of the shack to inspect the vehicle and its occupants.

"I've got five fresh fish in here," the driver said.

The blue-uniformed guard spat tobacco juice on the tire of the van.

"That young one in there is going to make some dude happy tonight," he replied. "Take them to the Control Center."

The shack guard signaled the tower guard to open a second fence gate. The patrol sped through and raced down a paved road. To the left I saw the prison's cannery and warehouse. On my right sat the Industrial Compound, a conglomeration of shops and a vocational school spread over a large area. It was the only part of the Main Prison complex that looked like a prison. The van came to a stop behind the laundry. The driver got out, walked to the back of the van, and opened the door.

I climbed out and looked at the prison buildings. They were dirty and dilapidated. Their lifeless gray color emanated a forbidding aura. It was a portent of the world we were entering — a world of racial strife and hatred; homosexual rape and slavery; protection rackets that provided a way for the strong to live comfortably at the expense of the weak; and widespread drug trafficking that brought its dealers tremendous profits and its users an escape from the bitter reality of their failed lives. It was a world where survival and status were achieved through the power of weapons: shanks, zip-guns, hatchets, swords, lead pipes, and chains. It was a fishbowl of pain, misery, and death.

The convict code ruled inmate behavior. It was a code of silence — see nothing, hear nothing, say nothing. The code's criminal values reinforce thievery as a way of life, violence as a means to an end, and an anarchic hatred of authority, particularly the police. "Honor among thieves" is the highest goal of the code. A man who betrays the code is an outcast. The convict code and the criminal ethic it inspires worship violence, lawlessness, and repression.

"All right, follow me," the guard ordered.

Like ducklings, we trailed behind the guard. I surveyed the prison layout. We passed the mess hall. It resembled a huge airport hangar. Scores of inmates lounged about outside, many sitting on the rails that ran down both sides of the Walk. It was fresh fish day. The wolves were observing the procession, stalking possible prey. The Walk came to a halt in the lobby of the Control Center, an area sectioned off by bars and gates as the check-in/check-out point for inmate traffic.

A bull-like guard stared at us through bullet-proof glass. He slowly got up from his chair, unlocked a solid steel door, and walked into the lobby. The patrol driver gave him the written information on us: our names and job/dormitory assignments.

"All right, from here on out, you're on your own," the bull said, glaring at the group. "Just catch the Walk and follow it to your dorm."

He paused, folding his arms. He was a menacing figure.

"Now I want each one of you to understand a basic rule," he continued. "My job is to keep you here, not wet-nurse you. You take care of yourself. If you can't hack it down the Walk, don't come crying to me for help. The only time I want to see your face up here is when you have some information to give me. Do I make myself clear?"

No one in the group said anything.

"All right, get the fuck out of my face and get down the Walk where you belong."

The old con led the way. He'd been through the grinder before. I followed his lead, carrying a pillow case of personal belongings over my shoulder. A reception committee greeted the fresh fish as we moved down the Walk. They lined the rails, eyeing us, forming a gauntlet of leers, wisecracks, and lewd laughter.

"You back again, Murray?" someone called out to the old con.

He was elated by the recognition. It conferred status on him.

"Yeah, I got a nickel this time," he laughed.

"You'll be down on one of them boys tonight," the boisterous inmate yelled to a chorus of laughter.

"Your mammy will," the old con retorted, feigning anger at the mocking laughter.

"Goddamn, look at that white boy," a black convict said to several other blacks as he pointed to Parks. "Those white boys gonna tear that pussy up tonight."

Parks pretended not to hear the remark. He looked straight ahead as he hurried down the Walk.

"What's happening, Billy?"

I recognized the voice before I saw the face. It was Billy Ray White. He had heard through the grapevine that I was coming to the Big Yard. He had put out the word that his "best friend" would be coming down the Walk. That guaranteed me social acceptance even before I set foot in the Main Prison. Billy Ray was one of the most dangerous inmates in Angola. His intense loyalty protected me. He had bragged to other prisoners that I was the only person who had written him after I was released. I sent him fifty dollars with a note after I got out of Terre Haute. The act met the highest ideal of the convict code: showing loyalty to a criminal friend.

After being acquitted of the double murder in New Mexico, Billy Ray was extradited to Louisiana, where he was convicted of a jewelry store robbery in Jefferson Parish and sentenced to twelve years.

"How you doing, Billy Ray?" I said, extending my hand.

He gripped my hand and pulled me to him in a friendship embrace — a signal to everyone watching that we were close friends, not just associates.

"I'm making it," he said with an easy smile — a deceptive trait in a man who could turn into a stone-hard killer in a flash.

"It's been a long time since those federal days," I said. "You haven't changed much — a few lines, maybe."

At twenty-nine, Billy Ray still had his boyish looks, although his eyes were harder and more intense. They could instantly turn venomous and menacing when he was braced for a fight or faced with the slightest challenge. His stare was as cold and deadly as a black mamba. But now he was laughing.

"Time will do that to you," he said. "You don't look too bad after spending all that time in a cell. I'm glad you beat the chair. I kept up with your case in the papers. Those assholes in Baton Rouge really wanted to juice you."

A sudden commotion behind us interrupted our conversation. I turned to see a group of black inmates surrounding one of the fresh fish.

"You're for me, nigger," a huge black inmate with a shaved head said vehemently. "You my pussy now."

The group of black inmates had the young black inmate jammed against the rail. The shaved-head goon had a knife pressed against the kid's side. Two other blacks stood close to the kid's face. A fourth inmate grabbed him by the hair and slapped him across the face. A guard stood at his post, no more than a hundred feet from the attack, watching.

"What's with the free man?" I asked incredulously.

Billy Ray burst into laughter when he turned to see the amazement written on my face.

"You've been out of circulation a while," he said. "This place is not like the Fed's. We run the joint. The screws just put in their eight hours and stay out of our business. If there's a killing on the Yard, they just come to collect the body."

Billy Ray slapped me on the shoulder.

"Get used to it," he said. "This joint is wide open. Half the guards are on the take. Hell, on this shift alone, I've got three running speed and grass for me."

I looked at Parks, who had slowed to stare at the black confrontation.

"What about him?" I inquired. "I'm surprised someone hasn't grabbed him yet."

"He's already spoken for," Billy Ray replied. "Blackjack already staked that claim. They'll let him know about it tonight. Why? You want him?"

"Hell no! I was just curious about him since we rode down together."

"If you want him, say so and I'll go take him for you right now."

"How are you gonna take him when he's spoken for?"

Billy Ray smiled.

"Easy. I take what I want in this joint," he said. "You'll see. It's just a matter of having the balls to do it. You sure you don't want that kid?"

I was struck by Billy Ray's casual power of life and death over Parks. I was face to face with what it meant to be a prison "slave." With a tug of conscience, I realized that I had the power to save Parks. I recalled the fear in his face when the old geezer told him that he would be a whore.

But trying to save Parks would have cost me my own well-being. I was not homosexual and didn't want to be part of a subculture with an inherent potential for violence. Had I taken Parks under my wing, I would have been forced to fight, even kill, to protect him from predatory homosexual studs who wanted him. In prison, sex is property. An inmate has an absolute duty to protect his property or he is considered weak — a condition that inevitably evokes a lethal challenge.

"No, I don't want him," I said. Parks would have to make it on his own.

"Okay. But if you change your mind, let me know and I'll get him for you."

We walked down the Walk to the Oak 4 dormitory. Loud music, a Ping-Pong game, and the slam of dominoes on a table top greeted us as we entered the dayroom section of the rectangular-shaped dorm. Sandwiched between the dayroom in the front and a TV room in the rear of the dorm was a large living area with four rows of army-style bunks. Each row consisted of fifteen bunks. Billy Ray took me to a bunk against the wall. It was unheard of for a fresh fish to get a wall bunk. I later learned that Billy Ray had forced its original occupant to move to a bunk in one of the center aisles.

Billy Ray escorted me through the dorm, introducing me to all the "solid convicts" — the power brokers who had status and influence in the prison subculture. He made a special point to introduce me to Big Mick, who, like Billy Ray, was one of the most feared and respected cons on the Big Yard. Italian despite his Irish nickname, Big Mick was a stocky, muscled man, who could bench-press 385 pounds six times. He stretched an extra-large T-shirt into a tight fit. It actually looked small on him.

"Billy Ray's told me a lot about you," Big Mick said, seizing my hand in a vise-like grip. "A friend of Billy Ray is a friend of mine. You're not going to have any problem in here. Billy Ray runs Oak 1 and I run Oak 4. Nothing goes down in here unless I say it goes down — and I say you're one of the Family now."

The Family was a gang of New Orleans inmates; most had been reared together in the Irish Channel. They controlled the heroin traffic and protection rackets in the Main Prison complex.

"I've been trying to get Billy Ray to move over here with the Family," Big Mick said.

"That's not my style, Mick," Billy Ray said. "I'd make half your Family catch out if I moved in here."

I sensed an underlying rivalry between the two men. They were like two bulls sizing each other up.

"Just take care of Billy for me," Billy Ray continued. "If he needs anything, make sure he gets it and I'll square it with you. He's my main man."

Big Mick's demeanor changed. The smile eased from his face.

"I thought I was your main man," he said.

I was uncomfortable. Big Mick was forcing Billy Ray to choose. Billy Ray stared hard at him.

"Let's keep it straight, Mick," Billy Ray said. "You're my friend. I'd die and go to hell for you right here on the spot. Just say the word and I'll go to the wire with you. But Billy and I go way back, long before you or anyone else in this joint. Nobody comes before Billy — nobody."

"I can dig it," Big Mick said. "Everybody knows how you stand with the dude. He's your main man."

I glanced several bunks down at young Parks unpacking his personal belongings. He was not as lucky. He didn't have a friend.

He was destined to be introduced to the brutal, violent side of prison life. It happened later that night when several convicts went to his bed and began talking to him. Their gestures made it clear that it was not a friendly conversation. I lay on my bunk watching the exchange. The clique was still there when the lights went out at 10:30.

Big Mick moved stealthily to my bunk.

"Something's going down in a few minutes," he whispered in a conspiratorial tone. "Several dudes are gonna take care of business with that new kid."

The inmates sitting around Parks' bunk were a crude, rough lot. A wild, desperate look touched Parks' face as one of them slammed a fist into it. He screamed like a frightened child.

"Shut up, bitch," one of the inmates whispered, forcing Parks' head into a pillow. "You fight it and I'll break your fucking neck."

The other two inmates stripped Parks naked. He didn't try to resist. He was subdued by fear. The other man eased the pillow over Parks' head.

I lay on my bunk powerless to help Parks as the rapist got in the bunk beside him.

"Watch for me," he said, undressing. "If the Man comes in, stall him."

"Turn over, bitch," he demanded.

I imagined Parks' face twitching uncontrollably as fingers packed in cold Vaseline. He screamed as his attacker penetrated him in a single thrust, driving into the boy's rectum, relishing the power it gave him.

"Shake back, bitch," the attacker moaned. "Give daddy a wiggle."

Parks felt a searing pain as one of the other inmates pressed a lit cigarette against his flesh.

"Give your daddy a wiggle, bitch," he demanded, choking off a laugh, "or I'll keep this fire on your ass all night."

Parks started crying as he pushed his buttocks back and wiggled his ass against his attacker.

Even as the last of the attackers pulled himself out of the abused boy's rectum, Parks was trying to push back harder. He was begging for more, and when they finally left him, he cried again —

not because he was hurt but because he liked what they had done to him. He knew his life would never be the same again. He wanted to recapture the pain and brutality of the rape. He had become its victim, and since he had been raped like a whore, he would relish the role.

I fell asleep as Parks headed for the bathroom to clean out his rectum. The young biker was dead four months later, stabbed to death by his homosexual lover.

16

INTELLIGENCE IS A RARE COMMODITY IN PRISON. An intelligent inmate can build a power base through a Machiavellian mixture of cunning and daring. But he must be careful as he moves through a violent community ruled by rumor, misunderstanding, and paranoia; a world in which the peasants are seconds away from revolting against the monarchs.

I was willing to take the risk. Utilizing my reputation as a jailhouse lawyer, I gained tremendous influence on the Big Yard within a matter of months. I relished the role. I was the man with answers to legal questions and solutions to personal problems. As I listened to inmates' problems and complaints, I offered legal advice and put seemingly complex problems into simpler form.

My role as a leader inspired intense loyalty. My responsibility became clear to me one day when Eddie Ralph, one of the prison's notorious gangsters, almost attacked an inmate he thought was threatening me. Eddie believed that I was his only hope of reversing a life sentence. He walked up as I was engaged in a minor argument with another inmate. It was no big deal to me but it was to Eddie. He went berserk. He wanted to kill the other prisoner even though it meant another life sentence.

I understood how easily I could provoke violence. Still, I was unwittingly brokering deals that set the stage for conflict between a new standard of inmate behavior and the traditional convict code. It would take the lives of my two best friends and put a target on my back.

The power and influence I amassed on the Big Yard quickly enabled me to transcend racial barriers. I was the only white inmate who could safely walk down to the "ghetto end" of the yard and move in and out of the black dorms. It astonished white inmates and angered white security personnel.

"You're walking culture shock," a black Muslim minister told me one day as I made my way through a black dorm.

"I've watched you, man," the Muslim said. "You're a phenomenon, that's what you are. You can rap to an Uncle Tom, or a Panther, or a redneck honky — even a New Orleans gangster. You can lead them all to riot. You speak all the languages. That's why the Man's gonna kill you."

"What?"

"The System, of course — the Ku Kluxers who run this joint. You've already sent shock waves through their world. You're a warden's worst nightmare. You not only have the ability to lead but you can't be controlled — and you're not afraid of authority."

"The System has to be changed," I replied.

"Just remember — if you ever get in a bind, the Muslim Brothers will stand by you. Our reasons and motivations are different, but our struggle is the same."

The Muslim minister was right. My influence transcended racial lines and crossed the subculture's class lines as well. I was vice president of the Angola Jaycees, secretary of Narcotics Anonymous, and president of the Dale Carnegie Club — three of the most influential inmate organizations in the prison. The administration first recognized inmate organizations at Angola in 1953. The number and nature of such organizations had grown dramatically over the years to the point that, by 1973, they played an integral role in the inmates' social life. Striving for and obtaining leadership positions in these organizations was the goal of every "inmate politician."

Solid convicts had traditionally viewed "prison politicians" as flunkies for the administration. They were considered no better than snitches. But solid convicts sought me out for counsel. I could instruct a Jaycee Speak-Up class and advise the Family about the consequences of warfare with a rival gang.

The legal victory in my death row lawsuit (to gain exercise privileges) had spawned a flood of litigation in the local federal court. Every jailhouse lawyer wanted a piece of the prestige associated with such a victory. In response to this dramatic increase in prisoners' rights litigation, Elayn Hunt, the new reform-minded corrections secretary, created an innovative Prisoner Grievance Committee. Comprised of thirty-seven inmates representing Angola's five thousand inmates, the committee was established to investigate and resolve as many prisoner grievances as possible without going to court.

It was a noble idea that marked the beginning of similar grievance mechanisms throughout the nation's prison system. Hunt's personal endorsement gave the Prisoner Grievance Committee unprecedented credibility. I dealt myself in on the power with a deal I cut with several other white inmate leaders and a black inmate faction. As a result, I was selected secretary of the committee, and a popular black inmate was named chairman. Then I spearheaded a subcommittee selected to draft the group's bylaws, making sure that most of the real power resided in the secretary.

The Grievance Committee gained immediate and widespread acceptance with the inmate population when it secured unheard-of privileges: permission to watch late-night television; TV sets in maximum-security lockdown; long hair; beards and mustaches; uncensored incoming and outgoing mail; a new disciplinary policy; a larger and better-equipped law library; restraints on security harassment; and hot meals, mattresses, and hygiene supplies for inmates in punitive segregation.

Most of the credit for these privileges went to me. As a result, I became subject to harassment. The predominantly redneck security staff considered me a troublemaker and an agitator. They believed I was leading the inmates toward an Attica-like rebellion — a major penal concern in 1973. Even Hunt, the reformist, believed I was the "most dangerous inmate" in her prison system because the inmates would burn the prison to the ground if I gave the order.

I chose to ignore the mounting flak, continuing to press such controversial issues as having security officers address inmates as "mister" and requiring them to divulge the names of informants before they locked an inmate up on the basis of "confidential information." I was the first inmate counsel-substitute to represent an inmate before the prison's Disciplinary Board. After I was allowed by the warden to appear at the hearing, the chief of security refused to attend. When the warden ordered him to preside over the hearing, the chief of security turned his chair around and sat with his back to me throughout the proceeding. I helped establish a disciplinary process that gave inmates the right to call witnesses, cross-examine adverse witnesses (including guards), present evidence, and appeal decisions made by the board. The prison's staunchly conservative security force reeled in dismay, shocked by the impact of these changes.

Top-ranking security officials made it clear they wanted me dead. Had it not been for my association with the Family, my friendship with Billy Ray, and my status with the general population, I would have been killed. I was warned repeatedly by an inmate informant close to security that a contract had been put out on me. The rumor served to make the Family wrap its protective ranks even more tightly around me.

It was through the Grievance Committee that I met and became close friends with a black inmate named Irvin "Life" Breaux. Life had been elected to the committee by cell block inmates to represent the maximum-security population. He was one of approximately two hundred black inmates locked up following the stabbing death of a prison guard named Brent Miller on the Big Yard in 1972. Prison authorities believed Life masterminded the guard's murder.

Breaux was sent to Angola in 1964 with a life sentence for a murder in New Orleans. Less than a year after his arrival, he killed an older inmate who made aggressive homosexual advances toward him and was given an additional five-year term for manslaughter. Two years later, he got another five-year term for assaulting an inmate who told him he should "get a man."

By the late '60s, Life was infected with the fever of militancy that was sweeping the nation's prisons. He was a walking time bomb, ready to explode at the slightest provocation. He was typical of the many hostile young black men who turned to militancy as a way of expressing their rage against the system during that era. Life believed violence was a legitimate form of political expression and a necessary tool for achieving social change.

Although we were markedly different in style and personality, Life and I developed a strong bond. We spent hours formulating political theories and debating ways to save the world. Because of our leadership roles on the Grievance Committee, we viewed ourselves as prisoner activists.

In a peculiar kind of way, the civil disobedience of the early '70s brought order to our prison existence. It gave us something to oppose. We were like the prisoners described by the McKay Commission in 1972 following the Attica revolt:

> Many inmates came to believe they were "political prisoners," even though they had been convicted of crimes having no political motive or significance. They claimed that responsibility for their actions belonged not to them — but to society, which had failed to provide adequate housing, equal educational opportunities, and equal opportunity in American life.

But Life had reached a more advanced state of "political prisonerhood" than the one described by the McKay Commission. He justified crime only if it was committed for the "struggle." He believed it was criminal to commit a robbery for personal gain. Unlike Huey Newton and Eldridge Cleaver, Life did not believe criminals had a place in the "struggle." That intense belief kept him in constant conflict with the criminal fraternity ruling the prison subculture. He thought the convict code perpetuated more oppression than the corrupt rule of the prison officials. Its favorite vice angered him the most — homosexual rape and its subsequent slavery. In the end, it would cost him his life.

17

I WALKED INTO THE DORM ONE AFTERNOON in March 1973 from a "crisis meeting" with Hunt and Warden Henderson. An early melt-down of heavy winter snow in the north and heavy spring rains had the Mississippi River poised to boil over its banks. Plans were being made for the mass evacuation of the prison, if it became necessary. The Grievance Committee was asked to allay growing inmate fears and concerns. While the "great flood" never materialized, the high water enabled prison officials to smuggle out several thousand head of cattle that were later said to have drowned. It was rumored they made their way to a politician's ranch.

As soon as I saw Big Mick lying on his bunk nervously stroking a set of beads, a habit he had when agitated, I knew that the river's raging waters were the farthest thing from his mind.

"What's happening?" I asked, sitting on the edge of his bunk. I had come to like Mick. He was using his drug money to put a physically handicapped sister through college. Most of the rest went to his mother.

"I lost three bundles of good dope today," he replied. "Major Norwood and his shakedown crew hit the recreation room this morning. They went straight to my stash."

Anytime Norwood went straight to a stash, he had a tip. Someone had fingered Big Mick's stash, as much to hurt his bankroll as to make him feel vulnerable. Three bundles of heroin, consisting of seventy-five individual bags, would bring more than two thousand dollars on the Walk.

"Who or what's behind the play?" I asked.

Big Mick sat up on his bunk. The tattoo of a dagger through a heart pulsated under an arm muscle.

"I pay good money for security protection," he said. "Norwood wouldn't hit me unless he was told to. And it had to be someone high up because my money goes way up the chain of command. Somebody's making a power play. Those Dixie Mafia motherfuckers have flooded the yard with weed and Valiums. They want it all — they're trying to put me out of business."

The term "Dixie Mafia" was coined by a member of the Dallas Crime Commission in the late 1960s. It was used to describe a loose-knit gang of professional thieves led by Kirksey McCord Nix, Jr., the son of a powerful Oklahoma appeals court judge. A 1971 Louisiana State Police intelligence report said the Dixie Mafia roamed across the South and Southwest pulling big scores and carrying out contract murders. According to the report:

> During the year 1967, it became apparent to law enforcement officers in the Southern and Southwestern United States that an organized group of criminals were operating from Florida to Texas, committing bank robberies, tie-up residence robberies in which ski masks were worn, murders for hire, burglaries, major thefts, confidence swindles, pigeon drop swindles and were also involved in gambling, prostitution, and business frauds.
>
> The method of operation of these subjects is for a local character to set up a score in his city, make all necessary plans, obtain the equipment, supplies, transportation needed for the job and have out-of-town gang members actually commit the crime. This MO has been quite successful for the organization, both in terms of jobs completed and avoiding

prosecution. However, this method seems to breed an unusual amount of distrust among the criminal associates, which resulted in the murder of numerous members of the gang.

Nix and two henchmen, Peter Mule and John Fulford, were convicted of murdering wealthy New Orleans supermarket owner Frank Corso during a shootout after he caught the gang burglarizing his home in 1971. Corso was shot five times but managed to wound Nix in the stomach in the exchange of gunfire. Corso's wife picked up her husband's gun and continued firing as Nix and the others fled to a getaway car. The intelligence report stated that a Nix associate in Dallas rented an airplane, flew to New Orleans where he picked up Nix, and returned him to a Dallas clinic. Nix was later arrested there. He survived the wound, although he refused to allow authorities to take out the bullet. It was subsequently removed by court order. Nix, Mule, and Fulford later received life sentences, following one of the most expensive and highly publicized trials in Louisiana history.

Four years before the Corso killing, Nix was the driver of the vehicle that ambushed a car driven by Tennessee's "Walking Tall" Sheriff Buford Pusser. While Pusser survived the attack, his wife, Pauline, was killed. Carl Douglas "Towhead" White, a longtime Pusser foe, had ordered the contract killing of the sheriff. The triggerman was Carmine Raymond Gagliardi, a Boston hoodlum and hired killer. Nix was called in as the wheel-man because of his driving skills and his knowledge of the state's rural backroads.

Pusser became obsessed with tracking down his wife's killers. Towhead was shot to death in a Corinth, Tennessee, motel in 1969. Gagliardi's body was later found in the Boston Harbor riddled with bullets. In his book *The Twelfth of August*, W. R. Morris, Pusser's biographer, said that Pusser had "discovered through his investigation that Nix was one of the assassins. He confided to me that he was not going to reveal the information to the authorities, because he had his own method of justice."

In 1976, Nix told me, during a conversation about some legal problems he was having, that he had killed Pusser's wife. He said a contract was put out on the sheriff, not because he was a "corruption fighter" but because he was a corrupt lawman "who got too greedy." A reliable Louisiana State Police investigator, however, told me in 1989 that Nix was just the driver of the ambush car, not the triggerman.

It made no difference to Pusser whether Nix pulled the trigger or drove the car. He wanted Nix dead. To escape Pusser's "own method of justice," Nix arranged, through his family's political influence, to get a two-year sentence in a Georgia prison where he would be safe. There he met John Fulford, a career criminal and ruthless killer who controlled the prison. Fulford hooked up with Nix's Dixie Mafia gang upon his release from the Georgia prison system in the late '60s.

Following the Corso conviction, Nix was sent to a federal prison for five years on an unrelated weapons charge. Mule and Fulford were sent to Angola. They quickly amassed considerable power and influence throughout the prison, particularly on the Big Yard. Their drug operations posed serious economic competition for the Family's narcotics operation. Bitter feelings grew between the two rival gangs.

"What's the next play?" I asked, knowing that Mick already had a plan.

"There were only two people who knew where my dope was," Mick said. "Me and Mouse. Mouse cut a deal with Mule. I'm gonna cut his fucking heart out tonight. The Mafia boys wanna play games, well, I'm gonna show them how to play this game."

Big Mick read my thoughts.

"Don't worry," he said. "You're not involved in this. I've got enough backup with Blue, Sancho and Mex. If it goes down bad, we'll need a lawyer, a mouthpiece to take care of us. We do the fighting. You do the thinking. Just keep a tool handy in case things get out of hand. We're gonna sling some mean iron in here tonight."

Mouse was a dangerous convict. He was a veteran of prison violence. A longtime drug dealer for the Family and a well-liked member of the New Orleans criminal fraternity, he had several close friends who would fight with him in the event of trouble. The dorm was full of weapons. They were necessary for survival in Angola in 1973. When a prison is out of control, the rule of the knife is law. "I'd rather for the Man to catch me with it than have my enemy catch me without it," was a popular inmate saying.

116

Any knife that was detected and confiscated was replaced by two more. Prison security eventually quit trying to control the proliferating weapons. Instead they tried to maintain a balance of power between the Family and the Dixie Mafia. The prison was run by security guards living on the prison grounds. They came from a village known as "B-Line." The redneck families that lived there — the Dixons, Butlers, Oliveauxs, Norwoods, and Bryans — had run the prison for several decades. The warden's job was simply an administrative position. Power and control of the prison was vested in the B-Line regime. They could make or break a warden, as they had often demonstrated.

This night, the die was cast. There would be death in the dorm. I went into the television room, where I removed a ten-inch double-edged homemade knife that was taped under a wooden bench. I placed the blade up the sleeve of my pajamas and walked back to my bunk, where I put the knife under my pillow. Then I sat back to await the bloody battle that was shaping up.

A quiet tension had settled over the dorm. Mouse and his friends were at the other end of the dorm shooting up speed. Big Mick lay on his bunk with a handkerchief across his eyes. It was as though he were planning the battle in his mind. Blue, Sancho, and Mex, all Family henchmen, sat at a table in the lobby playing cards, occasionally engaging in whispered conversation.

I had my own way of dealing with the nervous tension. I pulled a portable typewriter from under my bunk. I began a proposal for the Grievance Committee. A few minutes passed before I sensed the dorm had grown unusually quiet. No noise was coming from Mouse's corner. No one was talking and the radios had been silenced. The sudden pause in human activity was a signal. Death often makes its presence known in prison before it strikes. I grabbed a towel from the rack beside my locker, took the knife from under my pillow, and covered it with the towel in my lap. I looked around the dorm. Big Mick was lying on his bunk with eyes still covered. Blue, Sancho, and Mex were still in the dayroom.

Primed for a battle between Big Mick and Mouse, I was unprepared for what followed. Across the dorm I saw Blackjack standing by his bunk fully dressed. A man didn't walk around the dorm at night dressed unless he was about to leave or do battle. Blackjack headed for the TV room. He carried a knife with the handle in his palm and the blade pressed flat against the underside of his forearm under the sleeve of his shirt. He walked with a purposeful stride. There was no hesitancy in his step. A few days earlier he had caught Parks with another man. Normally jovial, Blackjack had become withdrawn and moody. His pride was at stake, and pride is the measure of a man in prison. Wounded pride has resulted in many prison killings.

Blackjack opened the TV room door. He stood for a few seconds scanning the entire room, taking in every potential enemy and every possible object that could be used as a weapon. At least two dozen inmates were sitting on benches and in chairs watching the *Carol Burnett Show*. Parks was laughing, clapping his hands together at a Harvey Korman and Tim Conway comedy skit.

Satisfied with the situation in the room, Blackjack gripped the handle of the knife and walked up behind Parks, unnoticed. In one quick motion, he reached over and drove the knife to the hilt into the kid's chest. Parks sucked in a deep breath, let out a gurgled scream, and rose from the bench. Blackjack quickly withdrew the blade and drove it into the kid's chest again. This time, Parks grabbed Blackjack's hand where it gripped the knife and pushed it back out of his chest.

Possessed with the strength of youth, Parks managed to break away from Blackjack and make a dash for the door. Blackjack caught him just as he opened it and drove the knife deep into his back. The force of the blow shoved Parks against the door and broke its window. He spat blood all over its shattered glass.

Still, the mortally wounded kid managed to get the door open. A man attacked by a knife can do desperate, seemingly impossible things. Parks staggered down the aisle between the bunks. Inmates watched with unfeeling eyes. Blackjack started after the kid.

"Hold it, Blackjack — the bitch is finished," one of his friends said, pulling him back into the TV room to help him remove his bloody clothes.

Parks ran a few steps, reeled, stumbled against a bed, and ran a few more steps. I sat on my bunk watching him stagger down the aisle. His eyes were wide open. He kept reaching behind his back with one hand as he waved the other in front of himself like a blind man, feeling his way without a cane. He tried to speak. Blood poured out of his mouth. As he stumbled past my bunk, it spurted all over my typewriter and ran down the half-written page.

Parks finally managed to make it to the dayroom, where he collapsed face-forward on the concrete floor, shattering his jaw. He heaved one last time before dying. A young guard ran into the dorm. When he saw the kid's body on the blood-splattered floor, he went into an epileptic fit. Hearing the commotion, a second guard from another unit came running into the dayroom. He knelt down to help his shaking, twitching fellow officer.

"For God's sake," he screamed, pointing toward Parks, "will one of you get a stretcher for that kid?"

"Fuck that bitch," Sancho said. "All she needs now is a hole to be dropped in."

Big Mick raised up on his elbow, the first indication that he was aware of the violence and chaos. He saw Parks lying on the floor and the frantic efforts of the guard to get his stricken comrade out of the dorm.

"The bitch finally got her issue," he said.

Big Mick got out of his bunk and walked over to Sancho.

"C'mon, let's get her out of the dorm," he said.

Together, they each grabbed an arm and pulled Parks' body out onto the Walk, leaving a trail of smeared blood behind them.

"God," my mind screamed, "how had I become part of their Family?"

I was no better than a counselor for the Mafia. I shared their food and drink and profits and, therefore, the responsibility for their crimes. I pulled the bloody paper from my typewriter, tore it into small pieces, and flushed it down the toilet. I threw my bloody blanket on a nearby empty bunk and retrieved another one. A kid was dead and friends of mine had just thrown his body on the Yard like a sack of garbage. I was angry — as much at my own helplessness as the callousness of Big Mick and Sancho.

A half-hour later, all the inmates in the dorm were escorted to the Control Center for questioning. It was the routine following a killing, done more to harass than to investigate. We were lined up against the wall and interrogated individually in the major's office. Security always got their man when more than two prisoners witnessed a killing. Information is valuable barter in prison. The code of silence and loyalty among convicts had already begun to erode by the 1960s as young street thugs and middle-class dropouts invaded the prisons. Silence prevails only when there is fear of retaliation, the kind to which the Dixie Mafia subscribed. To them, it was better to kill than to trust.

In this instance, Blackjack was fingered quickly. He didn't have the kind of status in prison to invoke fear of retaliation. He was escorted to maximum security. Even though they had their man, security continued to interrogate the rest of us for the remainder of the night.

"Goddamnit," Big Mick muttered as he stared at Mouse at the other end of the hall. "The asshole got away tonight, but he'll get his issue. He can go to the bank on that."

I thought about young Jamie Parks lying in the prison morgue. He would be remembered, if at all, as a "gal-boy." But I would always see him as a terrified kid, trying desperately to pull the knife out of his back.

18

THE BRUTAL MURDER OF JAMIE PARKS exemplified the violence, hatred, rape, and cruelty so prevalent on the Big Yard during the spring of 1973. I was tired of its madness and lawlessness. Everyone at the prison walked on the edge of paranoia. With the threat of the flood gone, violence regained center stage — each day an inmate was stabbed, killed, raped, or brutalized.

The level and intensity of the violence shocked even hardcore convicts. One day seventeen black inmates raped a white kid in the Education Department, waiting in line outside the classroom for their turn to sodomize him. Another inmate was stabbed to death because he wouldn't give up his Timex watch.

A brooding despair hovered over me, like the shadow of a rain cloud. I had returned to pills, taking handfuls of amphetamines. Speed at least kept the demon of despair at bay. There were too many demands, too much pressure, and too many crises to cope with. I occasionally smoked weed to take the bruising edge off speed.

Billy Ray, on the other hand, embraced the increasing level of violence. While other inmates armed themselves with knives and hatchets and Roman-style shields and slept with Sears Roebuck catalogs tied to their chests, he casually walked through the prison armed with two knives, always ready to extend one to any opponent. He slept bare-chested.

"It's time to separate Vikings from Christians," he said.

One day, as we walked around the Yard, the topic of prison violence came up.

"Violence doesn't bother me," he said. "I wish they would take all the guards out of here — just leave a few in the towers to keep us in. Then let the battle for absolute rule begin — I'd be one of the last Vikings standing."

"I wouldn't survive long in that kind of world," I replied. "I don't have the heart for the jungle."

"You don't need heart, Billy. I'm your heart. I would die for you."

And he would have. There was nothing that Billy Ray would not have done for me. His loyalty frightened me at times because I could not match its depth and intensity. One day, he walked into the Grievance Committee office. We were alone.

"I'm going to escape," he announced, as he sat in a chair in front of my desk. "It's something I've been . . ."

"You're going to do what!" I exclaimed.

"Just listen, Billy," he said, leafing through a stack of blank typing paper sitting on my desk. "I've been working on an escape plan for the last six months for James and Ronnie McLain. But Ronnie is getting weak. I could force him to go but he'd leave James stuck out, so I'm going with the dude. I owe it to him. We go back ten years; he's done a lot of good turns for me."

"I understand your loyalty toward James," I said, "but you don't have much time left — you discharge in a couple years."

Billy Ray had been doodling with the pen on the top sheet of paper. He stopped and looked directly into my eyes.

"It's not about time, or my loyalty to James," he said. His eyes softened.

"It's about us, Billy. You're changing this prison through the Grievance Committee. Your efforts have created a massive demand for change. A new order is being introduced into our world and I'm not ready for it. Word down the Walk has it that the committee will next integrate the Main Prison."

I now understood his escape plan.

"That issue is on our agenda," I replied with a slight sigh. "The committee has been told integration is going to happen — the only question is when and how."

Billy Ray reached across the desk, locking a fist-like grip on my arm.

"Don't you see where that puts us, my friend?" he said. "I cannot and will not accept niggers being forced down my throat. There's some other whites down the Walk that feel the same way I do. They will turn to me when the Man forces integration. I'll kill the first black motherfucker put with me. I'll have to, don't you see?"

Releasing my arm, he stood up.

"This integration thing will put us at odds, Billy," he said, leaning forward on my desk. "The committee will be asked to keep the peace. You will be the voice of reason, the one people will turn to for a solution. I will be the voice of resistance. Others will turn to me for a violent reaction. I'm a warrior, a prophet of death. One of us will be forced to compromise our principles or be put in a situation where we oppose each other. I won't ever let that happen."

Billy Ray turned and walked to the door.

"Escape is the only answer," he said, turning back to face me. "Besides, the convict world I've known is a relic of the past, like Stonewall Jackson; had that brilliant military strategist lived, we wouldn't be faced with a nigger problem today."

"Does your hatred really run that deep, Billy Ray?" I asked.

"It probably runs deeper than you can imagine," he replied. "I don't hate niggers because their skin is black. I hate them because, as a race of people, they lack values and principles. My values and principles are not those of a free law-abiding society, but they are what I live by, what I am committed to. Niggers are incapable of any kind of values."

Two days later Billy Ray White and James McLain rode out of the prison compound concealed in the false bottom of a pickup truck driven by a prison maintenance worker who did not know they were in his vehicle. When the driver stopped, as he always did, at the prison's ice house, Billy Ray and McLain crawled out of the truck and raced for the Tunica Hills.

Their escape, however, was short-lived. Neither man had physically conditioned himself to move through the deep ravines and rough terrain of the treacherous hills. Fatigue and dehydration soon exhausted them, allowing the prison's bloodhounds to easily track them down. But Billy Ray had enough strength to kill the first baying bloodhound that came upon him where he sat propped against a tree. The chase crew was enraged when they saw the dead dog with his grotesquely twisted neck lying at Billy Ray's feet.

"I oughta blow your fucking brains out, White," one of the guards said, placing a cocked .357 magnum against Billy Ray's forehead.

"Go ahead, asshole," he said, looking up into the eyes of the guard leaning over him. "You will have the new experience of killing a man who is not afraid to die."

The guard hesitated.

"Pull the trigger, motherfucker," Billy Ray said as he reached up and seized the wrist of the guard's gun hand.

"You're crazy, White," the guard said, yanking his hand free, staggering backwards. "Crazy bastard . . ."

Billy Ray stood up to face the armed guards.

"I'm not crazy," he said extending his hands to be cuffed. "I'm sick of assholes like you."

Billy Ray was placed in one of the prison's four maximum-security cell blocks.

Though surrounded by the Family and others who called themselves "friends," I was now alone on the Yard. I had served nearly eight years at Angola. Favrot had predicted that I would spend at least fifteen years in prison. I could not fathom another seven years in Angola. My mind focused on serving ten, perhaps twelve years. Something would happen, had to happen, after ten years. Traditionally, a lifer in Louisiana served no more than ten years, six months.

One night, as the moon's gentle grace sparkled over Angola's darkness, I lay staring at the ceiling, waiting for chemical relief. I had just taken three Valiums to bring me down from the mollies. It was a daily ritual — mollies in the morning, Valiums at night. Like

Billy Sinclair, approximately age thirty-two, at the Angola State Penitentiary.

Left: Billy Wayne Sinclair at eight years old.

Right: Billy Sinclair's parents, Bessie Jewel and John Sinclair, at an unidentified Army camp in California during World War II.

Right: Billy Sinclair, at age eight, with his older brother, Johnny.

Below: Billy Wayne Sinclair with two of his brothers and his sister: *(left to right)* Mary, Billy, Pat, and Daniel.

Billy Sinclair in the death house at Angola on March 17, 1981.

Above: Billy Sinclair at bat during an inmate baseball game at Angola. One of the prison's dormitories is visible in the background.

Right: Billy Wayne Sinclair walks across the yard accompanied by a guard at Angola.

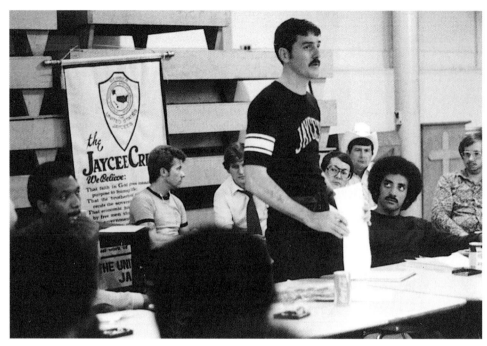

Billy Sinclair, president of the Angola Chapter of the Jaycees, addresses inmate members of the club during a meeting at Angola.

Billy Sinclair interviews C. Paul Phelps, secretary of the Department of Public Safety, for *The Angolite* circa 1980.

Right: Angolite editors Billy Sinclair and Wilbert Rideau in the main visiting room at Angola in the early 1980s.

Below: Sylvester Peters and Billy Sinclair in the visiting shed in the main prison complex at Angola. Peters, an Angola inmate, gathered information for *The Angolite* during the early 1980s in parts of the prison where the magazine's editors might be in danger from inmates jealous of the editors' privileges.

The staff of *The Angolite* in 1980. *Standing, left to right:* coeditors Billy Sinclair and Wilbert Rideau, Sylvester Peters (Pete), and Louis Ortega; *seated,* Larry Stegal and Tommy Mason.

Ashanti Witherspoon and Billy Sinclair attend an inmate meeting at Angola. Witherspoon, an Angola inmate, was close to pardon board chairman Howard Marsellus.

Lawyer Richard Hand, conferring with Billy Sinclair
(unseen behind the bars) on death row at Angola in 1971.

Jack Martzell, one of Billy Sinclair's
pro bono lawyers, on vacation in
Poplarville, Mississippi, in the spring
of 2000.

Ross Maggio, Jr., warden of Angola, in
his office in 1976.

Billy Wayne Sinclair meets children at a Catholic school in Monroe, Louisiana, during a speaking tour circa 1980. Billy and *Angolite* coeditor Wilbert Rideau frequently toured the state speaking at schools while C. Paul Phelps was head of the Louisiana Department of Public Safety.

Billy Sinclair, coeditor of *The Angolite*, during an interview at Angola with a Monroe, Louisiana, television reporter.

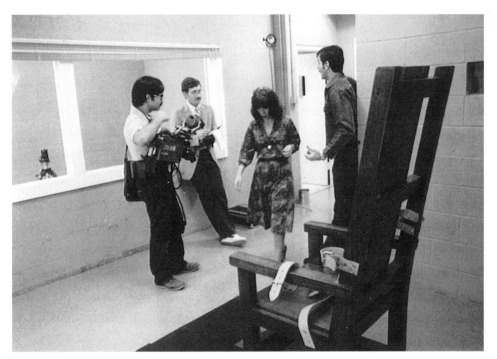

Jodie Sinclair prepares to shoot interviews in the death house at Angola, March 17, 1981, with a television news crew from Lafayette. Jodie Sinclair *(middle)* walks past Billy Sinclair *(right)* moments after meeting him.

Jodie Sinclair interviews Warden Frank Blackburn with Channel 9 photographer Susan Jackson in the death house at Angola on March 17, 1981.

My Beloved Brother Billy

Its not wrong of you to deney me the privilage of dying in your company ~~Billy~~ as I stand on the treshhold of freedom from this madhouse into the illusion of freedom ~~together~~ anywhere on this mad planet because your will is mine. In the name of your cherished friendship I will be a coward. My loyalty to you is such. I would be dishonorable to you and myself if I took my life now without your consent. However due to my selfishness I am asking that you ~~reconsider~~ reconsider and give me your consent. It would be the greatest favor you could ever possibley grant me. It has occurred to me that mabey Im wrong to ask this favor of you. Billy try to place everything in as proper prospective as you can and let me know—. My Brother I would proudly die for you and if its what you really want I will even live for you. As it wrong of me to ask you to let me go now? As it greedy? Help me under-stand.

                    You're not heavy, you're my Brother
                    My only Brother and I love you,
                    and my death won't seperate us.

Billy Ray White's second suicide note, which Billy Sinclair
pressed into an album of gummed paper.

Billy Ray White, a year before his suicide.

Billy and Jodie Sinclair at a prisoner's club banquet at Angola in 1983.

C. Paul Phelps with Jodie and Billy Sinclair at a prison banquet at Angola in 1984.

Billy and Jodie Sinclair at the Louisiana State
Police Barracks in Baton Rouge in 1987.

Jodie Sinclair, Houston, Texas, 1998. *George Wong, Houston.*

on the Row, death was everywhere. I had to escape its malignant presence. I could not take Billy Ray's route. I held fast to the belief that if I kept breaking the rocks, one day there would be no more rocks.

"Wha'cha doing?" I heard Mex whisper to Blue.

Blue was struggling with a pen and paper in the dim moonlight.

"Nothing — just justifying my existence," he said without looking up.

That was a hard thing to do on the Big Yard in 1973. A razor could not have sliced through the tension circulating at both ends of the Yard. Black inmates had split into three major factions — gangs from New Orleans, Baton Rouge, and Shreveport. They engaged in repeated clashes in an unrelenting power struggle to control the prison's homosexual slave trade — a slavery fueled by President Richard Nixon's "war on crime" that packed young blacks into the nation's prisons in ever-increasing numbers.

While the blacks fought over the homosexual slave trade, the Family found itself embroiled in a violent power struggle with a bolder, more aggressive Dixie Mafia. The Mafia had added a litany of B-Line security guards to its payroll. It was widely rumored that their drug operation was protected by three of the prison's five security majors. One thing was certain — the Dixie Mafia operated with impunity. Its members got the best inmate job assignments, allowing them the greatest freedom of movement and information. Well-placed inmate clerks delivered "snitch notes" and files on informants to the gang's leaders. They were given advance warning of security shakedowns and their "runners" were never searched at security checkpoints.

The extent of their corrupt, murderous influence was evident in the death of James "Gramps" Gwin after he was placed in segregation for his own protection. A career criminal, Gwin was a powerful drug dealer with close ties to the Dixie Mafia. But he had actually become too powerful after he cultivated a criminal relationship with several black power brokers.

"The Dixie Mafia boys are afraid of Gramps," Big Mick told me one afternoon. "They're going to set him up for a hit. They'll probably get someone off the Trusty Yard to do it. I don't care who does it, so long as the Family is not involved in it."

Gramps was a shrewd old con. He sensed the hit. He decided to "roll over" and blow the lid off corruption at the prison, including naming the prominent security officials who were protecting the corruption. After Gramps was placed in "protective custody," Dixie Mafia leaders Mule and Fulford were placed in the same cell with him. The next morning, Gramps was carried out of the cell dead. The cause of death was officially listed as a heart attack.

The state police conducted a criminal investigation into Gwin's death. A key state police investigator was convinced it was a contract killing carried out by the Dixie Mafia at the behest of a high-ranking B-Line security official who would later become Angola's warden.

Mule and Fulford were released from segregation following Gwin's death. Main Prison inmates were encouraged to believe that Gramps had been killed because he was prepared to "rat" on the Dixie Mafia. His murder was a warning that an informant could be silenced anywhere in the prison.

The greater the Dixie Mafia's influence became, the tighter the Family circled the wagons. The slightest encroachment into the Family's territory was met with severe retaliation. Big Mick wasted no time when he needed to retaliate. I walked into the dorm one day to find him in a powwow with Laredo, Sancho, and Blue. From their gestures and the tones of their voices, I knew a serious matter was under discussion, probably involving violence. I went straight to my bunk and laid out my things for a shower. I didn't want to know what they were discussing.

"Come here, Sinclair," Big Mick said, gesturing me toward the group.

I couldn't walk away. I needed them as much as they needed me. Their muscle protected me from a knife in the back.

"Look, we've got a problem," Big Mick whispered. "Laredo's gonna take out that dude Yates. If a bust comes down, we'll need you to hook up a defense for him, to help him beat the rap."

Yates was a henchman for the Dixie Mafia. The red-faced Alabama native stood six feet four inches tall and weighed 240 pounds. A professional armed robber by trade, he was a barroom brawler who had captured the prison's heavyweight boxing championship in a two-punch bout. He hooked the reigning black champ with a left to the midsection and a hammering right to the side of the face, shattering the former champ's jaw. Yates was a dangerous man to be talking about killing.

"What's this all about?" I asked.

"I sold him a bundle of dope," Laredo replied, nervousness creeping into his Mexican accent. "I was waiting for him to bring me the bread, but the motherfucker don't show. I go to him like a man and say, 'Man, where's my bread?' The dude doesn't even blink an eye. 'You're jacked, greaser. Get the fuck out of my face.' The dude caught me short, so I says, 'That's cool, Bro. Check you later.'"

"And we're fixing to check him," Big Mick interrupted. "Nobody jacks the Family."

"You got that right, Big Mick. I'm gonna cut that big hillbilly's heart out."

"You know what this is really about, Mick," I said.

Big Mick stared hard at me. Muscles rippled as he tied a red bandanna around his head.

"You bet I do. It's about fucking survival. It's about pride. It's about the Dixie Mafia pushing and pushing. Nobody pushes Big Mick! I made my name off bitches like them, and I'm fixing to show those assholes why I am the Big Mick."

Violence moves fast in prison. Big Mick and Laredo walked out of Oak 4 dorm followed by Blue and Sancho. Each man wore unmarked jeans and large unmarked shirts to conceal their weapons. They wore brogans and leather gloves with the fingertips cut off and wool skullcaps that could easily be pulled down over their faces. The gear was standard prison battle dress.

The clique found Yates sitting at a table in the dayroom of Oak 2 dorm playing poker. Seeing the Family, Yates quickly pulled a knife that was taped to his leg and slowly stood up to face the enemy.

"How's it gonna be, greaser?" he said, backing up against the wall. "Me and you — or me and you and all of them? I tell you what, fuck all of you."

Laredo pulled his knife, kicking the card table out of his way.

"You gonna die here today, Yates," he said.

"That may be, greaser," Yates said, calmly shifting his position and preparing for the Mexican's lunge. "But you gotta give ass to get ass. So come get this white man's ass."

Laredo was small but quick. He grabbed a chair, slinging it at Yates, who blocked it with his free arm. Laredo moved like a mongoose after a cobra, hitting Yates in the side with the knife. Yates didn't flinch. He swung his knife upward in a vicious thrust, only to see Laredo quickly dance away. Yates moved after him like a charging bull after a matador. He forced Laredo into a corner. The Mexican made a desperate lunge with the knife. Yates grabbed his knife hand and literally slung Laredo across the dayroom. The knife flew out of Laredo's hand, crashing against the wall.

"You're mine now, greaser," Yates said as he moved toward Laredo, who quickly jumped up in obvious panic.

"Fuck you," Big Mick said.

Stepping away from the clique, he swung a baseball bat, hitting Yates in the side of the head. The thud sounded like a watermelon being dropped. Yates sank to his knees, instinctively crawling toward the door.

Laredo retrieved his knife and charged after the mortally wounded Yates. He caught Yates just as he crawled out onto the Walk. Laredo began stabbing Yates, who kept trying to ward off the blows. A large crowd of inmates watched with mixed fascination and excitement.

"Please, Laredo, don't kill me," Yates hoarsely begged as the knife brutally ripped his flesh.

"Don't cop deuces now, bitch," Laredo cursed.

A security guard ran up to the fight, blowing a whistle.

"All right, all right, break it up," he ordered. "Get off him, Laredo — that's enough."

Kneeling over Yates, Laredo was a wild man. Blood was splattered all over his face and shirt.

"You want some of this action?" he said, looking up at the guard with his hand gripping the knife that was still buried in Yates' chest.

The guard backed up against the wall.

"You gonna die here today, motherfucker," Laredo said as he stabbed Yates several more times.

Blue and Sancho finally pulled him off Yates' limp body and

dragged him back into Oak 4 dorm. Yates had thirty-nine stab wounds in his chest and neck, thirteen of them through the heart. Blue and Sancho took Laredo's bloody clothes and gave them to a flunkie to burn. Sancho took the murder weapon and buried it.

Since a guard had witnessed the killing, it didn't take the goon squad long to haul Laredo off to segregation. I defended him before the Disciplinary Board but there was no defense to present. He was later tried for murder, convicted, and given a life sentence consecutive to the fifty-year armed robbery sentence he was already serving.

Even with everything I had experienced as a child and had already witnessed in prison, nothing in my life had prepared me for the kind of callous, ruthless violence so prevalent on the Big Yard in 1973. Although I had not lifted a hand in violence, I had embraced the criminal ethic that sanctioned and encouraged it. I took pride in being a solid convict and nurtured my reputation in the criminal subculture through my legal expertise.

But I had seen more than enough. I wanted to break my pact with the criminal ethic. I began searching for a way to live in the prison community without being criminal.

19

By THE SUMMER OF 1973, Louisiana prison officials were under intense pressure from the U.S. Justice Department to integrate the Main Prison complex. Rumors of integration inflamed in-group tension that spilled over into racial tension, creating a climate ripe for a "race war." This tenuous situation was exacerbated by the B-Line clique's adamant opposition to integration. B-Line guards fed the rumor mill with ugly predictions that a riot would occur if the Big Yard were integrated. A riot, of course, would have worked to their advantage, giving them a free hand to smash the budding black militancy at the prison.

The Grievance Committee requested an emergency meeting with Hunt and Henderson to discuss the integration issue with inmate leaders. Hunt brought two Justice Department attorneys with her to the conclave, which was held in the visiting room at the A-Building. It proved to be the committee's most significant meeting.

"The first thing I want each inmate here to understand is that Angola is going to be integrated," Warden Henderson said, rising from his chair to address his remarks to the group of a dozen inmate leaders. "Integration will be achieved even if we have to call in the National Guard. This administration accepts the legal mandate that the living quarters in the Main Prison must be integrated immediately."

Henderson sat down. Hunt gestured toward one of the Justice Department attorneys, a tall man with shoulder-length hair and a beard. He removed the pipe he had been incessantly puffing during Henderson's brief remarks.

"We feel that we have formulated a reasonable plan to integrate the prison," he said in a clipped northern accent. "Our plan calls for each dormitory on the Big Yard, as well as the Trusty Yard, to be integrated by placing a racial quota of whites in each dormitory. We realize there may be some problem with the numbers but that can't be helped — we only have 150 white inmates to more than a thousand black inmates on the Big Yard alone. That translates into five whites and fifty-five blacks in each dorm —"

The plan was a recipe for a race riot. I rose to interrupt the attorney.

"Let's get one thing straight up front," I said. "You're not going to put five whites in a dorm with fifty-five blacks —"

"That's exactly what I'm saying and that's exactly what we will do," the attorney retorted. "Our proposal is already on paper. It's reasonable and we . . ."

"Go get your National Guard, Warden," I said, speaking directly to Henderson.

The attorney was startled.

"What do you mean?" he stammered.

Blowing a cloud of cigarette smoke out of the side of her mouth, Hunt elected to say nothing. A nicotine-stained index finger detracted from the attractive image she presented with her thigh displayed under a tight-fitting miniskirt. She stared hard at me. Insolently, I stared back. I was not afraid of her power, and that made me dangerous in her eyes.

In 1972, when Governor Edwards named her to head the Louisiana corrections system, Elayn Hunt was hailed as a reformer with both the integrity and the courage to clean up Angola. She promptly closed the Red Hats.

Hunt's gesture in closing the infamous cell block was symbolic. Warden Henderson had already phased it out. While the closure of the Red Hats prompted the inmates to call Hunt a savior, it alienated the B-Line regime. The clique was not about to relinquish its power to "a bitch." Several powerful B-Line security officials promptly allied themselves with Henderson. Despite their previous objections to his liberal philosophy of penal reform, such as his adamant opposition to the death penalty, they preferred dealing with him to the new, radical woman director.

Hunt next suspended field work, announcing that the "sugarcane era" at Angola was over. It would prove to be her biggest mistake. The prison plantation revolved around sugarcane. The money that the crop generated, much of which found its way into the pockets of corrupt lawmakers, was the core of the B-Line clique's political power. During a ten-week period between October and December, every inmate at the prison was put to work cutting the twelve-foot-high stalks of sugarcane. Irrespective of their age or their health, they worked from sunup until sundown, seven days a week. Shotgun-toting inmate guards and their B-Line masters crushed resistance and rebellion. Nothing mattered except bringing the crop in on time.

As a reward for getting all the sugarcane cut before the winter freeze, inmates didn't have to work during the Christmas holiday season. The prison's rules against homosexual sex, gambling, and drugs were unofficially suspended during their "vacation." Hunt's order to stop the field work would haunt her to her grave. Idleness spawned a level of violence that turned the prison into a lawless jungle and ultimately forced a federal judge to take control of Angola. Without field work to bleed off their energy, Angola's inmates turned to drugs, gambling, and homosexuality. Violence was the inevitable by-product.

Within a year of her appointment, the inmates were cursing Hunt's name, booing her when she was introduced at the prison's annual rodeo. She never quite got over that humiliation, feeling betrayed by the prisoners that she had vowed to help.

The Justice Department attorney turned to her. "What is this man talking about, Ms. Hunt?" he asked, gesturing irritably in my direction.

She squashed out the cigarette in an ashtray. That cigarette, and the countless others she chain-smoked, would contribute to her death of pancreatic cancer in 1975.

"He's saying there's a problem with your plan," she replied in a masculine, grating voice.

"No, that's not quite what I'm saying," I said, leaning forward, both fists pressed against the conference table. "What I'm saying — and I think each of you would do well to listen — is that you're gonna have a race war, not a 'problem,' if you try to implement this plan. And I'm talking about a war, literally — not a gang fight between some racial malcontents. Those guys down the Walk are armed to the teeth. You know it, Ms. Hunt. Right now you're swapping transfers to satellite institutions for inmates who turn in pistols to you. So you know what kind of weapons they have down there — and you know your B-Line security force is not going to stop the violence. They want a race riot more than some of the inmates."

"Well, I can assure you, Mr. Sinclair —" the attorney tried to interject.

"With all due respect, sir," I snapped, "you can't assure me of anything. I live in this jungle."

A solemn mood settled over the room. Henderson toyed with a pencil, opting to let Hunt respond to my charges. I waited for other inmates to speak.

"Sinclair's right," Life said, rising as though on cue. "I understand and respect that you people have a difficult task facing you. But this place is still ruled with a Civil War mentality, and that makes things more complicated than the plan you have put on paper. We live in the real world — not a paper one. Our realities are violence and hatred."

Life paused, letting his words be absorbed.

"You're simply not going to implement a fifty-five to five ratio," he continued. "It's unrealistic to even propose such a plan. Being black, I wouldn't live in a dorm with fifty-five whites and only five blacks."

The two Justice Department attorneys asked for a few moments to confer. They walked to another table, engaging in an intense, whispered exchange. I lit a cigarette, staring at Hunt. She had one leg square-crossed over the other like a man. Inmate gossip linked her romantically with two Angola prisoners. One was Bill Brown, the editor of the prison's news magazine, *The Angolite.* The other was a New Orleans drug offender. She often checked the two inmates out of Angola to take them to her office in Baton Rouge. She also accompanied them on speaking engagements around the state as they praised her "prison reform" plans before civic groups, universities, and high schools.

"Well, gentlemen, do you have any suggestions?" the attorney asked when they returned to the conference table.

"Make it half and half — thirty whites, thirty blacks," I said.

"Parity is unacceptable," the attorney said.

"What's wrong with parity?" I asked.

"Apparently you're out of touch with racial priorities," the attorney answered, shrugging his shoulders.

"What about twenty whites in each dorm?" Life asked.

I looked at the other white inmates. They nodded in agreement. Life looked at the black inmates at the table. They also nodded in agreement. A compromise had been reached without a single word of protest.

"I would like to confer with Ms. Hunt and Warden Henderson for a few moments," the attorney said, signaling an adjournment of the meeting.

Fifteen minutes later, he called the meeting back to order, announcing that the Justice Department would accept the forty to twenty ratio.

"This volatile issue is by no means settled," Hunt added. "Your job has just begun. You must now sell this plan to the inmate population. You must persuade them to integrate voluntarily. I do not envy you your task. You have one week to convince them to accept this plan before we take the necessary measures to implement it. I will pray for each of you every night."

Life was the prison's most influential black leader. His presence on the Yard was essential to the success of the voluntary plan.

"We can make the plan work but only if you release Life from the cell block," I said, speaking directly to Henderson. "He's the only black leader who can sway the militants who oppose integration. He's the key to nonviolence."

Henderson toyed with his pencil a few moments before answering.

"Alright, I'm going to release Breaux, but if there's any violence, I'm locking both of you up — for a long time."

We walked away from the meeting jubilant. The black leaders congratulated me for securing Life's freedom from the cell block.

"If words were bullets, Sinclair, you'd put Machine Gun Kelly to shame," Treetop said.

Before he was released from the cell block, Life received a message from an inmate orderly that Billy Ray wanted to see him. He walked over to the white side of the cell block and stopped in front of Billy Ray's cell. Several white inmates cursed at him as he walked by. He said nothing, waiting for one of them to confront him directly. No one did.

"You wanted to see me, White?" Life asked, as he walked up to the bars in front of Billy Ray's cell, noting the pill-induced glaze in Billy Ray's eyes as he got out of bed.

"Yes, I have a favor to ask of you," Billy Ray said, gripping the bars as he looked directly into Life's eyes. The clarity of Billy Ray's voice surprised Life. He was accustomed to the slurred speech of pill addicts.

"What is it?" Life asked.

Before Billy Ray could answer, Life continued:

"Perhaps I should ask, 'Why me?'"

"We have only one thing in common," Billy Ray said, his voice turning as cold as a Minnesota winter. "Our friend, Billy Sinclair. I love him more than a brother. He's the only family I got. From what he tells me, and from what I've heard from other people, you're a good friend to have in a jam. Watch Billy's back through all this integration crap. He only sees what's in front of him."

Although he had heard of Billy Ray's many exploits, Life had never seen him up close. Except for the eyes, Life was struck by Billy Ray's boyish appearance. But his eyes made Life uneasy. They radiated an impenetrable glare of rage and defiance.

"You don't have to ask me to do that as a favor," Life said, recovering his composure. "I'll be the eyes in his back. You really don't have to worry, though. I've seen him operate under pressure and he's always in control. His greatest asset is controlling all the players in any situation."

While Life spoke, Billy Ray wondered how he would handle himself in a knife fight.

"I've often said any friend of Billy is a friend of mine," Billy Ray said. "But I can't say that about you. I've never called a black man a friend."

Perhaps Billy Ray was trying to provoke a confrontation. Everything in his world revolved around the insatiable need to meet a challenge.

"Like I said, I'll be the eyes in his back," Life said, unconsciously clenching his jaw muscle. "You and I are cut from the same cloth, White — we're haters. I hate what you are as much as you hate what I am. Without hatred, we are nothing. Hate is our life force, and, believe me, it will kill us both."

Billy Ray smiled, loosening his grip on the bars.

"But it's good, ain't it, Life? We live only for the moment, expecting nothing but the worst. Fucking-A, hate will kill us. And we won't be remembered for a goddamn thing — but at least we live each moment committed to what we are."

Life turned and walked away. The aura of fatalism about Billy Ray had unnerved him. Life was relieved when the order for his release from the cell block came later that same day.

For the next week, Life and I were constant companions. Fear, hate, and paranoia were running rampant, making it virtually impossible to secure any consensus among the prison's black and white power brokers. We held meetings with them that lasted for hours. We always stood together, side by side, as distrust and hostility shredded one proposal after another. We never gave an inch. I came to trust Life as much as I did Billy Ray. Their differences tore into my heart like a vulture's bloody beak. How could I bridge the chasm between them? There was no easy answer.

While most inmates were willing to accept integration as inevitable, the Dixie Mafia wanted violence. A violent confrontation would put the black militants and most of the Family in lockdown. The Dixie Mafia would then be in a position to control the prison's narcotics and protection rackets, leaving the black power brokers to fight over the homosexual slave trade. Life and I were determined to prevent their power grab.

"We have to put twenty whites in each Oak dormitory," I told a group of leaders one night in the Recreation Room. "Now the whites should decide which twenty are going to live in each dorm. We will come up with four lists of names. I suggest blacks come up with their four lists. We can select two whites and two blacks from each list. They must approve each name on the list. If they find any inmate on the list, black or white, unacceptable, that name will be removed and placed on another list.

"As a practical matter, we should designate one list for the undesirables. Put them all together. If there is anyone on the list who is totally unacceptable, we'll make him leave. It's that simple."

Bubba Red, a powerful black leader from New Orleans who wanted a piece of the Dixie Mafia's drug market, was the first to respond. What he said was too good to be true.

"I like the idea. We can make it work. Everybody will have a say about who they live with. We can even take it a step further. We can draw up a list of rules for each dorm. That would help each side adjust to the other. You know, let the brothers jive with *Soul Train* and let the honkies kick with *Hee Haw*."

The compromise worked. The Main Prison was integrated in less than a week without a single incident of violence. It was a miracle — the nonviolent integration of the prison during its worst period of violence.

I later learned that Big Mick and Bubba Red had cut a deal. Big Mick would supply the heroin and Bubba Red would control its distribution among the blacks. Although that racial alliance ultimately brought about the demise of the Family, it stalled the Dixie Mafia's attempt to control the prison's narcotics traffic, at least for a few years.

20

FOLLOWING THE INTEGRATION of the Big Yard in 1973, Life moved into the Oak 4 dormitory where I lived. We presented a portrait of racial unity. Oak 4 had remained the most powerful dorm on the yard, housing the strongest and most influential inmates. Following our lead, its residents successfully established a racial détente. Coexistence was preferable to war when the consequences were too costly for either side to bear. The certain annihilation of all combatants in the event of war is the best formula for peace.

But that was not the case in the other three Oak dormitories. The balance of power there quickly shifted in favor of the black majority. They controlled the dorm's vices: sex, drugs, gambling; the best beds, the TV room, and the dayroom. The power shift in the three Oak dorms mirrored the gradual shift of power taking place in Angola. Blacks began to get jobs previously reserved for whites. They assumed greater influence over the day-to-day operations of the prison. They moved into all-white inmate organizations, such as the Jaycees and Narcotics Anonymous. Being a majority, they easily elected officers to key positions. Only the Dixie Mafia remained all white.

Against the backdrop of shifting racial power, the B-Line regime targeted the Grievance Committee for harassment. It was losing its absolute control over the inmates as a result of integration. The regime blamed the committee for the winds of change that were sweeping the prison. In particular, they blamed me and Life. We were "radicals" with a communist agenda. The regime and the Dixie Mafia wanted us out of the way — either locked up or dead.

One day as I walked through the Control Center, an inmate I barely knew asked me to drop off his shirt at Oak 1 dorm. It was easy to do so I took the shirt. But I did not go straight to the dorm. Instead, I stopped at the Barber Shop for a haircut, hanging the shirt on a coat rack. When I left the Barber Shop, I forgot it.

As I walked out of the Control Center, Major Norwood and his shakedown crew converged on me. They slammed me against the wall and roughly kicked my feet apart. Norwood, a longtime player in the B-Line regime, searched me but found nothing. He was clearly agitated.

Later, I doubled back to the Barber Shop and examined the shirt that the inmate had given me. There was an open pack of Camel cigarettes in one of the pockets. The cigarette pack had eight joints of marijuana concealed in it.

Angered by the attempt at a setup, I went straight to Oak 1, only to learn that the owner of the shirt had just been taken into protective custody.

The setup attempt fueled my desire to resign from the Grievance Committee. I had grown tired of the inmate demands and fed up with harassment from security. Every time I walked through a security checkpoint, I was either frisked or strip-searched. The Grievance Committee office had been raided twice by the shakedown crew, who tore everything apart in search of "drugs and weapons." The B-Line regime kept the rumor mill churning with suspicions that Life and I were plotting an Attica-like rebellion. It was a peculiar time for the two of us. On one hand, we had the militants urging us to lead an uprising; on the other hand, key security personnel were feeding the belief that we planned to do it.

The executive council of the Grievance Committee repeatedly brought the harassment issue to the attention of Hunt and Henderson. But they were so embroiled in a power struggle that our complaints fell on deaf ears. Henderson had mounted a major effort to form a coalition of Cajun security guards and several key B-Line officers to wrest control of the prison from the B-Line forces. Meanwhile, Hunt was waging a political crusade in the state legislature to close Angola. She favored smaller prisons located nearer the community. While Henderson was trying to control the violence with his new coalition, Hunt was manipulating it to support her political agenda. She argued that the only way to end the bloodshed and corruption at Angola was to close the sprawling prison plantation.

My decision to resign from the Grievance Committee was sealed when I learned that Hunt had struck a secret deal with two members of our executive council. She promised them speaking trips and furloughs in exchange for spying on me and Life. When I told Life about my decision to resign because of Hunt's interference, he decided to resign as well. But he wanted to gut the committee.

"We cannot let the Grievance Committee become a pawn of the administration," he said. "It may not have much credibility after we resign, but I don't want to leave it intact for her pets to use. I risked my life to make the committee credible and I'm not about to let those Uncle Toms have it."

"What do you want to do?" I asked.

"Take the committee down. We have enough support to force en masse resignations. Let's send that dyke a real message."

We quietly put together a coalition favoring abolition of the Grievance Committee. Relying on the committee's bylaws, which I had written, Life and I called an emergency meeting to discuss the resignation issue outside the presence of the administration.

"We're all being used as pawns by the administration," Life said, addressing the full committee. "Elayn Hunt wants this committee to exist for her professional prestige, to enhance her image in the prison industry as a progressive, reform-minded administrator. The committee has become a political tool. We're no longer a legitimate, independent grievance mechanism. Hunt bought off two members on the executive council with speaking trips — Bird and Leotha."

There was a stir among the members. Whispered conversations grew louder. Life glared at the committee. He silenced them by slamming his fist on the podium.

"The way things stand right now," he continued, "we cannot do what we were elected to do — serve the needs of the inmate population. And if I can't serve the inmates, then I won't serve on the committee at all. I will not be a lackey for Elayn Hunt. Sinclair and I are tendering our resignations from the committee and we strongly urge each of you to do the same thing. An en masse resignation would send a clear message to Baton Rouge."

The room was as quiet as Tut's tomb.

"If you elect not to resign," Life warned, "I will let you explain it to the inmate population, and they will have all the facts. That I guarantee."

The threat was left hanging. I stood up next to Life, clapping. Several more members rose, taking up the applause. It grew, assuming a unanimous thunder of approval. The traditional us-against-them convict appeal had worked. No member wanted to walk out of the room identified with the Hunt administration.

News of the collapse of the Grievance Committee flashed throughout the prison. The committee had established unprecedented trust and respect among the inmates. Committee members quickly blamed Hunt for the collapse, saying she did not do enough to support it.

A few weeks later, Bill Brown, the editor of *The Angolite*, summoned me to his office. The convict editor was an avowed Hunt loyalist. In exchange for a cushy job and influence with the administration, he produced a low-key publication that reported on club news and social events.

"I want to talk with you about the Grievance Committee problem," Brown said as I sat in front of his desk. "More to the point, I want to know why you and Life orchestrated the resignations."

"Is this an interview or information gathering for your own use?" I asked.

"It's not an interview," he replied, extending a pack of cigarettes. I ignored the offer.

"The reasons we resigned are simple," I said. "Security was riding roughshod over us and Hunt did nothing to stop it, not to

141

mention the little side deal she cut with Bird and Leotha to get them to spy on me and Life because we wouldn't go along with her program."

"What's so bad about going along with the program?"

I was conscious the conversation might be recorded.

"I have a simple philosophy, Bill Brown," I answered. "You're either on one side of the fence or the other. You can't play both sides. I'm on this side, so I'm loyal to this side. If I wore a badge, then I'd be loyal to Hunt's side. I don't believe you can be a convict and a policeman at the same time."

While I still professed allegiance to the convict code, I was no longer sure of its values. Increasingly, I was being drawn into Life's radical political values. But I was too proud to back away from the code in front of Brown.

"You'll never get anywhere in this world if you don't know how to play both sides of every situation," he said.

"I don't ever expect to get out of this prison alive," I replied, "and ass-kissing this administration damn sure won't help my situation."

Brown continued to regard me calmly.

"Let's lay our cards on the table," he said frankly. "Ms. Hunt wants the Grievance Committee reactivated. She asked me to talk to you about helping in that effort. The committee is important to her."

The Grievance Committee was important to Hunt because it represented the last vestige of respect she had among the inmates. Its members had openly and defiantly rejected her leadership. The en masse resignation had become a political issue because a majority of the Grievance Committee publicly announced their support for Warden Henderson's policies.

"I have nothing to do with the committee anymore," I said. "My position is clear. My involvement with it is over. Hunt can re-activate it anytime she wants to."

"Be serious, Sinclair. Ms. Hunt knows the committee won't have any credibility unless you take part in it. Those dudes down the Walk are not going to believe in it. All she wants you to do is re-activate the committee. And if you decide to back away from it later on you can. Just help her get it back on its feet. You help her, she'll help you. I promise you that."

"What's she gonna do?" I asked. "Get me a transfer to a satellite facility?"

Brown cleared his throat, blowing air into his balled fist.

"Let me give you a piece of advice, Sinclair. I respect you. Those dudes you're standing up for down the Walk could care less what you do for them. You will either be killed or locked up. That's the way power works, my man."

Brown was right, and deep down I suspected it. Still, I rose to leave the office. I would not accept his deal. Unwittingly, I had set the stage for my own downfall. While I had mastered the art of physical survival in prison, I had yet to fathom the power that controls any administration. Ultimately, I would come to realize that the power of politics, not morality, ruled the free world and the prison. I stopped at the door, turning back to Brown.

"Tell Elayn Hunt to go to hell."

The decision to walk away from Brown's offer came back to haunt me. Had I gotten on board, I might have been a free man. As I passed through the Control Center on my way back to the jungle, Major Norwood stopped me.

"Alright, Sinclair, take everything out of your pockets and strip," he ordered.

I said nothing. A veteran prison guard, Norwood was needling me, trying to provoke insubordination. He had been the main instigator of harassment against the Grievance Committee. Stripped, I stood naked before him.

"Alright, open your mouth."

I complied.

"Wider."

I complied.

"Turn around and spread those cheeks."

I complied.

"Show me the brown eye."

I complied.

"Raise your feet."

I complied.

"Alright, get dressed."

Slowly, I began to put on my clothes. Our eyes locked. I refused to look away. We clearly saw the mutual hatred in each other's eyes.

"I'm gonna tell you something, Sinclair," he said. "If it's the last thing I do, I will put your ass in a cell, and you will never get out. I promise you that. I'm gonna break you, dude."

"You may get me back in a cage, Major," I said, "but you'll never break me. I'm a better man than you are any day."

Dressed again, I turned and walked back into a world of uncertainty and human madness. While there had been no major racial violence following the integration of the Big Yard, individual and gang-related violence continued to escalate. Leon Craft, a black inmate, had his head crushed with a cinder block by two drunken inmates. The killers dragged his body under a Walnut dormitory and buried it in a shallow grave. Security was so lax that guards listed the dead man as an escapee.

Rumors kept circulating through the inmate grapevine that Craft had been murdered and buried somewhere on the Big Yard. Security ignored them. But Warden Henderson did not like the ugly whispers. He ordered a thorough search of the entire Big Yard.

When a young guard crawled hurriedly out from under a Walnut dorm, ashen-faced and muttering incoherently, the horrible truth was known. A team of guards unearthed Craft's badly decomposed body. It had been buried for more than a week. The guards threw its horrible-smelling remains on a stretcher, covered it with a green army blanket, and rolled it down the Walk, past inmates lined up in the dorm windows anxious for a glimpse of the swollen, putrid mass.

Irritated, one of the guards pushing the stretcher angrily screamed at the inmates: "Get out of those windows, you sick sonuvabitches."

"Fuck you," came a chorus of response.

Shortly after the Fourth of July, a full-scale war erupted between the black gangs from New Orleans and Shreveport. Hundreds of inmates swarmed onto the Yard in full battle dress to fight and duel over ownership of a punk. They resembled the Roman Legion doing battle. One inmate was killed, another had his arm severed at the elbow when he raised it to ward off a hatchet blow, and dozens more were seriously injured. Only the seriously wounded were taken to the prison hospital. The rest hobbled off to their respective dorms where their punks or friends sewed them up. Inmates kept a stash of medical supplies for such emergencies. The injured simply took a handful of Darvons and passed out.

In late July, three of Big Mick's drug dealers on the Trusty Yard summoned him to the Education Department. The three — Rachal, Santana, and Monster — had decided to kill Mouse because he had humiliated Rachal by calling him an "asshole" in front of several people. Gang pride was at stake.

"We can't let this slide, Big Mick," Santana said. "Mouse has been pushing us hard lately because we have the best dope on the yard. He undercuts our prices. Hell, he's even jacked several of our customers. The dude is forcing this play, Mick."

Big Mick knew the time had come to settle up with Mouse.

"Who's gonna take him out?"

"Rachal — it's his beef," Monster said. "We're gonna be there to make sure the play goes down right."

"You better make sure he's dead," Big Mick ordered. "If you don't kill him, he'll come back and kill every one of you. And probably me as well. I know the dude. He'll die hard."

That same night Rachal crept up to Mouse's bunk. Mouse was sleeping on his right side. Armed with a large butcher knife, the Frenchman eased up behind Mouse and buried the knife three times in his chest. Mouse's death screams were heard across the entire Trusty Yard. They were not screams of pain but rage. They echoed like a demon rising from the depths of hell.

Though mortally wounded, Mouse struggled out of his bunk only to have Santana bash him in the side of the head with a thick oak walking cane.

Across the dorm, Iron Mike, one of Mouse's henchmen, jumped up in his bed. That was as far as he got.

"Don't get up, motherfucker," Monster told him as he placed a knife to his throat. "Just lay back down. You don't want any of this action."

Mouse managed to crawl several feet down the aisle. Rachal scurried back to his bunk while Santana walked over to Monster.

"I'll see you motherfuckers in hell," Mouse screamed as he heaved a death sigh.

"Get a stretcher, Santana," Monster said. "I know he's dead but I'm pushing him to the hospital to make sure. I promise he'll really be dead before we get there."

The very next night, Lee Oscar, a close friend of Mouse's and a criminal associate of the Dixie Mafia, stabbed Rachal to death as he lay sleeping. Oscar used the same kind of butcher knife that Rachal had used to kill Mouse. Santana and Monster were supposed to be watching over Rachal as he slept, but they had fixed several bags of heroin and were in a "nod" when Oscar struck the fatal blows. The Dixie Mafia had made good on its vow — a life for a life.

21

THE ESCALATING LEVEL of sexual violence among the black inmates forced Life to bring together several key leaders to deal with the problem. They founded The Brotherhood, an organization dedicated to saving young inmates from the sexual violence. The Brotherhood operated on the premise that a young inmate should have an opportunity to keep his manhood. If he wanted to be a punk and allowed himself to be turned out, The Brotherhood would not interfere. On the other hand, if he wanted to be a man, The Brotherhood would give him an umbrella of protection.

Warden Henderson sanctioned the formation of The Brotherhood. Realizing that the inmates had control of daily operations in the prison, he was powerless to stop the sexual violence. New inmates, mostly black, were being packed into Angola, which forced as many as eighty to be housed in sixty-man dorms. Henderson's coalition of security officers was not professionally trained. And he could not turn to the B-Line regime. They were unwilling to take control of Angola. Reducing the level of homosexual violence was not in their best interest.

The regime used homosexuality among black inmates as a means of protecting its interests in the drug traffic that the white inmates controlled. As long as the blacks were divided, fighting over territorial interests in the homosexual slave trade, the white drug trade went unchallenged. Some B-Line security chieftains bartered off prized young black kids to powerful criminal bucks — even performing marriage ceremonies in the Control Center to make the bondage official.

Henderson was forced to turn to inmates for assistance in his futile effort to reduce the violence. He had only one guard to each four-dorm unit — a ratio of nearly three hundred inmates to one guard. The B-Line regime accused Henderson of "selling out to the black militants." They pointed to the brutal murder of Brent Miller, saying Life led the assassination team of militants who slit the young guard's throat.

Ignoring resistance from the B-Line regime, Henderson gave Life carte blanche to carry out his organization's nonviolent objectives. Life made frequent trips to the Reception Center, where he lectured all incoming inmates about what to expect on the Big Yard and how to deal with it. Suave and articulate, he easily commanded the attention of the intimidated youthful offenders.

"The Brotherhood stands ready to defend you," he said. "If you want to be a man in this joint, The Brotherhood will protect you. But if you choose to become a punk, you're on your own."

Looking down at the young faces, Life understood their fear and terror. He had experienced the same thing eleven years before when he walked into the Reception Center.

"Let me tell you about the dudes in here," he continued. "You've heard the horror stories in jail about how bad they are, so you're afraid of the Big Yard. I don't blame you. I went through the same thing when I came here. But there's no need to be afraid. A dude walked up to me and told me I was for him. You know what I did? I sent the motherfucker home in a pine box. He won't ever try to fuck another man again."

Growing livid as he spoke, Life gestured forcefully to make his points.

"I hope none of you has to do what I did, but if it comes down to some asshole trying to take your manhood, then you get a knife, a ball bat, or a piece of pipe and kill the motherfucker. You hit him, and you keep on hitting him till he's dead. When a brother tries to deny a brother the right to be a man, he no longer deserves to live. You're black. Be proud. And be ready to fight and die like a black man — it's the only dignity you will ever have in this cesspool."

Most of the new arrivals had been nurtured on violence in New Orleans housing projects. It was a way of life in their world of dirty streets, filthy buildings, and rat-infested alleys. They had watched alcohol and drug addiction destroy their men and prostitution brutalize their women. These inner-city realities were etched in their brains. They fought, stole, and murdered their way to the human warehouse on the Mississippi River that was waiting to gobble them up and spit them out worse than when they entered.

Rance Moore had been one of the young men looking up at Life's lean, fiery figure with awe and admiration. As he lay on his dorm bunk one hot August night reading a book that Life had given him, he was grateful for the protection of The Brotherhood. Life had promised to get him moved to Oak 4. He did not relish the idea of spending another night in the Walnut dorm. He had not showered yet because he was too self-conscious to show his body. The thought of other men wanting to use him as a woman tormented him. He was tired of evading their lustful stares.

Glancing around the dorm, he felt sealed in a tomb about to suffocate.

"Man, that sure is a pretty thing," one inmate said, accompanied by exaggerated gestures.

"You can say that again," another replied, laughing as he slapped a thigh. "I'd like to get next to that stuff."

Their laughter rolled across the dormitory, only to be sucked up by the clamor of other sounds — the curses of men playing tonk; the boasts and laughter floating from the shower as soapy men tried to out-shout each other about the ironies and cruelties of the day; and the wail of a siren from the television set.

Inmates are loud, boisterous, physical creatures. A callous and insensitive breed, most have wasted their lives on crime and drugs. Given their lives of failure, they aspire to strength and power, criticizing and ridiculing weakness. Their social interactions consist of noisy boasting and bragging, exchanging embellished exploits about banks robbed, stores burglarized, whores pimped, and money made and wasted on the "good life."

Young and fresh out of Louisiana's Cajun country, Moore had no chance of surviving alone in Angola. He sat on his bunk looking out the dorm window into the darkness, trying to escape his fear. But every word and burst of laughter seemed directed at him. His paranoia ran wild. His heart was paralyzed with terror when two half brothers, Willie Carney and Gilbert Dixon, sat down on his bunk.

"You belong to us now, bitch," Carney said.

There was an abrupt cessation of noise and activity in the dorm. Nearby inmates began walking into the television room, a collective social signal that Moore was on his own. To preserve his manhood in prison, a young man must be willing to kill or die at any given moment. That moment had arrived for Rance Moore.

"We can do this thing any way you want to do it," Carney said, "but you're gonna be for us or we'll take it."

Dixon was the quieter, less aggressive of the two. He was always coming behind Carney to correct problems that Carney had created.

"Look, kid," Dixon said, "just pick an old man. If you don't, this will go on every night till you do. If it's not Willie, it'll be someone else. You've got to make a choice — fight or fuck. You're not gonna fight, so you might as well get used to being a bitch. You young dudes wanna steal and then come in here expecting a free ride. The game's not played that way, brother."

"Please, I just wanna be left alone," Moore whined. "I don't want any trouble."

"It don't go like that in here, bitch," Dixon replied, jamming a finger in the kid's face. "This ain't Sunday school. Get some heart or get a man. Don't force some dude to get a life sentence over that ass of yours."

Carney and Dixon walked away, leaving a terrified Moore on his bunk. Enough pressure had been applied for the moment. The dorm quickly resumed its boisterous activities.

Before the lights went out in the dorm, Moore made a decision to surrender to fear and give up his manhood. He didn't have the courage to fight or the will to die.

A general laziness pervaded the Big Yard on Saturday mornings. Most inmates slept late because they had stayed up late Friday night watching movies, doing drugs, or engaging in sex. But Dixon and Moore were up early. They worked in the kitchen and had to get up at four o'clock to prepare the breakfast meal. They sat alone at a dining table in the mess hall awaiting breakfast call.

"Don't worry about last night," Dixon said. "It's not the end of the world. It's the only way you can survive in this hellhole."

Moore nodded, shame and guilt tearing at his conscience.

"Like I told you, the best thing you can do now is get an old man," Dixon advised. "If you get hooked up with the wrong dude, he'll use you and let his friends use you. You're better off being with someone who will take care of you."

"Will you take care of me?" Moore asked. "I'd rather be for you."

Restraining a slight smile, Dixon felt good. He had won out over Carney and the others.

"Sure, I'll take care of you, baby," he said. "I'll be good to you. I won't let none of these booty-bandits mess with you."

A guard walked up to the table.

"Captain Dupre wants to see you, Moore."

Dixon went with Moore down the Walk to the Clothing Room, where Captain Dupre waited. Dixon slowed his gait when he saw Life waiting outside the Clothing Room. Carney and several inmates were standing about thirty feet farther down the Walk and Dixon joined them. Moore walked straight into the Clothing Room.

Life approached Carney. There was a heated exchange. The other inmates stood around, tense, waiting for the first sign of physical aggression. All were armed. The bloodletting was avoided when Dixon pulled Carney away. They walked back to their dorm to await Moore's return.

As soon as Moore emerged from the Clothing Room, Life grabbed him and walked him around the Yard. Several members of The Brotherhood trailed along behind Life as a protective shield. Captain Dupre, a veteran guard, went to Captain Joe Pittman to discuss the trouble brewing between the two factions. Moore had told Dupre he wanted a transfer to Oak 4 dorm to be with Life. Dupre, however, already had "information" that Carney and Dixon had "turned out" Moore.

Dupre and Pittman kept a watchful eye on Life and Moore. At approximately nine o'clock, they saw a large gathering of Brotherhood members. The two veteran security guards approached the group and searched every man. They found one knife on the ground several feet from the group.

"Alright, Breaux," Dupre said, "I don't know what's coming down but something's going on. Go in that dorm and get the kid's things. Take him to Oak 4. I want this matter settled, once and for all."

Things happened fast after that. Moore told Life he had been turned out the night before. The news enraged Life. He wanted a confrontation with Carney and Dixon, especially Carney. Life hated their criminal ethic. Brotherhood members tried to reason with him, explaining Moore had voluntarily given up his manhood. It was not their fight.

Life would not listen. He was obsessed with taking Moore from Carney. Armed with a knife and a cause, he was prepared to kill or die.

In the meantime, Treetop, a Brotherhood member, went into the dorm to speak with Carney.

"Back off this thing," he said. "It's gotten out of hand. You and Life are both men. You can't kill each other over a man's ass."

"It's not my play, Top," Carney replied, wrapping an Ace bandage around his left forearm, the one he would use as a shield. "Life has this thing about me. I'm not pushing the issue. I didn't take that boy's ass. He gave it up. I don't care about the jive your Brotherhood is peddling. If a boy decides to be for me, I don't want The Brotherhood in my business about it."

"Brother Carney, it ain't worth it. Two brothers shouldn't kill each other over an asshole."

"You think this is that simple," Carney spat. "We're talking about pride here. If Life thinks he's gonna walk in here and take my whore, he's crazy. One of us will die here today. No motherfucker takes something that belongs to me. And the boy belongs to me now."

Life and Moore were intercepted by several Brotherhood

members at the door of the dorm. They warned Life that both Carney and Dixon were armed and waiting.

"You're out there bad on this one," a Brotherhood member said. "The kid gave it up freely. Nobody pressured him. He belongs to Carney and Dixon — that's the law in here. You can't go in there and take the man's punk."

"Why can't I?" Life snapped. "I'll do it or die trying."

"We're not going with you on this one," the member replied. "You're forcing this play, and that's not what The Brotherhood is about."

"I've never asked any man to fight with me," Life said, his eyes sweeping the entire group. "I came here alone — I can damn sure die alone."

Without another word, Life turned and walked into the dormitory. Moore and a dorm guard followed him. Reaching the living area, Life saw Dixon off to his left, standing at the first row of beds. He hesitated, staring at Dixon. But Dixon was not the man he wanted.

Life and Moore continued down the aisle toward the kid's bunk. Carney was standing near the bunk, waiting calmly as Life approached. He was not afraid of the impending battle.

As he approached Carney, Life pulled a knife from his waistband. Carney likewise drew his knife and wrapped a towel around the forearm already covered by the Ace bandage. Moore ran for his bunk while the guard turned and ran for help.

Life moved in on Carney as both men slashed at each other. Neither landed a solid blow. They feinted for favorable attack positions.

Moore shattered the silence of the death duel by breaking a quart jar, turning it into a jagged weapon. Carney turned to see the kid approaching him from behind with the broken jar.

Dixon did not hesitate. He moved quickly to Carney's aid. Irving Harding, a friend of Dixon's, tried to hold him back, telling him it was not his fight.

"That's my brother," he yelled, breaking free.

Dixon snatched a mattress from a nearby bunk and moved between Life and Carney. Carney turned his attention to Moore. When Moore saw Carney coming at him, he panicked, grabbing a pillow. He warded off several of Carney's knife thrusts.

While Carney pressed the attack against Moore, Life focused his attack on Dixon. But Dixon was not an easy foe. He had survival savvy. Life was surprised by his speed. Dixon quickly maneuvered Life against the wall with the upright mattress, and with jungle quickness, reached around and scored two direct hits in Life's neck.

Blood spurted wildly. Gurgling, Life struggled desperately against the mattress pinning him to the wall. He managed to get free and clench Dixon. The two men fell on a nearby bunk. Dixon scored several more blows as the two men fought in the clench.

Realizing that Life was losing the fight, Moore broke and ran for the door. Carney didn't bother to chase him. Instead he ran over to the struggle between Life and Dixon and stabbed Life twice.

Still, Life continued to fight.

Two guards ran up to the fighting men and ordered them to stop. Carney backed away immediately but Life and Dixon continued their death struggle.

"C'mon, Gilbert," Harding said as he pulled Dixon off of Life. "It's over. Cool it."

One guard rushed up to Life. He was in a semi-kneeling position, struggling to get to his feet to continue the fight. His knife was still in his right hand.

"You sonuvabitch," Dixon cursed angrily, breaking free of Harding and rushing up to stab Life again. Life crumpled to the ground, dead from eight stab wounds. His knife slid across the floor.

The guards asked Carney and Dixon for their weapons. Aware that The Brotherhood was outside the dorm, the men refused to give them up. The guards escorted them out of the death-silenced dorm. A half-dozen Brotherhood members huddled together staring as they emerged from the dorm.

"Just remember," Carney told the group. "The Brotherhood is to blame for what happened here today. You wanna change the way we live and think! Well, go in there and get your brother and bury him. I'm going to be locked up awhile, but when I come back down this Walk, none of you had better tell me anything about owning a punk. I will own a bitch as long as I'm in this joint."

The Brotherhood walked into the dorm and picked up Life's

limp body. They placed it in a prison laundry basket and rolled it down the walk. Word of his death had already spread across the Yard. Black inmates lined the Walk in silence; some removed their skullcaps as a tribute of respect to the fallen warrior.

Life had fought and died for what he believed in — the simple principle that a young man had a right to be free of homosexual slavery. His was just another senseless, tragic death, like so many others during that bloody era.

22

I WAS SITTING IN THE LAW LIBRARY when someone ran in shouting that Life had been killed. A part of me ceased to be. I was too stunned to care about how or why. I had known that violent death awaited him. He would not back down from what he believed. He left a hole in my life that would never be filled. He gave me the courage to be different in a world that demanded conformity. He taught me to rise above the hate and prejudice that a warped, backwoods culture had imposed upon me. He had made a lie of Billy Ray's neo-Nazi racial beliefs. He showed me that leadership is wasted unless an uncompromising commitment to principles and beliefs accompanies it. Some called him a fool for trying to help a kid who ran out on him. But he died a hero trying to make a difference in the brutal, corrupt world that killed him. It was not long coming after me.

It happened on a hot Sunday morning in August as I lay in my bunk trying to find a reason to continue what was now a superhuman effort to survive. Someone stuck his head in the door and hollered:

"Sinclair, James Dunn wants to see you on the Yard."

I didn't know Dunn that well. He was a nurse's aide at the hospital and aspired to be a jailhouse lawyer. I had talked to him once about his case, offering him some passing legal advice.

I slipped on a shirt and walked out on the Yard to see him. He was standing on the side of Oak 1 dorm, casually observing the crowd of inmates watching the boxing matches. The boxing extravaganza had been scheduled for the Fourth of July but was postponed because of the war between New Orleans and Shreveport gangs.

"What's happening, man?" he greeted me with a smile.

"Nothing. What are you on the Yard for? The fights?"

"Yeah," he shrugged. "They want a nurse on hand in case one of them punch-drunk idiots gets hurt."

"What can I do for you?"

"Do you have a copy of the Criminal Code?" he asked. "I checked the Law Library and they don't know where their book is."

"Sure, I've got the book."

"Can I borrow it for a few days?"

"I guess so. Just take care of it."

"Sure, man."

I had no reason to be suspicious of Dunn. He was just another inmate seeking legal assistance.

I retrieved the book from the dorm. I detected a nervousness in Dunn's demeanor when I returned. He was anxious to get away. My paranoia clock began to tick, too late.

"Thanks, man — I'll get it back to you," he said, hurriedly walking away.

I turned to walk back to the dorm, only to freeze when I saw Major Norwood moving across the Yard to intercept Dunn. When I saw another officer moving toward him from an opposite direction, I knew something was going down. Norwood snatched the law book from Dunn as he walked up to him. The second officer frisked him while Norwood stooped and examined the grass around Dunn's feet. He picked up something. I couldn't see what it was.

Norwood led Dunn to the Control Center. I walked back to the dorm trying to figure out what had transpired.

I had been in the dorm only a few minutes when the shakedown crew charged through the door. Two guards seized me, forcing me to strip naked. The other guards rummaged through my personal belongings, scattering legal material all over the floor and my bunk. Destruction of an inmate's belongings was a favorite tactic of the shakedown crew.

With the search completed, I was escorted to the Control Center and into Norwood's office.

"This is for you," Norwood said, handing me a pink disciplinary report.

The report said Norwood observed me talking with Dunn several minutes before I passed something to him. Norwood said when he approached Dunn to search him, the inmate dropped something on the ground — three cellophane packets containing what Norwood suspected was LSD. The State Police Crime Lab later confirmed it. I was charged with "possession of contraband."

"This is a setup," I said, pointing to the report.

"Tell it to the Disciplinary Board," Norwood retorted. "I told you I'd get you back in a cell. Well, dude, you're going to stay there this time."

The day I appeared before the Disciplinary Board to answer the contraband charge, all other cases were rescheduled. Richard Crane, Hunt's legal counsel, attended the hearing, which lasted nearly five hours. I presented a "setup" defense. Associate Warden William Kerr chaired the hearing, an indication of the importance the administration placed on the proceeding.

"The board finds you guilty," Kerr said. "You are hereby sentenced to extended lockdown in Cell Block C. You have a right to appeal this decision."

Without a word, I turned and walked out of the room. I would later learn the setup had originated from DOC headquarters with the blessing of Elayn Hunt. A ranking prison official told me years later that it had been ordered for my own safety. Hunt and others feared that I would be killed like Life so they had me removed from the general population. I never accepted the theory. I was set up in retaliation for bringing down the Grievance Committee. Elayn Hunt never forgave me for that insult.

Prison officials turned the contraband over to the local district attorney, who filed a criminal charge against me. The court appointed Hamilton B. Willis, a former classification officer at the prison and now an attorney, to defend me. He conducted an extensive investigation, uncovering enough evidence of a setup to convince the district attorney to nolle prosequi the criminal charge. Willis told me that the DA was outraged because prison officials had lied to him. They had used him in an attempt to legitimize the setup.

Years later, I learned that Life's killing also had been orchestrated by a ranking security chieftain who issued a memo authorizing Life to go into any dorm to remove young inmates believed to be having homosexual problems. At the same time, the security chieftain got several black power brokers to spread rumors that security would crack down if Life and The Brotherhood were not put out of business. The extraordinary memo was issued with the official agenda of creating a violent confrontation.

While Life and I had helped usher in a new penal era at Angola by working to improve its quality of life and to insure its nonviolent integration, the effort seemed pointless after his death and my confinement to maximum security. The prison's violence had robbed me of a dear friend and its corruption had returned me to a cell. With the maddening cell block sounds reverberating in my brain, I felt as though I had reached the bottom of the earth the day that cell door slammed shut behind me.

But my pain and grief had only just begun. Next, I would lose Billy Ray.

23

June 8, 1974

To Major Norwood and the goon squad, all you pigs everywhere, and the high & mighty dogs everywhere who judge
men and allow institutional madhouses such as Angola to
exist. Suck my goddamn nuts and pray to the gods you
use as a crutch that I don't see you bastards in hell. In
the unlikely event that such a place exists, you can bet the
fat asses that you sat on I'll deflate them with the hottest,
sharpest pitchfork I can find. Incidentally, notice the smile
on my face and the pride with which I gladly take my life.
It's something you dogs have never taken from me despite
your fourteen years of effort. To hell with you, you cringing
cowards.

BILLY RAY WHITE #68685
LOUISIANA STATE PENITENTIARY

The proverbial moment of truth had arrived; a moment I had known would come since the first day I met Billy Ray White. Still, my pulse quickened, heating up an already sweating body. The June afternoon was hot. The sun bore through the barred cell block window with a vengeance, heating the two fifteen-cell tiers, stacked piggy-back atop each other like ovens.

Voices laughed.

I caught the tail end of a loud conversation: ". . . next to a fly, a dumb whore is the most useless critter on God's green earth."

I slowly folded the suicide note, staring intently at my hands to avoid looking at Billy Ray. He had stopped in front of my cell. I passed the note back to him through the bars. I had been in the maximum-security cell block for ten months. A familiar sense of caged isolation inherited from my six years on death row had returned, leaving me withdrawn and quiet. Between conversations with Billy Ray, most of which had turned to his desire to kill himself, I had returned to reading, consuming a book a day at times.

"I wrote it last night," he said. "What do you think about it?"

I lifted my gaze and forced myself to look into the deep blue eyes of a friend I loved in spite of what he was. A lock of hair drooped across his forehead, accentuating the youthfulness of his handsome, unlined face. Despite drug abuse and unspeakable violence, innate intelligence and human warmth still radiated in his eyes. The trace of a familiar smile played at the corners of his mouth. Billy Ray possessed a charisma that made him easy to like, even to love. He had an uncanny ability to charm. He could have been anything other than a Ten Most Wanted murderer.

But Billy Ray chose to be one of the most dangerous and feared men ever to serve time in our nation's prison system. An awesome fearlessness made him a criminal legend in prison subcultures across the country. It was demonstrated in escapes from the St. Louis police in a hail of gunfire, from a federal reformatory in Texarkana in a daring daytime break with bullets slicing the air about him, and from a county jail in Kentucky under a fusillade of hot lead. He added several contract killings to his criminal credentials in Missouri, New Mexico, and Louisiana.

An armed robber by profession, Billy Ray had been involved in several shootouts while plying his trade, emerging unharmed each time. In prison, he was involved in numerous assaults and knife fights. He killed men in both state and federal penal systems as he rose to the top of the inmate power structure. He was a man who could laugh at danger and death, who had survived every attempt to kill him during his brief thirty-one-year life.

Now the most feared and powerful man in Angola stood before me wanting to die by his own hand. Suicide had always fascinated Billy Ray. It became an obsession — "the ultimate test of courage," he often told me.

"It says pretty much what you want to say," I said dryly, pointing to the note.

I lit a cigarette, not really wanting one but needing distraction from the moment. I inhaled deeply.

With cat-like ease, Billy Ray squatted on his heels. He let his arms dangle across his knees with his fingers almost touching the floor. A somber silence separated us. He stared at the paint-peeled bars as though spellbound by their unfeeling strength. He looked up at me with a soft, steady gaze that locked into my stare. Never once had he looked at me with the brutal anger and contempt I had seen him so often direct at others. The years of talking about his suicide were obviously over.

"It's time," he said. "I'm ready to take myself out of this fucking life. I've come to terms with it. Like that nigger Martin Luther King said, 'God almighty, free at last!' That's probably the only thing the nigger ever said I liked. Death is freedom."

"Let's talk about it some more, Billy Ray," I replied. "There must be another way out."

Even as the words fell from my lips, I knew it was too late; he had reached the end of life's fragile cord.

"You promised," he reminded, fixing me with his gaze. "You gave me your word you would accept it when the time came. Well, the time has come and I'm holding you to your word. You know what this means to me."

Indeed I had promised. Two months earlier Billy Ray had set into motion a bizarre suicide plan. With a .38 caliber pistol he had smuggled into the prison, he planned to go to the prison's hospital, take several employees hostage, and demand a meeting with Elayn

Hunt and Warden Henderson. He would demand television coverage of the meeting. After reading a manifesto denouncing the nation's prisons as "breeding factories" of crime, he would kill Hunt and Henderson "with the whole fucking world watching." He would then put a bullet into his own brain.

The scheme made me realize that Billy Ray had stepped across the fine line separating the criminal ethic from psychosis. An excessive diet of Valium, Darvon, and marijuana over the last year had pushed him over the edge. A recent knife fight with a black inmate had left him embittered. It was a vicious duel between two men who hated each other. After being stabbed through the mouth, Billy Ray ripped open the black inmate's stomach and pulled out his intestines with his bare hands. He was sullen and angry because he had not killed the black prisoner.

After that fight, he kept trying to provoke fights with other black inmates on the tier. Most thought he was crazy, while others were too afraid to accept his challenges. He was as dangerous as a mortally wounded water buffalo.

In those dark moods of bitterness, Billy Ray talked only about suicide, of dying in an attack against prison authority. It took me two weeks to persuade him not to kill Hunt and Henderson. After exhausting every rational argument I could think of, I finally convinced him that, by being his friend, I would be implicated in the crime and end up with the death sentence again. That argument had a sobering effect on him.

"I would never do anything to directly or indirectly hurt you," he said. "Fuck Hunt and Henderson — they ain't worth killing anyway. But you've got to give me your word you will accept my death; that you will be there with me when it's time to leave this hellhole."

Now I could no longer meet his gaze. I turned my eyes away, looking across the hallway out a window into an empty yard.

I squatted, shifting my weight to my right leg, as I faced Billy Ray. A roach scurried across the floor between us. My mind raced feverishly for the right words that would convince him to once again reconsider his decision. But none came. He was ready to die.

"I know what this means to you, just as I know what it means to me," I said. "For God's sake, man, I have to be sure this is what you really want. I have to know it beyond any doubt."

Relief spread across his face like a morning sunrise.

"You have my word this is what I want. Believe me, I must do it. My whole life has come down to this final test. I've waited years for this moment. I want to meet the Devil face to face, stare the bastard down, and walk straight through the gates of Hell."

His eyes sparkled at the thought of the challenge.

"You'll see things different once you're out of this joint," I argued. "There's beauty, and happiness, and love — there's meaning in life. You must believe in it. Life is not all bad, Billy Ray."

He shook his head vehemently.

"I don't and can't believe it," he replied. "Life itself is an accident — everything it produces is nothing but a bullshit illusion; the light at the end of the tunnel is really a train."

I ran a finger through a small puddle of sweat between my legs. Torn by uncertainty, I scanned my own caged existence, thinking perhaps Billy Ray was right. I was a mass of bone and flesh wasting away in a prison cell, alone in a world of burned-out cons who hopelessly grasped at any straw to attach meaning to their failed lives. The used sock in the corner, stiff from last night's jaded fantasy, reflected the starved nature of my existence. A brooding sense of despair was etched in every scar and crack of the dirty green walls that surrounded me. Hopelessness stalked me in my cell with a relentless cruelty. I was tired of dealing with it, worn to the bone with trying to make sense of it.

Still, I was not prepared to accept Billy Ray's existential belief that life is absurd; that we're born from nothingness, live in nothingness, and perish into nothingness. I had studied and rejected that Sartrean philosophy. I chose to believe that there is more to life than a process of suffering, with death the only reward for having endured it.

Billy Ray sensed my troubled thoughts.

"Don't you understand, my friend — Nietzsche's little madman was right. God is dead!"

"But what does that have to do with us? What does it have to do with me being part of your death to prove my loyalty and friendship to you? You ask a helluva lot when you ask me to understand your death wish, but that's not enough — you want me to be part of it. I told you I would do it when the time came, but I can't — I just can't do it. Call it cowardice, or whatever, but I can't do it."

Tears trickled down my cheeks. I could not go along with Billy Ray's last wish that I allow him to die in my presence, holding my hand in a bond of friendship.

"I understand," he said solemnly, "and I accept that. It doesn't change anything between us. You're still my ace. It's not cowardice. You simply can't see this thing as clearly as I do. But if you can't let me die in your presence, then at least understand why I must do this."

Anger flashed through me. My eyes bore into his.

"You ask me to understand! Goddamnit, understand what? You're my friend — you're closer to me than a brother. How do you expect me to understand that you're about to kill yourself? Why do this to me? Why do you have to make me a part of this . . . this madness?"

"It's something I need," he explained. "There are obligations attached to friendship. I'm just collecting on ours. I've always given you loyalty. Now I ask the same in return. It's important to me that you understand why I must take myself out. Fuck what others think! All I want is for you to know I have to do this. I really have no choice but to do it."

The sound of two cons fighting over a gal-boy invaded our conversation. We ignored it.

"Billy Ray, I understand a man wanting to take himself out of this hell — I've had those same thoughts in darker moments. A man does not spend as many years in a cell as I have without thoughts of suicide, but it's not the answer. What bothers me is that I have no way of knowing if it is what you really want."

"I give you my word it is," he said, reaching through the bars and clasping my hand. "You have my solemn word on everything I hold sacred that it's what I want, that I want to die, and die by my own hand. You know my word is my bond. I would not even utter such a thing if it was not true."

It was a hopeless situation. Our allegiance to the convict code and to each other bound me to his death wish. Reporting it or rejecting it would have been an unforgivable act of betrayal.

"Let me say this," he added. "I've told you I would never leave you stuck out, and I wouldn't. I'll hang with life and fade the bullshit till you're a free man — but I give you my word the precise moment you walk out of prison I will blow my brains out. If you force me to live and be part of your struggle, my obligation to our friendship ends the moment you step out of those prison gates. I'm asking you as one man to another to free me of the obligation of our friendship. Let me do this without any doubts. The only obligation I have in life is our friendship, and I'm asking you to free me of it."

I said nothing, staring past him through the window.

Releasing my hand, he rose, called out to the guard to open his cell door, and walked away. I heard him greet his gal-boy, whom he affectionately called Monkey, as he stepped into the cell next to mine. He had deliberately dropped the decision of whether he would live or die in my lap. I don't know why he did it, and I probably never will. The minutes, then hours, crept by. Shortly before dusk he passed a note through the bars to me. It began:

> My beloved brother, it's not wrong for you to deny me the privilege of dying in your company as I stand on the threshold of freedom from this madhouse. In the name of your cherished friendship, I will be a coward. My loyalty to you is such I would be dishonorable to you and myself if I took my life now without your consent. However, due to my selfishness, I am asking that you reconsider and give me your consent. It would be the greatest favor you could ever possibly grant me. It has occurred to me that maybe I'm wrong to ask this favor of you. Try to place everything in as proper perspective as you can and let me know. My brother, I would proudly die for you and if it's what you really want I will even live for you. Is it wrong of me to ask you to let me go now? Is it greedy? Help me understand. You're my only brother and I love you and my death won't separate us.

I was tired, too emotionally exhausted to care anymore. There had been too much grief in my twenty-nine years of life. My decision was swift and certain. I walked to the corner of my cell. Night had fallen and the senseless cell arguments had given way to the loud mixture of different television programs. I called Billy Ray to the front of his cell. With my shaving mirror taped to the bars of my cell, I had a full view into Billy Ray's cell as he did into mine.

"Do whatever you feel is right," I said. "I'll understand."

"Thank you, my friend," he said finally. "I'm free now. There's nothing to hold me to this hellhole any longer."

A brief silence passed between us.

"But there is one last thing."

I was afraid to ask what it was.

"What is it?"

"I want you to give me your word that once I'm dying, you won't call for the Man or let anyone else call for him," he said. "I don't want any second thoughts stopping this thing. I'm in it all the way, and you must give me your word you will cover for me."

"You have my word."

I lay down on my bunk. The heat was stifling and the swamp mosquitoes murderous. It struck me that I did not even know how Billy Ray planned to kill himself. We had not discussed a method. It never seemed important. I didn't think it would ever reach a point of no return. I checked my watch. It was 8:30 P.M. I realized that Billy Ray would be dead before morning. I no longer held out any hope. He had dealt himself a hand he could not fold even if he wanted to. He was that kind of man.

Occasionally the voices of Billy Ray and Monkey drifted into my cell, although I could not understand what they were saying. I wondered how Monkey would react, being in the cell with Billy Ray.

Billy Ray called to me. I quickly moved to the bars.

"What is it?"

"Me and Monkey have been talking this thing out, and I've decided to take him with me. The kid wants to go — he wants to die with me."

Billy Ray had stepped beyond the irrational. I smelled the marijuana before I heard them taking deep drags off the cigarettes.

"Don't do this, Billy Ray," I said angrily. "That kid has the mind of a twelve-year-old. He's not responsible. He worships you and he'll say anything he thinks will please you."

"But it's for his own good," he replied, his voice quite serious.

167

"The little Monkey ain't ever getting out of this joint — not with two life sentences. If I leave him behind, who's gonna take care of him? Some asshole like Blackjack or Monster will get him and fuck him over. They'll have him sucking every dick on the Yard. I can't leave this helpless little bastard to face that hell."

Billy Ray's assessment was right. Monkey could not survive on his own. He could only serve the predatory needs of a strong con. He had no hope of getting out of prison. He had raped a sixteen-year-old girl and robbed and killed her boyfriend. He had similar charges pending against him in other states. He was a pathetic wretch destined to spend the rest of his life as someone else's property.

"That may be true, Billy Ray," I said, choosing my words carefully. "But you don't have the right to decide whether he should live or die. If dying is so important to you, then do it alone. Don't kill that kid. I'm not buying the mercy bit — he may not share your notions of mercy. Give him a break."

There was a long pause. I could hear them talking.

"Okay. Monkey says it doesn't make any difference to him. If I want him to do it, he will — but if I want him to stay behind, he will do that too. I'm not going to kill him — it wouldn't be right. But you have to promise me something else."

"What is it?"

"Take care of Monkey for me. I know you don't want to be shackled down with a gal-boy, but take him under your wing until you find him an ole man who will treat him right and take care of him. Find someone who will be good to him."

"I'll find the right dude for him."

"Good. Now I'm gonna fuck him one last time."

I was on the floor staring through the bars. The darkness seemed so peaceful. I was removed from the rest of the world. I was sick of death — sick of seeing it, hearing it, and talking about it. Every rational fiber of my being screamed "I'm finished with this friendship!" and urged me to step away from it. But I didn't. Loyalty made me part of Billy Ray's suicide pact.

He did not speak again until after midnight.

"I wanna get Monkey out of this cell," he whispered through

the bars. "I can't be sure he won't panic and call out for the Man. He's been crying and I think he's too fucked up to handle this. I want him out of here."

"Send him through the hole," I said.

I removed several cinder blocks from the wall separating our cells. Four of the cells housing white inmates had cinder blocks that had been loosened so they could be removed. One cell had two bars that had been cut through. It would allow all the white inmates to get out on the tier at the same time in the event of racial trouble. After he was completely into my cell, Monkey went to sleep in an upper bunk after I gave him a Valium. Billy Ray reached through the hole and grasped both my hands.

"I love you," he said.

"I love you, too, Billy Ray."

"I'll let you know when the final moment gets close," he whispered.

"How you gonna do it?"

"Razor blades."

"The jugular?"

Billy Ray shook his head.

"No, that's too quick. I'm going with the wrists. I want to fully experience this thing."

It was 1:00 A.M. before Billy Ray called me again.

"It's time," he said. "Get your mirror and watch this."

With my left hand, I stuck a piece of mirror through the bars, holding it where I could see inside Billy Ray's cell. He had packed his personal belongings in a box. He moved to the back of the cell and sat on the edge of his bunk facing the toilet. He rested his left arm across his left leg, and with a stainless steel razor blade, he slashed his forearm open with two deep gashes. Blood gushed forth, flowing downward to his hand and onto the floor. He then slashed his right arm in the same manner, but he had some difficulty with that arm because his left hand was bloody. The blade kept slipping.

Clearly agitated, he thrust his right arm up to his mouth and chewed his veins out, spitting a mass of tissue and blood into the commode. He didn't even flinch. He turned his head toward me, looking over his shoulder to see if I was watching. Blood covered

169

his mouth and chin. He smiled. It was a fiendish, repulsive sight. I yanked the mirror back in my cell and slid down the wall. The cell block was quiet. Not even a whispered conversation could be heard.

Billy Ray whispered my name.

"I'm here," I said, not moving.

"It's done."

"How long will it take?"

"I don't know. I'll keep pumping my fist to keep the blood from clotting. I've got a bucket of warm water to stick my wrists in every now 'n then."

"I hope you find something better on the other side." My voice trembled.

"I won't. But if there is anything and if there's any way to get word back to you, I'll do it. So if you don't hear from me, don't invest too much in the life-after-death stock. I know there's nothing over there."

It was impossible to think of Billy Ray dead. He was too strong, too vibrant to die. I felt that somehow he would defy death.

"Read these," he said, passing me several pieces of legal paper through the bars. "It's something I wrote a couple of years ago." He had a towel wrapped around his arm to keep the blood from dripping on the floor. The notes were splotched with it.

One note read:

> My most important pressing goal is to make the most of my capabilities. I've laid around too long. I must employ strict self-discipline, gather new and stronger determination and concentrate more on strengthening my motivations. I believe self-discipline is the most important key, the master key that fits the door to any goal.

The second note, titled "Excuses for my Greed," revealed the contradictions that tore Billy Ray's life asunder:

> The main reason, I think, for my anxiousness to gain material securities is that I feel I must be financially independent if I'm ever going to be able to devote the depth and amount of time I feel would be necessary for me to satisfactorily ex-

plore the whys, wheres, whos, and hows of my existence. Then once I've found out how I want to live in relation to the big what, I can whistle along until unconsciousness, maybe? In the meantime, I must keep struggling to put better substance in the throw-away container that I am, but without blowing my mind over ways and means, at the same time become as financially independent as I want to be so as to hasten the day I can really explore what at present is the highest rung of my pursuit-of-happiness ladder. I firmly believe I can accomplish this goal. It all depends on how the bludgeoning of chance affects me. In the meantime I gotta tighten up and figure out better and faster ways to go over, under, around, or through the obstacles that are blocking or may block the path of my goal.

I read the notes several times, trying to find in them a better understanding of my friend. It seemed so tragic that the sum of a man's life could be reduced to nothing more than scribbling on a few pieces of bloody paper.

"Pursuit of happiness" was the key phrase. While he often laughed, I can't recall a time when he was truly happy. He never talked about happiness. Death was his only happiness.

He whispered my name again. His voice had weakened considerably.

"I don't know how much time I have left, but I need to tell you something."

"What is it?"

He paused. I heard him gasp.

"I want you to think about me — my life of crime and the failure it made of me. I want you to reject the code. This is not your world. You have too much potential to stay in this life. If you stay in it, it will do to you what it has done to me. It will destroy you."

"I have to survive in this life," I replied.

"Survive you will, but at some point you must make a decision to reject the convict code. It won't be easy. You will be scorned and rejected for it, but you've got to do it. You've got the courage and character to do it. Don't worry about the friends you'll lose. Believe me, you don't need that kind of friendship. Turn your back on them."

I said nothing. He moaned. I heard his feet shuffling as he stood up.

"I'm gonna lay down a few minutes," he whispered. "I feel weak and dizzy — it's almost over."

I had nothing to do but pace the floor of my cell like a fresh-caged animal. At times I could hear Billy Ray rambling — cursing life, praising friendship, and talking about the need for real love. I tried to make some sense of what was happening. A friend was bleeding to death no more than six feet from me and there was nothing I could do about it. While a call for help would have been considered an act of betrayal, my silence amounted to the same thing. I betrayed my obligation to do the right thing and stop the suicide.

That conflict tore at my brain. Instinctively I realized that my allegiance to the convict code was over. What kind of code of ethics forces a man to let a friend die? Only a code antipodean to what is normal, decent, and responsible. I had wasted my life at the altar of a false idol.

As the hours passed, I sensed death's presence, almost like I could touch it. My chest was tight, my soul cramped and smothered. My heart ached from the crushing weight of despair. Tired of walking, I stood at the bars, staring unseeing into the night.

Why had Billy Ray forced me to let him die? Why did I feel obligated to take part in his ritual of death? It was a debt I owed for his loyalty. He would have died for me. He expected me to share in his self-inflicted death. I could not have turned him away any more than I could have turned him in.

Around four in the morning, Billy Ray's condition worsened to the point of near-death. His words were slurred and his voice was terribly weak. He spoke in spurts, saying things that had meaning only to him. I felt a rush of guilt when, at one point, I wished the end would hurry. The emotional strain was tremendous.

A guard passed Billy Ray's cell, making a routine count. He never looked directly into the cells. He wanted only to see something that remotely resembled a human being.

"Wha'cha doin', White?" he asked as he passed Billy Ray's cell.

"Nothing, chief — just dying," Billy Ray answered, barely audible.

The guard didn't give Billy Ray's comment a second thought. He then passed my cell. It was my last opportunity to save Billy Ray's life. My mouth opened. I wanted to speak, to cry out, but no words came. The silence of the cell was deafening. The guard disappeared. I knew beyond any doubt that Billy Ray was going to die.

It was 5:45 A.M., June 9, 1974, when the words finally came.

"I'm ready now," Billy Ray said. "Get the Man."

I awakened two inmates in the cell next to me. I told them Billy Ray was dying and we needed to get the Man on the tier. We started shaking our cell doors. The noise brought the entire cell block to life.

"What's going on down there?" one voice called out.

"I don't know," another replied.

A disgruntled shift lieutenant walked down the tier. He knew some kind of trouble was brewing.

"Alright, what's all the racket about?" he shouted over the noise.

"Billy Ray's dying," I said.

The lieutenant walked casually to Billy Ray's cell. He aimed his flashlight inside the cell. With a jolt, he staggered backwards.

"My God," he said in a horror-stricken voice. "He's . . . Lord, get a stretcher — get a stretcher back here!"

While one hall boy ran to get a stretcher, two others carried Billy Ray out of the cell and laid him on the floor in front of my cell. He had on only a pair of blood-soaked underwear. His hair was matted with blood and his arms were a bluish swollen mass of mutilated veins and dried blood. His feet were turned outward, his underwear grotesquely pulled down below one side of his ass. His left arm was sprawled out across the concrete floor. His eyes were closed. His lips moved, perhaps trembled, but no words came out. His right forefinger twitched slightly and went still.

"How long has he been like this?" the lieutenant asked.

"I don't know, chief," I answered, staring at Billy Ray. His body looked so sunken, so weak. "Probably all his life."

The third hall boy rushed up with a folded canvas stretcher. He quickly unfolded it and the two other hall boys struggled to lift Billy Ray's slippery body onto it. One hall boy dropped one of Billy Ray's legs — some of his waste fell out on the floor. I knew he was dead.

All the hell, pain, and violence of his life had come to a brutal end. I watched as they carried him away. Downing four Valiums with a cup of water, I lay down on my bunk and lit a cigarette.

On the horizon, the first rays of dawn appeared, softening a dark world — a softening that did not touch me as tears of regret and shame rolled from my eyes.

24

I SPENT NEARLY TWO YEARS in maximum security. Major Norwood released me in June 1975 after I gave him my word that I would not "lead the inmates to riot" or stir up any kind of organized resistance against the prison system.

It was an easy compromise. Billy Ray's suicide had made me withdraw deep into myself. There were moments when guilt almost crushed me. "If only I had stopped it," my conscience whispered insistently. Sleep was often invaded by a brutal army of nightmares. There were other moments when I hated him because he had made me part of his death pact. His last act in life had been his most selfish.

But I would come to understand that my rehabilitation evolved from Billy Ray's suicide. Perhaps, just as he wished. It gave me the determination to examine my life and a reason to change my belief system. Even though I had been developing moral values in the years before his death, Billy Ray's suicide snapped the umbilical cord binding me to the convict code. In that sense, I believe, he died to save me.

I had become a criminal because I admired and respected cons like Billy Ray White. Their code of behavior made it natural for me to walk into that convenience store on Greenwell Springs Road and attempt to rob it. I had adopted their criminal values before I had an opportunity to develop a strong, independent belief system governed by law-abiding, responsible principles. The convict code does not allow freedom of choice. You either subscribe to its values or you are an outcast.

Over a period of a decade, between 1968 and 1978, I systematically examined and gradually rejected the code, formulating my own moral and ethical judgments to replace it. I determined for myself, as Life had done, what was right and wrong. A society of foul-mouthed, tattooed goons could no longer dictate how I should think. I was neither physically afraid of them nor emotionally bothered by the social ostracism they would surely subject me to.

By the end of 1975, I was nearly thirty-one years old. I had been in prison for ten years, eight of them in a cell. I quit smoking and started a rigorous weight-lifting routine. Drinking a quart mixture of protein powder and evaporated milk each day, I quickly added muscle and weight to my thin frame. I also quit taking pills and smoking dope. Nineteen seventy-five was the last year I took any form of narcotic or mind-altering substance.

While there were still a few Family members and a heavy concentration of Dixie Mafia inmates in Oak 4 where I lived, I remained aloof from them. I spent most of my spare time in the law library or on the weight pile. I had no friends or close associates. Most thought my antisocial behavior was attributable to my being "fucked up" over Billy Ray's death.

The Dixie Mafia had gained complete control of Angola by 1975. Their criminal enterprises of narcotics trafficking and extortion touched every segment of the inmate population. Through an unholy network of inmate politicians, corrupt classification personnel, and B-Line security guards, they controlled transfers to satellite institutions, trusty status, and choice job assignments. They sold these precious commodities to inmates with enough money to buy them. Their power was so pervasive they could (and did) buy parole and pardon board decisions.

Conditions got so out of hand that a local federal court declared the entire prison system "cruel and unusual punishment." In the wake of federal court intervention, Warden Henderson resigned to become head of the Tennessee Department of Corrections. Elayn Hunt died of pancreatic cancer in late 1975.

The Henderson resignation and Hunt's untimely death set the stage for a complete political upheaval at Angola. In March 1976, C. Paul Phelps stated that his primary penal objective was to regain control of Angola and make it responsive to the Department of Corrections. He gave that awesome task to Ross Maggio, along with the necessary authority to accomplish it.

Maggio swept into Angola with the force of a hurricane, confronting inmates and personnel alike. He cracked down hard on violence and narcotics trafficking, locking up scores of gang leaders and drug dealers. In a matter of months he broke the corrupt hold that the Dixie Mafia had on Angola, virtually eliminating violence and corruption from the prison's day-to-day operation.

Beefing up his security forces and equipping them with a variety of electronic devices, Maggio instituted strict security measures that disrupted the routines of Angola's criminal culture. He removed all known passive homosexuals from the general population, placing them in their own cell blocks or camps. Aggressive stud homosexuals were taken out of circulation and placed in lockdown.

Maggio deliberately upset and rearranged the entire power structure within the prison. Not only did he lock up gang leaders, he also removed inmate politicians from sensitive clerical positions and replaced them with free employees. As a result, inmates could no longer buy transfers within the prison or to other facilities; nor could they have disciplinary reports torn up or snitch sheets delivered to them.

Within a year, Maggio had transformed the nation's bloodiest prison into its safest. He cleaned up not only the violence and corruption but the prison complex itself: buildings were renovated or painted, grass was cut and manicured, and the fields were cultivated again. Maggio put fifteen hundred idle inmates back to work. Many of them had bought "light duty" status from a prison doctor who was an ex-con on the Dixie Mafia's payroll. Now every capable inmate was required to put in eight hours of work. Only the truly physically infirm were exempt.

Not everyone embraced the massive changes. Civil libertarians criticized Maggio's tough, authoritarian rule. Paradoxically, these were the same prison reformers who vehemently criticized the tyranny of violence and disorder under the Hunt/Henderson regime. These well-meaning liberals did not understand that the criminal ethic worships strength. When inmates rule a prison, violence proliferates. Rehabilitation, in their eyes, is synonymous with "pussy."

Maggio inherited a prison controlled by these criminal terrorists. To establish the rule of law, he resorted to the only methods they understood — force and intimidation. He cracked heads and kicked butts, but he brought law and order to Angola — something it had never known.

"No inmate will go to sleep in my prison afraid of being raped or killed," Maggio said. "I believe in feeding inmates good food, taking care of their medical needs, and providing them with safe working conditions and a clean living environment. I support recreational and rehabilitation programs, but rehabilitation begins with the individual — not me. I will give a man every opportunity to help himself but I will not try to get inside his head and understand what's wrong with him."

Nicknamed "Boss Ross" by the inmates, Maggio became a legendary figure at the prison. Tales of his exploits were told and retold. He replaced Billy Ray White as the most feared man at Angola. Even his enemies respected his fearlessness, determination, and sense of fairness. His presence was seen and felt in every section of the prison. He was the first warden to walk on the Big Yard alone. When warned of the possible dangers, he said:

"This is my prison — and if I can't walk alone in it, then it ain't my prison."

"But what if they take you hostage, Warden?" a security guard asked.

"Shoot me, then shoot the sonuvabitches who took me hostage," he replied, chomping down hard on his trademark cigar.

Because of Maggio's no-nonsense style, it was inevitable that the criminal power brokers would challenge his authority. They moved against him in May 1977 by staging a "work slowdown." Inmates performed their jobs as slowly as they could and walked slowly to and from work. It was rumored that the slowdown had been orchestrated by John Vodicka, a prison rights activist and a Maggio critic who headed the New Orleans–based Louisiana Coalition of Jails and Prisons.

The work slowdown was in its second day when a group of black inmates approached me as I worked out at the weight pile on the yard. They asked me to lead the protest, to articulate their grievances and demands to the administration.

"What are the grievances?" I asked between sets of arm curls.

"Harassment," Treetop said. "This dude Maggio ain't about nothing but harassment, and if you complain about it he'll kick off in your ass."

Continuing my workout, I listened as the group reeled off a litany of complaints. I paid particular attention to Willie Bee. He was a cowardly instigator who preferred to remain in the background — the "right-on, motherfucker" man. I had seen so many of them in my activist days.

"We need you to speak for us," Treetop said. "You're the best when it comes to getting down with the administration."

"Is Vodicka behind this thing?" I asked, replacing the weights.

"All I can say is that we have outside support," Treetop said, evading the question.

Laying a steel weight bar on the bench within easy reach, I turned to face the group.

"Let me tell you how it is," I said. "I'm not part of this slowdown thing. I'm not being harassed. I have no problem with Maggio. I believe this whole thing has been instigated by Vodicka, and like always, he's using inmates as pawns in a political game he's playing with Maggio. I've been down this road before so get someone else to speak for you."

"I told you, 'Top," Willie Bee said. "He ain't going to do nothing for us — that cell broke him."

Scotch anger surged through me.

"You got a problem with me?" I spat at Willie Bee.

"Cool it, Brothers!" Treetop said. An awkward pause ensued. I fought down an urge to pick up the weight bar and splinter Willie Bee's knee cap, Billy Ray style.

"You're out there bad, Bee," Treetop said. "Sinclair and Life were on the front line of the struggle when this place was really rockin' 'n rollin'. He's paid his dues. He can take any position he wants."

"That's just it, 'Top," I said. "I have no position. I'm just doing my time — not yours or anyone else's, just mine."

"I can dig it."

"Let me give you a piece of advice. Don't jack with Maggio. He's going to come down hard on this slowdown. He has to establish that this is his prison."

Two days later all Main Prison inmates were locked in their dorms. From our dorm windows we could see the prison's "tact unit" that Maggio had created and trained unloading riot-control equipment from several trucks. My work supervisor called Maggio requesting that I be given a chance to report to work. He told Maggio that I had not been part of the slowdown. A security major opened the door to Oak 4 dorm and yelled:

"Sinclair, you wanna go to work?"

A spontaneous hush fell over the dorm. I sat up in my bunk, realizing every inmate in the dorm was watching me. In a very public way, I was being made to choose between them and Maggio. While I had not participated in the work slowdown and had ignored the boycott of the mess hall, the inmates still considered me one of them. I had enough influence and standing on the Yard to get away with ignoring the confrontation they were forcing with Maggio. But this was different.

A Family member in the bunk next to mine whispered:

"Don't do it, Billy."

I stood up and put my shirt on.

"I'm going to work, Major," I said.

I turned and walked down the aisle toward the door.

"You may as well rat while you're out there, asshole," a bitter voice called out.

My back stiffened, braced for a knife thrust as I walked past the inmates sitting on their bunks.

"I'm coming too, chief," Big Mick said. Jumping to his feet, he followed me to the door.

The two of us walked out the door and down the Walk. We could hear the taunts and jeers of the other inmates behind us.

"Thanks, Mick," I said.

His action had saved me from being stabbed that morning.

"Don't thank me," he said. "Thank Billy Ray. Two days before he died, he made me promise to stand with you if you ever faced trouble."

He slammed his fist into his palm.

"Damn, man, what's wrong with you? Do you think those dudes would have let you walk out like that if I hadn't stood up with you? Let me tell you something. The debt's square with Billy Ray. You're on your own now."

That afternoon, Maggio made his move. The tact unit herded all the inmates, one dorm at a time, between the two fences separating the Industrial Compound and the Big Yard. They were surrounded by guards holding automatic weapons. The show of force was oppressive. The inmates were held between the fences during the heat of the afternoon and into the night. The swamp mosquitoes had a blood feast. The pressure of waiting, of not being able to speak, subdued the mass of prisoners.

From the loading dock of the kitchen, Big Mick and I watched the standoff. At 9:00 P.M. Maggio lined up several guards in front of the double fences. He opened the gate, walked in among the inmates, and randomly picked several of them.

"These are your spokesmen," he said, addressing the rest through a bullhorn. He led the spokesmen out of the holding area and made them kneel before the heavily armed guards.

"I don't negotiate," Maggio told the inmates who were forced to look into the glare of bright lights. "Go back in there and tell them to take off their shoes and roll their pants up to their knees. Get everyone together by dorm. When I call a dorm, I want everybody to trot back to that dorm. Now get out of my face."

Dorm by dorm, the inmates were made to high-step through a gauntlet of tact unit guards wielding nightsticks. The guards rapped them across their ankles and shins as they trotted past. Inmates who stumbled or fell were beaten back in line. Maggio crushed the rebellion with physical and psychological humiliation.

The next morning, without being given a chance to pack their personal belongings, more than one thousand Big Yard inmates were herded into waiting cattle trucks to be moved into Camps C and D, mini-prisons recently erected at different parts of Angola. Maggio ordered all the ringleaders of the slowdown and other suspected troublemakers placed in Camp J, a newly opened, ultra-maximum-security outcamp where some were beaten and reportedly tortured by the tact unit.

I was one of the several hundred inmates left on the Big Yard. I did not have to worry about retaliation for walking out on the slowdown. Maggio had broken the back of the Dixie Mafia, the Family, and other inmate gangs. There was no fight left in them. The inmates remaining on the Big Yard were so thankful they had not been caught up in the massive transfer that they did not cause problems for anyone. They simply wanted to lick their wounds.

In the ensuing months, Maggio faced more criticism from the ACLU and Vodicka for his suppression of the rebellion. The Louisiana Attorney General's Office and the FBI conducted separate civil rights investigations, but the warden weathered the controversy.

By crushing the rebellion and breaking the collective will of the criminal power brokers, Maggio bought the prison a decade of peace and stability. He set a new security standard for Angola: no negotiation under threats. He made it clear that the consequences of repression would be greater than the threat of rebellion. It is the only way to run a prison. Negotiation with terrorists invites more terror. Anarchy cannot be tolerated in a penitentiary; it must be repressed.

Those of us who had opposed the criminal gangs and had tried to free the inmate population of their violent terrorism embraced Maggio's new order of management. I was now outside the prison subculture. My break with the convict code was complete.

While I would never again be accepted within the criminal ranks, I still had to live cheek by jowl with those who rejected me because of my new ethic. There were hidden enemies, cons who still wanted to "catch back" because of my walkout on their work slowdown. But I refused to be intimidated by the danger. My pride and free will were at stake. I had been forced to make a public choice and I had made it. I had watched others make hard choices when they stood up for their beliefs. J. C. Bodden died trying to stop a robbery. Pat sacrificed himself for a friend. Life was murdered for his principles. Billy Ray chewed out his veins to save me.

25

For THE NEXT TWO YEARS, I walked a fine line on the Big Yard. My reputation as a jailhouse lawyer gave me some protection from a knife in the back, but violence toward me remained a real possibility. Inmates have long memories for "traitors." Smoldering resentment on the Big Yard against my walkout on the slowdown could ignite at any moment. I was living on high alert. Still, I continued my steps toward rehabilitation. The administration, however, made no move to accept me.

Then, in the summer of 1977, Wilbert Rideau asked me to join the staff of *The Angolite*. Rideau had been its editor for two years. *Angolite* staffers were considered administration lackeys, and inmates detested them. I already had enough ostracism to deal with. On the Big Yard I lived separate and alone. I had betrayed the convict code in an unforgiving environment. I didn't need the additional ostracism *The Angolite* would bring. But Rideau was persuasive.

"I need you, I really do," he insisted. "The magazine could use your skills and I need someone who will watch my back."

Rideau had saved me from freezing to death in a Baton Rouge jail cell years before. He was an easy man to trust. A slender man who dressed impeccably even by free world standards, he had a talent for making people around him feel important. Nothing was ordinary in his world. He had always nurtured the belief that he was born for greatness — he dreamed of being a "rocket scientist" as a child. He wove a web of importance around people who entered his world, and I was no exception. Rideau easily pulled me into his orbit, a realm of exceptional power. He had been given carte blanche to gather and convey information in a world ruled by ignorance and innuendo.

By 1977, Rideau had a budding reputation as a writer. He had written a column about prison named "The Jungle" for a chain of black newspapers in Louisiana and Mississippi and had published a piece about incarcerated veterans in *Penthouse* magazine. The *Penthouse* piece helped establish him as an author — a title that gave him prestige and power.

Rideau had first gained recognition as a writer in the prison community after he assumed control of the *Lifer* magazine in 1974. The *Lifer* was a small bimonthly magazine published with administrative approval by an organization for inmates serving life sentences. The *Lifer* quickly rivaled *The Angolite*, an all-white publication then edited by Bill Brown. The *Lifer* staff was all black. A racial rivalry developed between the two publications which spilled over into the general inmate population.

At Rideau's urging, I had written an article for the *Lifer* in 1975. Inasmuch as I had been one of the white inmate leaders who had successfully integrated the prison in 1973, Rideau believed an article by me in the *Lifer* would ease the mounting racial conflict generated by the two competing publications. But it didn't.

Rideau's success with the *Lifer* eventually won him a position on *The Angolite*. When Bill Brown was paroled in 1975, Rideau was named the new editor by Warden Henderson. He took all the *Lifer* staffers with him to *The Angolite*. The Lifers Organization felt betrayed. Its membership felt that he had used their publication to gain a position on *The Angolite* where he would have more personal influence with the administration. Most black inmates thought Rideau "sold out" to the white system. Some would never accept him again.

In 1976, Phelps decided to use *The Angolite* to help with the massive changes he had planned for the prison. He reasoned that it would be better to have facts circulating through *The Angolite* than have rumors percolating on the inmate grapevine. Rumors could explode into violence. If the magazine were a reliable source of information, the inmates would be less likely to resist the changes. He told Rideau that *The Angolite* had to become more than the club newsletter the *Lifer* had been.

Between 1976 and mid-1977, Rideau worked to make *The Angolite* a professional and credible publication. Phelps, Maggio, and *Angolite* supervisor Peggi Gresham embraced his efforts. They gave him access to information and an investigative freedom never before bestowed on an inmate editor. It enabled him to transform *The Angolite* into one of the best penal publications in the nation.

Still *The Angolite* did not gain easy acceptance among the inmates. Its legacy of carrying the "party line" lingered in the inmate subculture. As a result, the inmates didn't believe the magazine could address the real issues affecting their day-to-day existence. When it was delivered to the dormitories every other month, more copies went into the trash unread than into the hands of inmates who bothered to leaf through its pages. White inmates hated the magazine because it had an all-black staff. Black inmates rejected it because they didn't trust Rideau. To them, he was "Phelps' nigger."

The slur, however, did not bother Rideau. He methodically cultivated the image. His exemplary behavior and writing expertise had indeed attracted Phelps' interest. Rideau was the "model prisoner" that he praised most frequently, both in public and in private. Phelps pointed to Rideau as the premier example of rehabilitation. Through his special relationship with Phelps, Rideau became the most powerful inmate in the state's prison system.

Articulate and self-educated, Rideau was a talented, creative black man in a southern prison. He used that unique appeal to cultivate contacts within the state's news media. He took delight in outsmarting some reporters with exaggerated tales of death row, laughing in private at how gullible even the most case-hardened scribe could be. He was especially fond of telling the story of how he smuggled a *Playboy* magazine into death row to learn how to read, because inmates weren't allowed anything but a Bible. In reality, condemned inmates had access to books, magazines, newspapers, radio, television, and even college correspondence courses. Death row was a hellhole, but it was not as deprived as Rideau led some reporters to believe.

As the convict editor's local fame grew, Phelps began to pressure him to put a white inmate on the staff. Rideau began shopping around the prison for a suitable candidate. He settled on me because I had the credentials he needed: I could write, I had legal skills, and I enjoyed substantial credibility among both white and black inmates.

More importantly, I understood the social intricacies of prison in a way Rideau did not. He had never served much hard time. He became a trusty just one year after he was released from death row. The change in status took him from the Big Yard to a far less dangerous environment where he became an inmate clerk in the classification department. He believed my knowledge and reputation would help *The Angolite* gain acceptance. And since I was still persona non grata to much of the administration, I posed no threat to his position of power on the magazine.

Against that backdrop, Rideau went to Maggio. At first the warden refused to consider me for *The Angolite*. Rideau persisted.

"If you give him a chance, he'll be loyal to you. Sinclair has a reputation for loyalty."

At a staff meeting of all prison wardens and top security officials, Maggio asked each for their opinion about assigning me to *The Angolite*. Everyone argued against it. They said I would compromise the integrity of the magazine with criminal or political behavior.

Several days later, Maggio called me to the *Angolite* office. Dressed in a cowboy hat, blue jeans, and a denim shirt, he was sitting behind a desk when I walked through the door. He stared intently at me as he motioned for me to sit down.

"I'm assigning you to *The Angolite*," he said. "I want you to know every warden and ranking security officer here says I'm making a mistake. I'm giving you an opportunity to prove them wrong. If you screw up, I'll break your back, and I mean that literally."

Our eyes locked across the abyss between keeper and kept. I had no doubt that he would do exactly what he said.

"You have my word, Warden."

For a brief moment, his stare seemed to soften. Then his impenetrable mask reappeared.

I was under tremendous pressure when I became a staff writer on *The Angolite*. The Board of Pardons had just denied my first clemency application. The Bodden family and the Baton Rouge football fraternity had mounted massive opposition to my release. And I had to face the ugly reality that a number of powerful B-Line prison officials wanted to see me fall. They orchestrated two major setup attempts in a concerted effort to oust me from the magazine. Somehow, I survived both.

In addition, I was working with an editor who had an established relationship with the administration. Rideau was *The Angolite*. Gresham spoke only to him. All her calls and those from Phelps went to Rideau. I was the new kid on the block and few in the neighborhood liked me. Phelps ignored me when he occasionally dropped by the office. I would later discover that one of his close personal friends was a member of the football fraternity involved in the politics of my case.

But Maggio was different. He included me in conversations and listened to my views. I developed tremendous respect for his intellect and his character. I would later learn that he had attended Istrouma High School, graduating two years after J. C. Bodden and the other football heroes. He not only bucked the prison system to appoint me to *The Angolite*, he also bucked the politics.

In December 1977, I was devastated when Maggio announced he was leaving Angola to become warden at the Hunt Correctional Center, a new prison being built in a community near Baton Rouge. Frank Blackburn, a psychologist and minister who had been warden for treatment under Maggio was named the warden. He would never quite measure up to Maggio's bold style. But in Blackburn we had a warden who also supported *The Angolite*. In assuming the helm of the prison, he became "managing editor" of the best prison magazine in the nation.

By early 1978, I had become frustrated with *The Angolite*. I was in no man's land — rejected by both the inmates and the administration. Most white inmates quit speaking to me altogether. Blacks kept their distance.

Meanwhile, *The Angolite* was drifting. I had worked on three editions. But the magazine had taken no significant stand on penal issues except for an editorial I wrote in the November–December 1977 edition criticizing prison reform activist John Vodicka. Vodicka had recently written a letter to the Louisiana Bar Association asking its ethics committee to rule that law firms with "intimate connections with the governor" be barred from representing inmates before the state's pardon board because it created an "appearance of impropriety."

Since Vodicka could not produce a single case of wrongdoing to substantiate his charge, the *Angolite* editorial reasoned that he had unnecessarily infected the clemency process with politics and had prejudiced the inmates represented by law firms with close ties to then governor Edwards. The editorial sparked massive inmate interest, some of it hostile, because it challenged an established "prisoners' rights champion." It gained even more attention when I filed a lawsuit against Vodicka charging that his actions had violated my right to a fair clemency review and infringed upon my right to have an attorney of my choice since I was represented by one of the law firms he had cited in his complaint.

In response to the lawsuit, Vodicka told the *New Orleans Times-Picayune* that he knew his complaint "would cause some hard or ill feelings among that segment of prisoners at various institutions who either are represented by these two firms or are doing sentences of such length that the pardon system is virtually the only way of gaining freedom."

The militant, politically active inmates were incensed at my lawsuit and the *Angolite* editorial that I had written. I received overt threats from those who remembered I had turned my back on their work slowdown.

But other inmates saw the editorial and the lawsuit as an effort to help them. Most were long-termers who comprised half of the inmate population. The pardon process was their only way out of prison. They gave *The Angolite* their support.

The editorial and the lawsuit propelled me into a stronger position on *The Angolite*. The magazine had gained attention through the stand it had taken. It had put prison reformers on notice that the magazine would not kowtow to anyone, even the penal movement. That established the magazine's independence.

"We have a unique opportunity here, Wilbert," I said one night as we discussed the Vodicka editorial and the future of the magazine. "Phelps has been touting the 'free press' line. We forced him to back it up with the Vodicka editorial. Now, let's see how far they'll let us go."

"Some subject matter is taboo." Rideau replied. "There are issues neither the administration nor the inmates will let us deal with. The inmates will deliver their letters to the editor in person through that door with baseball bats in their hands. I don't know if we can face another Vodicka issue."

Rideau was a cautious man. He calculated the risks involved in any decision.

"We can if we convince the inmates and free people alike that this is their magazine," I pressed.

Rideau's brow furrowed. I had pricked his professional curiosity and his desire for acceptance.

"How do you propose we do that?" he asked.

"Easy. I have some story ideas — stories that will give the readers a side of prison life they've never read about before. I want to write about old-line prison guards. It will make their exploits larger than life. If we can get them to accept the magazine, the administration won't dare try to shut us up."

"You write the stories and I'll convince Gresham to let us run them," Rideau said.

Rideau and I interviewed virtually every veteran guard at the prison. Initially, some were reluctant to talk to us because they didn't trust the magazine. Gresham ran interference, convincing hard-nosed guards with the promise of a "fair and balanced story."

With an article titled "The Vanishing Breed" (May–June 1978), the guards got more than they bargained for. It praised their spirit, courage, and determination. The edition became a prized possession. Every guard at the prison wanted to read the article. One told us he traded his copy for a "piece of tail."

"I don't know how you two will top that one," Gresham said after the article appeared.

"The Vanishing Breed" introduced me to the downside of working with an established writer. An alternative New Orleans–based newspaper, *The Figaro*, ran a piece about the article, saying that it had obviously been written "by editor Wilbert Rideau." I was furious at the assumption, slinging the newspaper in the garbage. Wilbert promised to correct the record. It slipped his attention.

The *Figaro* piece inspired me to write "Anatomy of a Prison Suicide" (July–August 1978). It was an account of Billy Ray's death. There was no doubt about who wrote it. It was so popular, inmates circulated xerox copies so everyone would have a chance to read it. For weeks, it was the talk of the prison community, overshadowing even "The Vanishing Breed" and the Vodicka editorial.

The recognition I received for these articles triggered Rideau's competitive spirit. He wrote the next feature, "Conversations with the Dead" (September–October 1978). It told the long-termers' story and proved to be immensely popular with them. It became their bible.

Those three 1978 editions earned *The Angolite* a finalist spot in the 1979 National Magazine Awards competition and won it a 1979 Robert F. Kennedy Journalism Award. I was promoted from staff writer to associate editor after the Kennedy Award. "Conversations with the Dead" garnered a 1979 ABA Silver Gavel Award for Rideau, marking the first time a prisoner had ever won the award.

In 1979, *The Angolite* produced three major award-winning articles: "The Other Side of Murder," an in-depth piece about capital punishment, for which I won the 1980 George Polk Award; "A Prison Tragedy," a piece about Life's killing, for which I won the 1980 ABA Silver Gavel Award; and "Prison: The Sexual Jungle," a penetrating look at sexual violence in prison, for which Rideau also won the 1980 George Polk Award. I became coeditor after the Polk Awards.

In 1980, at Rideau's suggestion, we began to submit all articles to award competitions under a joint byline. The celebrated black/white writing team was thus born. The magazine would win three more major journalism awards under the Rideau/Sinclair byline: the 1981 Sidney Hillman Award for "Louisiana Death Watch," a piece I wrote about capital punishment; a 1981 ABA Certificate of Merit for "Career Criminal," a piece I wrote about recidivists; and a 1982 ABA Certificate of Merit for "Louisiana Death Watch."

The awards brought national and international recognition to *The Angolite*. The magazine became the flagship for the nation's penal press and the benchmark for investigative journalism in Louisiana. The stories we wrote seared away sham and conventional beliefs about keepers and the kept. We wrote the truth about cell madness, guards turned pimp and killer, midnight suicide, and self-mutilation. We chronicled the scalding shame of homosexual rape and wrote of paranoia, the psychological mind-set necessary for survival in prison. We carefully crafted our words to temper our bitterness and purge any bias in our stories about the casual atrocities of life behind prison walls.

With the blessing of Phelps, Blackburn, and Gresham, who were enamored with traveling to glamorous places to pick up our awards, we became criminal justice "experts." We traveled the state with an unarmed security escort lecturing about the criminal justice system at universities, civic groups, high schools, and churches.

The *Angolite* Experiment, as it had been dubbed by Rideau, was effectively over by the fall of 1981. There would be no more major awards for the magazine under the remainder of our tenure. Rideau and I would write more good articles and be the subject of more print and television reports. But Louisiana's first Republican governor in one hundred years had taken office. Dave Treen had rigid views of crime and punishment and they did not include a free penal press.

The *Angolite* Experiment was a flash in the darkness; a brief but valiant effort by two prisoners who shared a simple desire to enlighten the free world about prison life. Censors began picking over its carcass within a few years of its birth.

26

IN EARLY MARCH 1981, Louisiana was just weeks from its first execution in twenty years. The state's death law had finally passed constitutional muster. It had to be rewritten after the United States Supreme Court overturned the death penalty nationwide in 1972 in *Furman v. Georgia*. A drifter and drug addict named Colin Clark was set to die on April 8. He was the first man scheduled to be executed in Louisiana's electric chair since Jessie James Ferguson in 1961.

Clark was convicted of killing a Red Lobster restaurant manager in Baton Rouge in 1978. His impending execution was big news statewide. *The Angolite* planned a major feature story, "Louisiana Death Watch," for its July–August edition. Wilbert and I were scheduled to go to the death house at Camp F on March 17 to see the electric chair and take pictures for the magazine. Two Louisiana television news crews, one from Baton Rouge and the other from Lafayette, would also be at Camp F doing stories on the death penalty.

A patrol van picked us up at the Main Prison complex for the ride to Camp F. The metal security screen separating inmate from driver rattled incessantly as the blue-uniformed driver raced to keep from being late. Rideau and I did not have to ride behind the screen like other inmates. It was a symbol of the unprecedented trust that the administration placed in both of us. Oblivious to the clanging racket and the reckless speed of the abused vehicle, I shuddered as the dank smell of a death cell rushed back into my brain. I was about to face the death machine that had haunted me for six years before *Furman v. Georgia* rescued me.

The patrol van passed one of the several dozen farm lines whose inmates were hoeing grass from the banks of the many deep ditches that snaked through the prison's cultivated acres. Most of the inmates looked up as the van passed. A few waved with huge grins. Others stared at us with hate and resentment. I heard one muttering in angry tones, "Dere go dem two jive motherfuckers." Rideau and I had learned to live with their hate. He watched my back and I watched his.

The van covered the three miles from the Main Prison complex to Camp F in record time. It stopped at a cinder block complex not unlike the prison's other outcamps. Outside, flags snapped in the breeze as the wind sent ripples across a small lake and birds wheeled in the air above newly plowed fields nearby. I saw the familiar sign at the entrance of the building warning that only those on official business were allowed inside. The prison van arrived late. Not even orders from the warden's office could make the vans run on time. Blackburn and Gresham greeted us at the door of the building that housed the death chamber.

"I want you to talk to Jodie Bell," Blackburn said. "She's that Channel 9 reporter, and a good Baton Rouge story wouldn't hurt you."

My stomach tightened when I faced a television interview. I was especially self-conscious of my deep southern twang, but once the interview was under way, my nervousness quickly disappeared. Blackburn led us into the death chamber where the electric chair sat, cold and ominous. I experienced a terrible sense of loss as I stood staring at the chair in utter fascination. A decade before, nightmares about it had regularly invaded my sleep. The dreams were always the same. I was alone in a small cell. The final moment was drawing near. I was tortured by gnawing questions that had no answers. Why had I brought my life to this end? How had I ended up killing Bodden? Death beckoned. I was alone and terrified.

"Please don't let me wet myself," I prayed.

The warden approached. His face was hard and his eyes were full of hatred.

"It's time," he said.

The guards led me down a dark corridor. Suddenly, the chair jumped out at me, a brilliant apparition in the dark. I fell to my knees, forcing the guards to drag me to the chair. I couldn't breathe as they strapped me down. I saw a hand on the switch. It was my father's. I screamed and wet myself.

I turned toward the group in the death chamber. A small, delicate-looking woman walked in with a news photographer and laid the television lights that she was carrying on the floor. As she glanced up, she looked directly into my eyes. I felt the breath leave my body. She was the most beautiful woman that I had ever seen. I leaned against the wall trying to look studious and professional. I didn't want her to catch me staring at her, my mouth agape. But I kept sneaking glances at her. She moved like a dancer as she got things ready for her interviews — issuing instructions to her photographer, testing her tape recorder, and talking to Blackburn. The sight of her spawned a tornado in my head.

In prison, a man is forced to do without a woman. He only has two sexual outlets: homosexuality or masturbation. As I looked at Jodie, I ached with the desire to know her as a woman.

"Jodie Bell, meet Billy Sinclair," the warden said, stepping forward to introduce us. The first words we spoke were the usual pleasantries that society prescribes for introductions. I gave no sign that I noted her sex. My manners were a practiced art, necessary camouflage in Angola's unpredictable environment.

Jodie's photographer indicated the chair that I was to take for the interview. She had placed Jodie's facing mine. The chairs almost touched. The physical proximity necessary for television interviews challenged my concentration. As Jodie sat down, her left knee inadvertently brushed my thigh. I had to glance away to regain my composure.

"Are you asking me about the various methods of execution?" I asked, repeating what I thought she had said.

"Yes."

I settled into a practiced answer.

"I prefer the firing squad. With the firing squad, you're going to be dead within thirty to forty-five seconds. The electric chair can take up to forty-five seconds for the first volt to reach maximum output. You are talking about a process that may take up to two or three minutes to kill a person. In the case of Ethel Rosenberg, it took six charges of electricity to actually kill her. The gas chamber can take up to twenty-seven minutes to kill and hanging up to twenty minutes if the neck doesn't break."

Jodie listened to the deadly timetable, seemingly unaffected. I tried to look past the impenetrable curtains of her eyes for some reciprocal feeling. I saw nothing.

"You had the death sentence. What is your opinion of capital punishment?" she asked.

I loved the sound of her voice. It was so precise and distinctive. Her question was a natural one. Virtually every reporter in the state who was doing a piece on capital punishment wanted to interview the two convict editors who had spent years on death row.

"Some will say I should have been put to death. The sentence I have now, life without parole, is not mercy. Only a person who has not spent a day in prison could say that life without parole is more humane than death. If society is going to keep me locked up for the rest of my life, then it should do the humane thing and take me out and execute me."

Two years before, the Louisiana Board of Pardons had recommended that my life sentence be commuted to forty-five years, a decision that would have freed me had Governor Edwards approved it. But Edwards bowed to the opposition in my case — a powerful political force led by District Attorney Ossie Brown, the same man who had once been appointed my lawyer. Emotion slipped into my voice as I thought about the denial.

"Had I known I was gonna go through all this," I continued, "I would have demanded the death penalty as Gilmore did."

In the background Blackburn's two-way radio crackled out a message. Somewhere a cell door slammed shut. The sound of

Rideau's hard heels on the tile floor disrupted my thoughts. He had concluded the second interview and the reporter wanted to interview me next. My heart wasn't in it. I kept straining to hear Jodie's voice or catch a glimpse of her. I was glad when the second interview was over so I could turn my attention back to Jodie. She was still talking to Rideau. He looked at her, head slightly cocked, one round black pupil clearly visible, the other half-hidden by a drooping eyelid.

"People operate under the mistaken notion that imposing a life sentence on people is a form of charity. But it's just another form of death, one that is more excruciating because the only peace a man's gonna know is the peace of the grave. I see no sense in prolonging suffering like that."

An ironic smile played at the corner of his lips. He was bitterly aware that mercy was a newcomer in his world. He had denied it to his victim as she knelt before him pleading for her life. Now he was begging for mercy himself from the pardon board and the governor.

"When I lived on death row for thirteen years, my pleas for mercy falling on deaf ears, it made me realize what my victim must have felt. I did the same thing to her. I ignored her pleas. You know, it was sort of like a role reversal, and in that came an appreciation for life and the thin line that separates the living from the dead."

At the age of nineteen, Rideau held up a bank in downtown Lake Charles that was next door to the Singer Sewing Company store where he worked as a janitor. He took three hostages, two women and a man. They worked at the bank and knew Rideau. In a wooded area outside of town, he tried to kill all three. He shot two, also stabbing one of them in the throat. The man managed to run away. The woman, bleeding from a cut in her throat and a gunshot wound, feigned death. He turned to the third hostage with his knife and cut her throat as she begged for her life.

"Why did you cut her throat?" Jodie asked, recoiling at the thought.

"I think I ran out of bullets."

I was glad when Jodie's interview with Rideau came to an end. The camera crews began packing their equipment. Blackburn ush-

196

ered her toward a foyer in the lobby. I walked over to offer a farewell. I had been looking for a way to maintain contact. Blackburn drifted away. Jodie and I began talking like two reporters anywhere, comparing notes on the difficulties of covering stories. Suddenly, she shifted conversational gears.

"How would you like to make a lot of money?" she asked, deliberately taking me by surprise.

"Well, I . . . Sure I would." It was almost a stammer.

"Look, you can write. You've won a bunch of national awards. How would you like to write for soap operas? You know how much it pays?"

She smiled up at me. I wanted to talk to her for the rest of my life.

"Look," she said, "I've got these friends in New Orleans, they're head writers on a soap. You know they get five hundred dollars for one lousy thirty-minute script? I mean, five hundred dollars for that. And most writers don't want the work. They think writing for soap operas is disgusting. But God, it's great money. Want me to talk to my friends?"

"So why ain't you writing soaps, then?"

"Boring . . ."

She mouthed her answer up at me, smiling as she stretched the word out, making the sound last as long as a sentence. I looked down at her with my heart in my eyes. I was close enough to catch the scent of her perfume. I fought down an innate desire to touch her cheek: to let my fingers trace the soft outline of her face like a blind man and absorb its memory in my mind's eye. Instead, my brain photographed her image. I would see it for days.

"Do you know who the greatest fans of soap opera really are?" I asked her. She pleaded ignorance. I was triumphant at knowing something she didn't.

"Death row inmates. It's how they get people in their lives."

"Did you do that?" she asked.

"No, I wore headphones to keep from going crazy."

The sudden shouts, the slam of metal against metal reverberating up and down the tier, country hits, soul, chow carts, guttural conversations — I had blocked them out with headphones during the day, and I felt grateful for the few hours of relative silence after midnight.

The others began walking toward us. My moment alone with Jodie was over. Efforts to resist the feelings that she aroused in me were futile. They went deeper than sexual desire. Jodie made me feel alive. She was everything I longed for. I wanted to be with her all the time, to be woven into the fabric of her life. I wanted to watch her drink coffee in the morning and cover stories all day. I wanted to possess her at night and then fold her in my arms and protect her until morning. Jodie was the dream that had always dwelled in my heart. I knew it — and it frightened me more than anything else in my entire life.

She reached out to shake my hand when she realized that Rideau and I would not be joining the reporters and the warden for lunch at Camp F. I watched as the warden led her and the rest of the entourage to the Camp F dining room for a special meal reserved for visitors. Like Faust, I would have sold my soul to Mephistopheles to have her feel what I did. When she was out of sight, Rideau and I sat in chairs in the lobby to wait for the patrol van driver to bring us a "stick-out" tray — food in a white Styrofoam container. As usual, it was cold and mixed together. Jell-O had melted into the beans. Normally, I would have searched out tidbits in hopes of salvaging a bite. Instead, I put the tray on a nearby table. My stomach was churning and my heart was still racing. I was helpless to control the feelings that Jodie aroused in me.

Outside, the sun rode a high quadrant in the sky and a soft wind riffled the grass as Camp F's inmate cooks lounged in the kitchen doorway, their day's work done. Bright light glinted off the small lake across the road. Rideau and I hunched our shoulders against the wind and pulled our jackets closer as we walked toward the prison van.

Back at the *Angolite* office, I went straight to my typewriter and typed a short note of appreciation to her. I kept it professional. The intense emotion I felt might frighten her. And I wanted to keep a line of communication open. I put her business card in a safe place. At least I had a memento. I put the note in an envelope and put it in the prison mail. Then I began a roller coaster ride. Would she write back or throw my note in the trash? Was I a fool to think that I could have a relationship of any kind with her?

It was too late to worry. I needed her in my life. There had to be a way. I had gone to Camp F to face the death machine that I had feared for so many years. I left irretrievably in love.

27

THAT ENCOUNTER REPLAYED IN MY HEAD for days. I added Jodie's name to the *Angolite* mailing list, a symbolic step perhaps, in my quest to attach her to my world. I spent my time trying to concentrate on daily tasks, but it was a futile effort. I kept waiting for a letter. Instead of writing, she called.

Rideau and I were sitting in Blackburn's office watching him toy with a battery-operated electric chair that he kept on his desk. He responded to our interview about the death penalty more like a psychologist than a warden. The more we pressed him for a specific position, the more he played with the toy electric chair and the more I wanted to grind it under my shoe.

The warden's secretary stepped tentatively into Blackburn's office.

"You have a phone call, Billy," she whispered, uncertainty making her terribly uncomfortable. "It's Jodie Bell."

Blackburn started laughing. The chuckle rose from an ample

stomach and then expanded into a roar. He put the electric chair down and turned to his secretary.

"You know *The Angolite*'s arrived," he said, "when its editors get phone calls in the warden's office. Be sure to tell Jodie Bell hello."

In 1981, under the Blackburn administration, reporters had easy access to *The Angolite*, and guards competed for the opportunity to escort the Rideau/Sinclair team on interviews and speaking engagements. It gave them a chance to meet "important people" and perhaps be on television. Even so, I had never known a reporter bold enough to talk her way through Angola's phone system to find me. But I kept a tight lid on my feelings as I stepped into the secretary's office to take the call.

"Billy, I need some help. How far is it from the Front Gate to Camp F?" she asked in her clear, self-assured voice.

"Four, maybe five miles." I managed to stammer, wanting to shout "She called me! She called me!"

The brief conversation left me shaken.

"Well, aren't you somethin'," the secretary said. "Getting a phone call from a reporter in the warden's office. That's never happened before."

I turned and stepped back into Blackburn's office. He was playing with the toy chair again. The warden gave me a penetrating stare.

"Jodie wanted to know how far it was from the Front Gate to the death house," I said. "She's working on her series. When she was here I offered to help. She said to tell you hello."

Blackburn relaxed.

"Good," he said. "Got to keep the media happy."

Rideau and I resumed the interview. I wrote Jodie with more information for the series on the death penalty that she planned to air in May. We began a casual correspondence. She dropped me notes as she ran across information about my case. My name surfaced almost inevitably in her Baton Rouge interviews about the death penalty. Personal information began creeping into our letters. She had asked about my family and my favorite memories of home. I had few, I replied, and they didn't seem real anymore.

I saw her again two weeks later at Phelps' office at Corrections Headquarters in Baton Rouge. Rideau and I were there to interview him about the death penalty. Jodie was there for the same reason. She was standing at a bulletin board with her glasses pushed back over her forehead into wavy hair that hung almost to her shoulders. Desire flooded through me again.

That night, I couldn't fight my feelings anymore. I headed down the Walk toward the phone on the wall outside the dormitory which inmates had permission to use at assigned hours for collect calls. I had her number memorized. I generally left the *Angolite* office at 11:00 P.M. Since all the other inmates were locked down for the night, Rideau and I had no time limit on our calls. It was one of the special privileges that we had carved out for the staff of the magazine. As I went down the Walk, I thought about what I would say. She answered on the second ring.

We had talked only a few moments before a torrent of love and desire burst out of me.

"I don't care how you cut it or shape it or dice it, I'm in love with you," I blurted.

She listened as I groped my way through the maze of the English language trying to tell her what she made me feel.

At the end she responded only by saying, "I will never hurt you, Billy."

I had to see her again. I persuaded Gresham to allow me to have "special visits" with her. They would be in the "attorney-client" conference room in the Main Prison's A-Building. They were another sign of my special status in the prison community as an *Angolite* editor. Rideau accompanied me on the first visit. It was a condition the weekend major had imposed. Already there were suspicions that our relationship was more personal than professional.

I would learn everything I could about Jodie during the next few months. Knowing the details about her life was almost like possessing her. Every new fact fleshed her out, body and soul, in my mind. I explored the contours of her experiences, fingering the details, lingering over the time lines and contradictions like a lover undressing his beloved for the first time.

She was living in Baton Rouge when we met. She kept an

apartment there, traveling to New Orleans on the weekends to see her family. Her father's family came from South Louisiana. Her great-great-grandfather was a founder of New Iberia. Her grandfather was a successful Houston developer. A cousin was a conservative congressman.

Her father was a black sheep. He was a brilliant if erratic personality full of nervous energy, who pulled up stakes in a flash if he perceived a better business opportunity elsewhere, no matter how many thousands of miles away.

Jodie was born in Houston. At the age of six she moved to Fort Worth, where her father manufactured a national brand of dog food. His business was a fabulous success. An article in *Life* magazine in 1949 called him "The Golden Boy with the Midas Touch." He retired to Mexico in 1950 at age thirty-seven, lost his fortune, and recouped it selling oil deals to movie stars for tax write-offs before losing all his money for good. He died a pauper in a veteran's hospital in Houston at the age of sixty-one.

By the time she was nineteen years old, Jodie spoke three languages. As a child, she lived in a log cabin in Anniston, Alabama, and on a chicken farm in Brookshire, Texas, before the family moved to Fort Worth, then Mexico City and Acapulco, and finally to Beverly Hills before returning to Houston. She went to school in Mexico, Italy, and Switzerland. Her life included memberships in country clubs and Christmases with no toys when her father was broke. She knew World War II expatriates in Mexico City; Hollywood actors, nightclub dancers, and cliff divers in Acapulco; and nuns and servants who took care of her during her parents' frequent absences. Her upbringing left her with an unorthodox world view. Jodie knew at an early age that virtue wasn't confined to the right side of the tracks and sometimes it wasn't found there at all.

She also knew fear. Her father had an explosive temper. Beatings for childish missteps were frequent and unpredictable. Jodie and her three sisters tiptoed through a childhood punctuated with violence, as her parents fought a losing battle with alcoholism. She learned to hide fear and keep up appearances. She was at home in almost any social setting, but she never lost the feeling that she was an outsider no matter where she went.

But nothing in Jodie's background prepared her for the world she was entering. She would not only have to deal with the restrictions of prison but with a man who knew virtually nothing about relating to a woman like her. She was from a world of privilege. By any standard, I was trailer trash. But I knew from the moment I saw her that she was my natural mate. I waited for our first visit with a mixture of fear and anticipation, oscillating wildly between the two extremes. When the day arrived, I bolted on a plate of armor to cover up my feelings and almost ruined the visit.

She walked into the A-Building, where a guard in a caged-in office pressed a button unlocking the first of two barred doors. She stepped inside, signed the visitor's register, and stepped to the second cell-like door, waiting for the signal that it too had been electronically unlocked. Another guard ushered her around a corner and down a short hall to the attorney-client conference room where I stood, my back against the wall, not knowing how to act. I nodded in her direction when she stepped through the door but I didn't let my guard down. She had not told me that she loved me. I still had no idea where I stood.

She turned to Rideau. "Good morning, Wilbert."

He smiled a relaxed, easy grin. "What you got there? Everything but the kitchen sink, huh?" He cocked his head at Jodie's large purse like some bright bird, his look both quizzical and amused, eyebrows furrowed in a characteristic frown as he tried to bridge my silence. Jodie was my visitor, yet I had made no real move to greet her. Uncertainty shredded my confidence. I remained across the room, arms folded across my chest, my face devoid of expression.

Jodie forced herself to face me as she crossed the room. She extended her hand, her professional facade in place, as she looked up at me.

"Hello, Billy."

She miscalculated the distance she would have to reach to shake my hand and stumbled over my foot, scuffing the high shine on my boot. She blushed and stammered out an apology.

"I've ruined your shine. I'm so sorry."

My boots and their high shine and the neatly pressed jeans that I wore were a way of demonstrating that I was different from the average inmate. As much as I could, I dressed like a free man, bartering cigarettes to other inmates in exchange for pressing my clothes and maintaining the mirrorlike polish on my boots.

"That's all right," I managed to get out. "It didn't hurt anything."

Jodie was dressed for Saturday errands or casual encounters — neat, clean, in Levi's and high heels. She was very beautiful.

Fingering a notepad, I sat silently, an ancient, brooding look on my face.

"Hey, you know what?" Jodie asked Rideau, giving up the idea of conversing with me. "I heard only your best friends can call you Wilbert. Yeah, I heard you're so tough, nobody calls you anything but Rideau unless they've known you all their life."

A Channel 9 photographer had told Jodie the story, his eyes wide with the Rideau legend as he spoke with a sort of reverence for the editor's notorious reputation.

"You can call me Wilbert, now that you're associating with him."

He smiled and jerked his thumb toward me.

"Well, it would sound funny if I didn't. I mean, he calls you Wilbert. Excuse me, I mean 'Wilbuh.'"

Jodie cut her eyes at me as she mocked my deep drawl. I couldn't suppress a grin. Outside, there was a knock on the door. Coffee arrived in Styrofoam cups. Our waiter was a tall, thin black inmate with a wide grin.

"Pete couldn't stand it until he could get in here to meet Jodie Bell," Rideau said. "Pete's *Angolite*. He does a lotta stuff for us."

Pete was the magazine's runner, an errand boy who could put his ear to the ground deep inside the prison, talking to sources about story material in places where Rideau and I were considered sellouts — rats who informed on illicit activities in return for comfortable jobs on the prison magazine.

"Hey, Pete," Jodie said. "Nice to meet you. How are you?"

Pete bent and bobbed at her greeting, his big grin even wider than when he came in with the coffee.

"Say," he said. "You're not so tall, you know. I thought you'd be, you know . . ." He indicated a spot higher than mid-chest against his six-foot frame.

Jodie laughed. Television made her four-foot-eleven-and-one-half-inch frame look a lot bigger.

"Most people think that. TV makes me look about five foot six. And then everybody's so shocked when they meet me . . ." her voice trailed off.

Pete wasn't listening anymore. His grin had receded. An anxious look replaced it.

"Well, I gotta get back, you know . . ."

He made a vague apologetic gesture as he backed away. Jodie had no sense of being watched, but Pete's gesture indicated that guards were calculating the amount of time he spent inside. She winced at the sound of keys and the reverberating slam of metal. She was at a loss in Angola's strange environment, unable to predict its expectations and demands from the visual cues and sounds that she heard. Despite the casual play she made of conversation, it was clear these clumsy intrusions bewildered her. The sounds outside subsided. Jodie glanced at the books in Rideau's hands. He noted her interest.

"You ever read any Ayn Rand?" he asked.

She was a favorite of his, he said. But Rand was just a name Jodie remembered from college.

"No, I'm not a reader, just the newspapers every day and some news magazines. That's it. I'm not an intellectual, I guess you could say."

Jodie had read voraciously before the age of thirteen — everything she could get her hands on — devouring the pages even by flashlight under the covers on school nights after she was ordered to bed. Adolescence and rebellion against her father's alcoholic rule called a halt to her budding intellectualism. Jodie escaped into marriage at age nineteen to the son of an Oklahoma farm boy and a doctor's daughter. He was a graduate of Rice University and the youngest editor in the history of the *Houston Post*. Motherhood required most of her attention. She enrolled in college at the age of thirty-six when her youngest child was ten. By then, the family had lived in New Orleans for a number of years where her husband was a journalism professor.

"Hey, I do have a book for you. Ever read *The Mind of The South*? W. J. Cash's book? It's a classic. History. The definitive work on the South. It reads like Faulkner. I'll send it to you. You've got a hole in your world without it."

"We got a lot of holes," Rideau replied. "Education on death row was kind of catch-as-catch-can. Of course, we had a lot of time for reading. When I first came to this place, I wasn't illiterate but I was ignorant. The governor was going to sign my death warrant and I didn't know who he was."

I followed their conversation silently, watching Jodie from my vantage point across the table, fascinated by her grace and intellect. I felt ready to join the conversation.

"By the way, sirs, let me warn you about something! That New Orleans writer who wants to write a piece with you was bad-mouthing you at a press club party down there last week. He just wants a ride off your byline because no national magazine is going to publish him on his name alone. Fuck him."

The term often peppered Jodie's language. It was common around the newsroom and she worked hard at playing the tough reporter because she had started in the news business so late.

"That doesn't even sound like cussin' when you say it."

Rideau's remark amazed her. It was her turn to be embarrassed.

"You see," he went on, "you got a congenital problem. You were born too high up to sound low down."

I nodded in agreement.

"Well, my ears aren't as tender as you might think, Mr. Rideau. I hear a lot when I'm out on stories with some of those photogs from Channel 9. One has the dirtiest mouth of any kid I ever met. He likes being the tough guy. I met his mother once, a very proper lady from Shreveport. The country club set, you know. His manners were perfect that day. She'd cut him out of the will if he ever slipped."

"Billy, you ready for them stick-out lunches?"

It was Pete, his close-cropped head and wide grin were all that were visible as he stuck his head around the door.

"What's a stick-out lunch?" Jodie asked.

"It's a lunch you get when you stick out," I said, rising as I spoke.

"Stick-out?" she repeated.

"When you stick out, you don't go to the dormitory for the count," I said.

"For the count?" It was a new and equally confusing phrase.

"Yes," I continued patiently. "They count before they feed. But some inmates get to stick out of the count if their job assignment . . . if they have permission to be someplace else."

Angola's inmates were counted several times a day. Rideau and I did not have to make the count. We stayed in the *Angolite* office. Most of our meals were stick-out trays delivered to us by kitchen personnel.

Pete handed in three lunches stacked on top of each other in Styrofoam containers. Jodie watched as I lifted the lid of the top container.

"We got fried catfish. You like catfish?"

"Yeah," Jodie answered, "but not this stuff." She winced at the soggy mass in the container. "What's your favorite food?" She directed the question at me.

"My favorite food? I like cold, boiled shrimp," I responded. "We used to have it years ago in New Orleans. And I like that salad bar they have at Burger King. Wilbert and I enjoyed that on speaking trips when they used to take us around to schools to talk to kids about staying out of crime. We don't get salad here. Just cooked vegetables."

"What?" She appeared incredulous. "You never get salad or fresh vegetables?" she asked. "Well then, they give you vitamins to compensate, of course."

"No, I'd have to get up at four in the morning and go to sick call at the hospital," I told her. "I'm better off sleeping."

"Well, you sure don't get much variety here," she said, pushing her beans around the white plastic container, their oily juice oozing from one of its sections to another.

"Sometimes that's a blessing," Wilbert said. "You might run up against something like broccoli. But we just get greens and stuff like that."

The tension was gone. Our remarks were relaxed and easy.

"Know where Rayville is?" I asked.

Jodie had never heard of it.

"North Louisiana, where I was born," I said.

"Geography was never my best subject."

She burst out laughing.

"Pray tell," she teased. "You hide it so well."

"Hey, I found out something about you," she said a moment later. "Did you know that an investigator in Ossie Brown's office, Leonard Spears, was a childhood friend of J. C. Bodden?"

I gave her a startled look. She had more than pricked my interest with the mention of my victim's name and the man who had once been appointed to defend me.

"Um hm, Spears grew up with Bodden," she went on. "He's been an investigator with Ossie's office for years. God, they're thicker than thieves down there in Baton Rouge! How did you get so many enemies?"

"They say I shot Bodden in cold blood. That I was calm and cool. Back in '66 at the time of my trial, my attorney never could find the people who saw me running away with Bodden chasing me. I didn't get the suppressed police report till 1980."

Jodie's eyes followed the length of my arm. She grimaced at the sight of my hand, curled around an imaginary gun.

"He was running after me. He was a big man. I knew if he ever got his hands on me, he'd kill me. I fired the shot backwards, I fired the shot," I extended my arm behind me again, "to scare him, to make him stop chasing me. I never knew he was hit. The last time I saw him he was sitting on the sidewalk in front of the store, yelling for the police. I didn't mean to kill him —"

The smiles and laughter were gone. I leaned forward, eyes alive with special intensity.

"You gonna stick with me?"

It was urgent and personal. Jodie looked up at me, sadness filling her blue eyes.

"I don't have any choice. It's not right for you to be here anymore. You've paid."

I focused intently on her words, alert to every nuance.

"I . . ." she struggled. "I . . . have to have a certain order in the world. I have to believe that I'm living in a universe that's not just chaotic. It's got to be a better place than that. I couldn't rest easy in my head knowing you were here. Knowing you've paid enough, and agonized enough, and changed enough. Knowing I should have extended a hand and didn't. It would sour everything."

The words came from her deep conviction that wrongs had to

be righted no matter the cost. As a child she had stood up to her father, challenging his unfair behavior, even though she always got a whipping for standing up to him during one of his rampages.

"A lot of people say we ought to be out, Jodie. Then they go home and we never hear from them again."

"I'm not a lot of people," she replied.

"This is a brutal world, a brutal world."

I hissed the words at her.

"I know."

She looked at me, too tired to cover up her feelings.

"Wilbert . . ." I turned to look at Rideau.

He rose and left the room without a word. Jodie stared at the table. I took her by surprise.

"Jodie . . ." I said as my hands enveloped hers. "Oh God, Jodie! I wanted to touch you for so long. You're so beautiful."

The words exploded past the barrier I had bolted in place.

"Oh God," I said as I touched her face in awe, repeating the phrase in a whisper. Then, I wrapped her in my arms, rocking her like a baby as I repeated the words.

"Oh my God, so long."

I brushed my hands across her face again and again like a blind man; across her lips, her eyes, and her cheeks, trying to memorize the feel of her flesh.

"This is a brutal world, baby, a brutal existence," I said, continuing to rock her and stroke her face. "This will be so hard for you."

"Billy . . ."

Every time she tried to say my name, I kissed her.

Suddenly I jerked upright, slapping my palms flat on the table at the sound of heavy keys banging against a thigh and the crackle of a two-way radio in the hall. In less than an instant, I was hyper alert, listening, assessing the potential.

"That's rank," I whispered.

Jodie was rigid with fear. She searched my eyes frantically for what it meant, shocked at my subservient reaction.

After a light tap, the door opened and Rideau stepped inside, his slight smile indicating that nothing was amiss.

"Rank just passing through," he said.

He brought two cups of coffee to the table. Jodie shook with relief as she lifted the cup to her lips. She was ready to cry. We were like children caught in a terrible game, with no right to touch, forced to steal what pleasure we could, listening all the while for the slightest sound, the signal to suddenly spring apart. Heart thudding in her throat, Jodie was still trembling. I saw the fear and bewilderment in her eyes.

"It's all right, baby," I said. I smoothed her hair as she relaxed against my shoulder. "It's all right. They come through from time to time. Nothing to worry about. It's all right."

There was no expression on Rideau's face. In prison a man learns not to see. I lifted Jodie to her feet. Her head was barely higher than mine as she stood by my chair. My hands encircled her waist as she bent to kiss my face.

"I didn't want to wait so long to touch you, baby," I said. "I couldn't read you. Until I pushed it, made you tell me, I didn't know."

She smiled and leaned against me. Awkwardly, I patted her cheek. I still could not believe that I was actually touching her.

"It's time to go," I said.

At my nod, Rideau stepped outside the door, shutting it quietly behind him.

"He can stand guard one, maybe two, minutes."

I spread my legs, inched my back down the wall, and lifted Jodie onto my lap. I kissed her, then cradled her head on my shoulder, rocking her gently for a time before I put her down.

"Somehow, I will find a way for us to see each other," I said.

She turned at the door to signal a final goodbye. Tears welled up in my eyes as I watched her go.

28

THE FAT BROWN PACKET almost filled Jodie's mailbox. She had been waiting on stories about me from the *Times-Picayune* in New Orleans. The newspaper clippings that tumbled out of the envelope left her reeling. I was no first offender. The carnal knowledge charge hit her like a balled fist in the gut. I was a sex offender! And a car thief! And an armed robber! She sat on the edge of her bed staring at the newsprint.

The facts stared back at her, ugly and unavoidable. There were no redeeming stories. The man for whom she had felt such passionate and instant rapport was decidedly criminal. My illegal escapades read like the Sears Roebuck catalog of crime. Tears of betrayal filled her eyes.

In a burst of anger, she grabbed the phone. It was nine o'clock, too late to call Angola. Fury fueled her resolve. She would do it anyway. The telephone's ring had a faraway sound, more like a buzz than a standard ring. She thought of the prison, circled with lights and razor wire in the dark shadows of the Tunica Hills.

"Main Prison Control Center," the security guard snapped, annoyed at being distracted as he tried to decipher a whispered transaction between two inmates outside in the lobby.

"This is Jodie Bell with Channel 9," she said, cold and imperious. "I need to check something with Wilbert Rideau."

"Hey, Pete," the guard called. "Get Rideau down here. Telephone."

A cacophony of prison noises filled the wire as Jodie waited — strains of a country and western song from a radio somewhere; vulgar shouts and raucous laughter; metal slamming against metal; and the crackle of a message over a two-way radio. The Control Center was as busy at nine o'clock on a Thursday night as it was in broad daylight. The guard inside the cage manipulated a series of gates controlling inmate traffic while another guard checked off inmates leaving various "callouts." A misplaced check or the failure to check would lead to a "bad count." That would require a recount. If the recount did not produce a "good count," there would be a "roll call count" of every inmate in the Main Prison complex, an affair that could take an hour or more.

"Hello," Rideau's unmistakable voice sounded above the background noise.

"Wilbert, this is Jodie Bell. Do me a favor, please? Tell your little friend Billy Sinclair that I found out all about his record."

"That's all?"

"Yes," she said crisply.

And then, "Wilbert why didn't he tell me about all that when we met? Why did he just talk about his murder conviction as though the rest didn't exist? Well . . . just tell him . . . tell him, I found out. Thanks, you hear?"

When Rideau stepped through the door, I sensed a problem. He could never conceal concern or apprehension.

"I think you better call Jodie," he said, pouring a cup of coffee. "She's upset — something about your record."

I stood up behind my desk, saying nothing. I pulled the curtain back and watched the last of the stragglers going down the Walk toward the dormitories. I masked the fear coursing through my brain as I turned and walked toward the door.

"Everything all right?" he asked as I walked out.

213

"I don't know," I replied, pulling the door behind me.

Jodie had been giving me information about my case that she turned up as she talked to Baton Rouge sources for her series. I had learned a lot about my case when I discovered the suppressed police reports in 1980. Jodie was filling in the blanks, fleshing out the people involved in my opposition. I had asumed she was familiar with my record.

As she undressed for bed, she decided she was finished with my bewildering criminal world. Angola's inhabitants had to be viewed in an inverse relationship, with light and dark reversed, like negatives instead of photographs. Face-value judgments were dangerous. She had wanted to believe in me. A profound tide of understanding had seemed to flow between us.

My telephone call interrupted her preparations for sleep.

"AT&T operator. Billy calling collect. Will you pay?"

I pictured her sitting on the edge of her bed, uncertain what to do. It had only been a scant quarter of an hour since she had talked to Rideau.

"Will you pay?" asked the impatient operator.

"Yes."

"Jodie, Wilbert told me what you said."

"So . . ."

Her voice was as cold as a Minnesota winter.

"I thought you knew."

"How would I know? How?"

"You're a reporter. You've been getting all those facts in my case."

"That doesn't make any difference. You could have told me the day we met. You could have made sure that I knew. If you're so honest, clean-cut, and forthcoming, why did I have to look it up?"

"I made a dumb assumption."

"That's hard to believe."

"Jodie, I've met so many reporters . . . been interviewed so much, I . . . Why wouldn't I assume you knew? It was in the *New York Times* piece."

"You're a sex offender." The words sliced the meat to the bone.

"It's not what it seems," I said, stumbling over my words like a wino. The social connotations of the carnal knowledge charge had always riddled me with shame. They made me feel like a sex pervert.

"Carnal knowledge of a juvenile. Well, what the hell is it, then, if it isn't having sex with little girls? Just tell me what the hell else it means."

She twisted the knife into the wound.

"She was my girlfriend. She was sixteen, five weeks short of the lawful age. I was eighteen. Six of us got busted at a beer party. My mother called the police. I was on probation for stealing a car. I didn't have a lawyer. My probation officer told me I would get six months on the pea farm if I pled guilty . . . he said I would then be sent to a federal reform school for rehabilitation."

The phone was silent. She waited for more. There was no more. When a federal judge revoked my probation for the car theft in 1963 after the state convicted me of carnal knowledge, he was disturbed by the harsh three-year sentence that a Louisiana court had handed me on the sex charge. He asked the state to release me into federal custody. The state refused. Louisiana and the federal government were not on the best of terms in 1963 because of the civil rights movement. The federal judge appointed a lawyer to represent me before the pardon board. He secured a recommendation for a pardon on the carnal knowledge charge but the governor never approved it. I ended up serving two and one-half years in the state and federal prison systems.

In 1977, the Louisiana legislature amended the carnal knowledge statute to require that there be greater than two years' age difference between the consenting parties. I was just fifteen months older than my girlfriend when I was sent to prison for having sex with her in 1963. The conviction continues to haunt me in the state's criminal justice system — just as it frightened Jodie into a rush to judgment.

"What about the armed robbery charges?" Jodie demanded, her words pouring out like acid. "What in the hell were you doing holding up places? You walked into those places with a gun."

There had been the two-month "crime spree" in the fall of 1965 that culminated tragically in Bodden's death. I was a terribly embittered young man when I was discharged at the age of twenty from the federal prison system in July 1965. I had been thrown on the Big Yard at Angola in 1963 for having consensual sex with my sixteen-year-old girlfriend. I had two choices on the Big Yard — and there was no middle ground — fight and accept the criminal code or submit and be another's man's pussy. I chose to fight. I entered prison a confused car thief and left an angry young criminal. The scenario has been repeated time and again in the nation's prison system.

Alexander and I committed four armed robberies together. In three of those robberies, I was not armed — I was the lookout. In the fourth robbery, I carried a .22 caliber pistol that Alexander had bought in Dallas.

"How stupid!" Jodie spat.

"Yes, it was — tragically stupid. I don't have a juvenile record. Prison made me a criminal. I don't say that to shirk responsibility for what I did. It's what happened. I embraced the criminal code as a substitute for the social acceptance I had never known."

The phone was silent. I sensed that Jodie was thinking about what she had been told.

"You're looking at a couple months in my life, Jodie. I stole a car with a friend to go joyriding when I was seventeen. We got caught. A few months later I got caught fucking my girlfriend. Those are not crimes of violence, but the system wanted to teach me a lesson. It did. It taught me to be criminal, and for two months of my life in 1965 I was undeniably criminal."

Jodie was not forgiving.

"But you escaped and tried to rob another store!"

"Yes. I was a twenty-one-year-old facing the electric chair for a killing I didn't intend. I escaped in 1966 and tried to rob another convenience store and bungled that attempt too. But look at the last sixteen years! Not a blemish. I've traveled the state as a trusty. I never once tried to escape or did anything to compromise the trust placed in me. Look at the whole record — the positive, decent things I've done. If you judge me solely on the two months in my life when I was truly criminal, then there is no hope for me . . . for us . . . for anything."

"I'll think about it. I just . . . It's very upsetting. It's a lot . . . a lot to get hit with."

"Just think about it . . ."

Jodie was terrified. She was falling in love with a convict, a murderer. The thought made her shudder. "What-ifs" jumped into her mind at every unoccupied moment, interrupting the natural feelings of a budding love. She sifted and resifted the evidence, agonizing over the bits and pieces of her convict lover's life. The pull from both directions left her paralyzed during the early months of our relationship. Resolution involved a brave leap of faith. Jodie decided to accept me for what I said I was. She made peace with my past and plunged headlong into an uncertain future believing that right would ultimately correct my situation.

29

JODIE'S REACTION TO MY CRIMINAL HISTORY left me badly shaken. I loved her with all of my being, but gnawing fear came with that love.

Fear of rejection stalks every prisoner who loves a free woman. A wife's inability to cope with separation, or a girlfriend's whim, is a knife that cuts to the bone. Inmates facing long years behind bars are powerless to ward off the "Dear John" letters or divorce papers that are bound to arrive. The fear began stirring in my soul soon after Jodie and I met. The episode over my criminal history set it roaring.

As coeditor of *The Angolite*, I had more control over my life than most inmates. My job assignment gave me some freedom of thought and action. I decided what to write, when to write it, and how to write it. Yet it did little to protect me from the fear of losing Jodie. The pursuit of fame — and Rideau and I diligently pursued it — became secondary. The need to make Jodie a permanent part of my life began to consume me.

She had promised to stay with me. She believed that I would be free one day. But her assurances did little to quiet the storm of fear raging in my heart. It made marrying her the primary goal in my life. Yet the idea of proposing marriage intimidated me. I could shrug off Angola's dangers, but asking Jodie to marry me left me weak in the knees.

The difference between our worlds was staggering. Jodie was a sophisticated woman, an educated professional from a noted Houston family. I was a bumpkin who made it big in prison. Worse yet, I was convicted of murder. While Jodie respected my awards and accomplishments and believed in my rehabilitation, I could not be certain that she would bind her life to mine in an act that was sure to cloud her future.

There were terrible disadvantages in marrying me. Louisiana prisons do not allow conjugal visits. Couples suffer from the emotional and psychological brutality of love that cannot be physically fulfilled. Prison marriage greatly strains a woman's financial resources. The cost of collect calls, lawyer's fees, gasoline, and motel bills demands constant sacrifice. Jobs are often lost when an employer learns that a woman is married to a convict. She suffers what amounts to "shunning" if neighbors and fellow employees find out. Jodie might reject me even though she cared for me.

There were few prison marriages at Angola. An inmate's opportunities to meet women were limited. But religious groups who came to the prison sometimes had single female members. And pen pal correspondences could blossom into romance. Occasionally, prisoners fell in love with a female member of another inmate's family who came to the prison to visit. Sometimes these relationships led to marriage. But "scammers" clouded the picture. These predatory inmates enticed lonely, well-intentioned women into their webs and exploited them financially. While scammers gave a bad name to prison relationships, most were not interested in marriage. Angola's visiting policy permitted just one female visitor at a time on an inmate's visiting list. It was easy to remove a girlfriend. But it took proof of a divorce to remove a wife. To make money from their women victims, scammers needed to quickly rotate them on and off their visiting lists.

Whereas Warden Frank Blackburn generally favored prison

marriages, the prison's head chaplain did not. He was a hard-bitten man who disliked inmates. He liked women who loved them even less. Prisoners and their prospective brides had to attend counseling sessions with the chaplain. The meetings were outlets for his bias and hostility. The chaplain invariably recommended against the marriage, forcing Blackburn to overrule him.

As a high-profile coeditor of *The Angolite*, I knew that marriage to a Baton Rouge television reporter had no chance of being approved. It would give a reporter who could not be censored access to the inside of Angola, to the reality of daily prison life. It was enough to stand a warden's hair on end. But I was determined to marry Jodie.

I practiced popping the question for days. A million mental rehearsals only increased my anxiety and fueled a gnawing sense of inferiority. As a child I had been conditioned never to "cross the tracks." I had been reared to accept my place. The social conditioning left me with a deep sense of inadequacy. I felt driven to accept any challenge as an opportunity to see how far I could push myself to succeed. But the gigantic leap I was about to make was the biggest challenge I had ever faced. Finally, I took the plunge.

Jodie and I were sitting in the attorney-client conference room on a hot summer morning in 1981. I traced the lifeline on her small palm as she talked. Then I locked my hand over hers, mindful that this action would be disturbing to anyone who peered in through the small window in the door. Jodie was more beautiful each time I saw her. I absorbed each expression, memorized each gesture, and savored the sound of her voice.

"I have something to ask you," I said, gently interrupting the flow of her conversation.

She cocked her head and gave me a quizzical look. Each passing second seemed like a torturous minute.

"Well . . . " she said after an eternal pause.

"Will you marry me?" I blurted out.

I waited in an agony of apprehension.

"Yes," she finally answered.

"Jodie," I said tenderly, "you have made me the happiest man alive."

And she had. I had never known pure joy or the new feeling of life that was rushing through me at hearing the answer I had hoped for. Jodie had brought me peace. She was my true home. Love was mine. I reached up and brushed wisps of hair away from her forehead, a habit that I had developed to express my tender possessiveness.

I didn't want to subject her to the chaplain's rude questions and the indignity of a wedding ceremony at Angola. I found another way to marry her. In June 1981, I read an AP story about a man and a woman who got married even though they were thousands of miles apart. It was a story about love and persecution in the Soviet Union: The stepson of a Russian dissident married his Soviet sweetheart while he was in the United States and she was in the Soviet Union. Aleksei Semyonov was the stepson of Andrei Sakharov, the Soviet physicist. When authorities began persecuting Sakharov's family, the dissident advised his stepson to move to America. But Semyonov's fiancée, Yelizaveta Alekseyeva, was not allowed to leave. After a year in the United States, Semyonov flew to Butte, Montana, and married Alekseyeva by proxy. The story said that Montana was one of only two states in the U.S. with proxy marriage laws. As luck would have it, Texas was the other. Jodie could go to Texas and marry me when her divorce was final.

In September 1981, Governor Dave Treen fired Phelps, citing "philosophical differences" in the operation of the corrections department. The governor had been in office seventeen months when he moved against the corrections secretary. Phelps' longevity was a tribute to his formidable reputation in the Louisiana corrections industry. But he was a liberal thorn in the conservative governor's side who frequently criticized the governor's strict penal policies in public.

Phelps was replaced with John King, a political crony of Treen's who had no experience in corrections. Blackburn was the next to get the ax. Treen replaced him with Maggio, who returned riding high in the saddle. Angola would once again be run in his familiar tightfisted manner. On his first night back, Maggio visited the *Angolite* office.

"It's good to see you, Warden," Rideau said.

"I told y'all never to count me out," Maggio replied.

He surveyed the office from the doorway and then walked over to a cabinet, opened its door, and inspected its contents. It was his way of saying the office belonged to him.

"The office is a little bigger but not as plush as I heard it was," he commented.

"Who said it was plush?" I asked.

"It doesn't matter. I was told y'all had carpet on the floor, all new furniture, a refrigerator, color television, and wall movies. There's a perception among a lot of people that the prison is run by this office."

"It sounds like we have some enemies," Rideau said.

Maggio bit hard into his cigar.

"Let me tell you how it's gonna be," he said. "There are some powerful people in the administration who want me to put a padlock on the *Angolite* door. They want the magazine out of business. I'm going to do everything in my power to keep y'all in print but there's gonna be some changes. You won't like them but at least y'all will be in business."

My special visiting arrangement with Jodie ended with the next swing of Maggio's ax. Maggio, or someone in the administration, conducted a secret investigation into our visits. When no evidence of wrongdoing could be found, word that Jodie was coming to see me was leaked to a reporter at WBRZ-TV, Jodie's rival TV station. The BRZ reporter quietly told a friend in Jodie's newsroom, who took the story to her news director at WAFB-TV.

The news director beat his fist on the desk in frustration. "Damn it, Jodie, why couldn't you fall in love with a state senator? That's a conflict of interest we could handle."

Jodie was the station's capitol correspondent. Covering the governor and the legislature were her primary assignments. But she had gotten too close to an unacceptable source. Reporters had a professional duty to uphold the public trust. They had to avoid even the appearance of a conflict of interest. But AFB had kept a reporter who paid under the table to have his traffic ticket fixed and overlooked the drug addiction that put another in a rehab clinic. The station's double standard made me gag. Bribery and drug abuse were acceptable. Jodie's love for me was not.

"Jodie, I hate this. You were on my A team. But I've got to take you off the air," he said.

She hadn't done a story about me or used her influence to help me with state officials. But it didn't matter. Management dropped the hammer anyway. She was offered "something to do with the secretaries upstairs."

Instead, she resigned. And with that, her carefully constructed world blew apart. She lost a job she had fought for against the long odds that an older, inexperienced woman could be hired in TV news at all. Her home was in New Orleans but she could not return. Her husband was a well-known college professor at Loyola University and her marriage of two decades was at an end. By the time we met, she had been living in Baton Rouge for fifteen months. She visited her husband and teenage children in New Orleans on weekends. But she had no intention of resuming traditional family life. Now she was forced to face a new life before she was ready. And she would have to go it alone.

Jodie was a midlife adolescent, like most women who grew up in the 1950s. She had been taught that a woman's place was in the home. In return for a husband's protection, women were to fill out their lives with a network of errands and responsibilities that secured a place for them in the family firmament. But Jodie had come unstuck. The free fall left her dazed.

Alone and afraid, she forced herself out of bed early every morning. She rewrote her resume and packed her belongings in cardboard boxes she scavenged from a grocery store. She made resume tapes with the station's permission, dubbing off her best stories from Channel 9 near midnight so that no one would see her. She convinced herself that she was embarking on a great adventure in Texas after fifteen years in Louisiana. But no amount of manufactured self-confidence could quiet the panic that took hold of her in the middle of the night. Station management had assured her she would never work in news again. She had gambled on me and lost. I bled inside each time we talked.

Jodie left Baton Rouge for Houston on a bitterly cold Friday morning in January 1982, all her belongings loaded in the back of her compact car. A blue norther had blown in the night before. The sky was so clear that it glittered. She could see for miles as she headed west over the Mississippi River Bridge toward an uncertain future in Texas.

And then, unbelievably, just two months later she received the job offer of a lifetime. KGO-TV, the ABC affiliate in San Francisco, wanted to hire her. As a new reporter, she would have to work on weekends for up to a year. But Saturday and Sunday were the only visiting days at Angola. She begged Maggio to let her in the prison to see me every three or four months on a Monday or a Tuesday.

He was curt.

"I can't have the appearance of special treatment in this prison, especially not for a member of the *Angolite* staff. Those guys are hard enough to protect as it is."

Jodie pleaded with him, explaining the significance of the job offer.

"Warden, reporters just don't get offers from big markets like San Francisco straight out of little places like Baton Rouge. This is a huge career opportunity. The network owns this station. And I'll be making three or four times the money I made in Baton Rouge."

He cut her off before she could say any more.

"That's it," he said. "My decision is final."

So was Jodie's. She turned down the San Francisco job to stay with me. It was the chance of a lifetime, a fitting crown for all her efforts to succeed in the news business. She never got an offer like it again. I reeled in disbelief when she told me on the phone. I had been sure she would go. Loving me had already cost her so much.

She married me four months later. We didn't bother asking Maggio. He was sure to deny a marriage request from a coeditor of *The Angolite*. A proxy ceremony was our only choice.

I sent the necessary legal papers to Jodie through Richard Hand. They included a certified copy of my birth certificate and two notarized forms, one designating my stand-in — her brother-in-law, Allen Abbott — and another certifying that I did not have syphilis. She took them to a justice of the peace at the courthouse in downtown Houston. He checked her brother-in-law's identification, swore him in as my proxy, and pronounced Jodie my wife. She had a recorder so she could tape her vows and play them for me that night over the telephone.

"Oh, I don't do vows." The justice of the peace smiled and gestured at her brother-in-law. "I would feel kind of stupid saying 'Do you take this woman,' when another man does." He shrugged. "I just sign the papers if they are okay. And that does it."

It was over in minutes, like applying for a driver's license or signing the papers for a loan. I swore that if I were ever free, we would say our vows in a church.

The marriage infuriated Maggio, or so we were told. Utter and complete control of the prison was a point of pride with him. Nothing took place at Angola unless he sanctioned it. Yet I had gotten the prison hospital to give me a blood test, and the prison notary to certify my consent to marry, and had spirited the documents out of Angola through the legal mail — all without Maggio's knowledge.

The prison grapevine hummed for days after word leaked out about our marriage. A member of the pardon board asked the state attorney general's office to check its legality. Surely, she thought, a frontier-type Texas law was not binding in Louisiana.

When I learned that my marriage was being questioned, I went to the prison law library to research the issue. The U.S. Constitution provided the answer. It said that states must respect each other's valid laws. A New Orleans lawyer gave Jodie the same opinion. As Edward F. Bukaty III wrote her in August 1982:

> I cannot find any specific statute and/or case dealing with the question of whether Louisiana courts recognize a marriage performed by proxy in Texas. However I did find voluminous case law to indicate that Louisiana, pursuant to the full faith and credit clause of the United States constitution, Article 4, sec. I, is commanded to recognize marriages legally performed in another state.

For the first five years of our marriage, Jodie came to Angola every two weeks, driving the 275 miles from Houston to Baton Rouge every other Friday night. She stayed in a cheap Baton Rouge motel and drove the fifty miles to the prison early Saturday morning. She drove back to Houston on Sunday mornings. She had never driven on the highway alone for any distance until she married me. I knew the trips scared her. She didn't know anything about engines or how to change a tire.

She spent extra money maintaining the car, traveled with sealant for flats, and religiously changed the oil every three thousand miles. She said extra prayers every time she pulled out for

Baton Rouge and pretended that she was just driving to the next town. But good maintenance was no cure for bad drivers on the five-and-a-half-hour pull to Baton Rouge in the dark. She was forced onto the shoulder more than once over the years.

Otherwise, the route was monotonous — pastures, rice fields, and piney woods on land as flat as a board. But it played into the games she invented to keep from being frightened — she imagined that she was a lone tree in a pasture, a cloud scudding along on the wind, a spiral of dark birds rising from newly planted fields of rice. Music pumped her up when she was tired or night blindness temporarily obscured the road. She listened to rock and roll, symphonies, and sitars. Familiarity finally put her at ease on the road. And then a hurricane caught her unawares.

It blew up out of the Gulf of Mexico in late October 1985. Hurricane Juan started as a trough of low pressure over the central Gulf on Thursday. Two days later, it was a tropical storm. From the beginning, its movement was erratic. Shifting steering currents made its course hard to forecast. Just after midnight on Sunday morning, it drew a bead on the upper Texas coast. By then, Jodie was asleep in Baton Rouge on her way to see me. A weather check before she left Texas had said the storm appeared to be no threat.

She arrived at the prison under cloudy skies. By mid-morning, a steady rain was falling. We held hands in the visiting room oblivious to the weather. By the time she left at three in the afternoon, a steady downpour was soaking the Big Yard. But there was little or no wind. Jodie covered the fifty miles to Baton Rouge in less than an hour and turned the car west toward Texas. By then, I knew she might be in trouble. The evening newscasts were full of reports about the approaching hurricane. I prayed that she would stop in Baton Rouge. But the wind wasn't bad and she didn't need gas. She kept going toward Texas.

"I'm not worried, Billy," she said as she kissed me goodbye before she left. "What's a little rain?"

It was a terrible assumption. Jodie was driving straight into the teeth of Hurricane Juan. It was already raking the western edge of Louisiana on its way to Baton Rouge. Night fell on Interstate 10 between Lafayette and Lake Charles. By then it was too late to turn back. A howling wind was shaking her small car; towns along the way had no power and torrential rain hit her windshield in sheets. She was afraid to exit into one of the dark, flooded towns, and equally afraid that the water washing over her car would kill the engine, stranding her on the highway where she might be hit by another car in the blinding rain.

Gripping the wheel in terror, she took shelter behind an eighteen-wheeler traveling due west toward Texas. The truck was the only other vehicle on the road. It was plunging directly into the storm at thirty-five miles an hour, the best speed it could manage. Jodie's eyes burned as she tried to keep its taillights in view. It was all she could see in the dark, highway signs having become virtually invisible in the blinding rain. Her shoulders ached from fighting to hold the car on the road. It took her nearly three hours to drive the seventy-eight miles from Lafayette to Lake Charles. But she clung to the belief that she would make it through the storm. A waitress at a truck stop in Lake Charles gave her the news.

"What's with this weather?" Jodie asked the woman behind the counter.

"Lady, we been having a hurricane," was the laconic reply.

Jodie left Louisiana with the worst behind her. Thirty miles to the west, on the Texas side of the border, the skies were already beginning to clear. I had been calling her apartment repeatedly for hours praying that God would spare her if she were on the road. When I finally got her on the phone, she was ready with a jaunty reply to soothe my anxiety and allay the guilt I felt that she was in danger because of me.

"Billy Wayne, I'm from the Alamo State," she said. "We never give up."

Hurricane Juan killed twelve people. Damage along Louisiana's coast amounted to more than $1 billion. Its eighty-five-mile-an-hour winds and twenty-foot waves toppled offshore oil rigs, forcing workers into the storm-ravaged Gulf. It capsized rescue boats, drowning rescuers and rig workers alike. It rampaged back and forth along the coast for four days, sucking up strength from the warm Gulf waters. Because it came so late in the season, people paid little attention to Juan until it reached hurricane strength on the very afternoon that Jodie began her drive back home.

30

In 1982, JOHN KING, Louisiana's corrections secretary, mounted an assault on the state's penal press. *The Angolite* operated under the constant threat of censorship. Two other Angola publications — *The Challenger*, a sports publication, and *The Epistle*, a religious publication — were shut down. Publications in other penal institutions were either shuttered or forced to report news that the administration had sanitized. While *The Angolite* closed out 1981 as the best penal publication in the nation, its bold and unique standard of prison journalism was under continual siege.

King's real objective was control of *The Angolite*. It had consistently opposed criminal justice measures that the governor was advocating — double bunking as a way to relieve prison overcrowding; the use of inmate labor on prison construction projects; and a harsh clemency policy that ignored merit and rehabilitation.

After Phelps was fired, King was determined not to let *The Angolite* shape public opinion on these and other key criminal justice issues. Although he was a novice at corrections, King was acutely aware of *The Angolite*'s credibility and the status it enjoyed in media and criminal justice circles.

"Be careful," Phelps warned us the day before his tenure ended. "You're dealing with a new brand of animal now. This administration operates under a siege mentality. It circles wagons on every issue."

"How do we handle them?" Rideau asked.

"Do what y'all do best," Phelps replied. "Be creative."

We were. We began to practice a new brand of prison journalism. We identified broad, timely criminal justice issues and built articles around them using research and creative writing to compensate for the restrictions the Treen administration placed on the magazine. In 1982, *The Angolite* produced six issues on violence and gun control, suicides in jail, incarcerated veterans, growing old in prison, lifers and the politics of clemency, and a historical perspective on rehabilitation. I wrote six of the features in 1982 and two of the four in 1983.

Rideau was depressed. His freedom effort was in a holding pattern. It affected his editorial effort. The two features he wrote during that two-year period (1981–1983), "Strange Bedfellows" and "The Fiscal Crunch," were not vintage *Angolite*. I found myself carrying *The Angolite* while Rideau spent his time cultivating personal relationships and media contacts who could aid in his freedom effort.

The diminished effort received mixed reviews. The blood and guts journalism, as inmates called it after "Anatomy of a Prison Suicide" and "Conversations with the Dead," was gone. Administrative cooperation was needed to produce those kinds of hard-hitting investigative features, and that cooperation was fast disappearing. We faced a repressive atmosphere in which few people were willing to talk openly about sensitive subjects — an integral component of investigative journalism. And when we were able to get interviews, our articles were often censored.

In early 1982, Rideau and I were summoned to the warden's office for an "editorial conference." Maggio was concerned about the "provocative" nature of some of our articles.

You're going to have to tone it down," he said. "You simply don't understand the depth of animosity toward the magazine — the powers that be would love to see the both of you brought down. I could win a statewide election by crushing this magazine."

The discussion grew heated. We were probably the only two inmates in the prison who could, or would, argue with Maggio — and I pushed our luck to the breaking point at that particular meeting.

"I don't trust Dave Treen and I don't trust John King, and sometimes I don't trust you, Warden," I interjected at one point during the exchange.

A death-like silence fell over the room. Maggio bit down hard on his cigar. He stared hard at me with menacing eyes.

"Let me tell both of you something," he said, removing the cigar from his mouth. "You're still in business because of me — nobody *but* me. You can't imagine the flak I've taken keeping *The Angolite* going. I'm telling you not to push your luck — you're nothing more than a tick on an elephant's ass."

It was that simple. A free penal press existed only as long as the system was willing to tolerate it or had the courage to permit it. A padlock can be placed on an inmate editor's door with the ease of swatting a fly on the wall.

Rideau and I made the trip back to the *Angolite* office in somber silence. It had been an emotionally exhausting meeting.

"You almost pushed it too far with Maggio," he said, sitting down behind a desk littered with mounds of paper.

"We're always on the edge, Wilbert — a knife in the back down the Walk or a kick in the gut by the administration. We pushed it too far by creating this fucking monster — we now have our professional pride and reputations at stake. We've got to push, always a little more than we should."

"I have no problem with pushing the system. I've pushed against the odds all my life. But there's more at stake here than the journalistic integrity of the magazine."

"Your freedom?" I asked.

"Yes, my freedom. That's more important to me than anything or anyone. This magazine is my key to freedom — and I'll do what's necessary to keep it operating, to keep that padlock off the door."

A silence passed between us. Rideau and I had always worked well as a writing team. I respected his talent for diplomacy and his skill as a writer. But he was never a friend like Life or Billy Ray.

"Look, Treen is a one-term governor," he said, breaking the tension. "Let's just focus on keeping the magazine in business. You've got to carry it. I've got to work on getting out of here when Edwards comes back. You can push. Just don't push us off the cliff."

"I have no problem with carrying the magazine. I owe it to *The Angolite*, even to Maggio. But there will be some problems walking the tightrope of compromise. How do you maintain journalistic integrity under the siege of censorship?"

"You can handle it, Billy. Gresham once told me that you've paid more dues than anyone on the magazine. She was right. You can deal with pressure."

The pressure was tremendous. The King administration cut out travel to the free community to interview officials for stories. We were thus forced to conduct interviews over a telephone routed through a tape recorder in Gresham's office, where her secretary taped the conversations for us. The recorder frequently malfunctioned. The tape would somehow wind up erased or the quality of its sound was so poor that it could not be transcribed. Several times we had to arrange second, even third, interviews with the same person. We lost valuable information to the sudden plague of equipment failures, something that had never been a problem before.

The magazine experienced other problems as well. The photographs we took for stories were frequently lost en route to or from the developer. Or they were delivered to us days after the magazine was sent to the printer. We frequently asked, even begged, employees that we knew to pick them up in Baton Rouge because the prison delivery system was so unreliable.

The printing of *The Angolite* was taken over by Prison Enterprises, a new administrative section created by the King administration. While the quality of the magazine should have improved, it suffered. Time and again, printing ink bled through the paper, forcing us to throw away hundreds of ruined pages. Sometimes we were short hundreds of copies of one page, reducing the number of magazines we could circulate to the inmates. Boxes of printed pages disappeared from the print shop, necessitating a second printing. At one point, Gresham placed a security guard at the print shop to oversee the printing process. Rideau and I believed the problems had one objective — to make producing *The Angolite* difficult, if not impossible.

231

The sabotage notwithstanding, *The Angolite* was named the best prison publication in the nation in 1982 and 1983 by the American Penal Press, a competition sponsored by the School of Journalism at Southern Illinois University. Of all the awards *The Angolite* had received, these were probably the most significant, given the conditions under which it was produced.

Censorship of *The Angolite* was initially couched as a difference in "perception and style" between its editors and the Treen administration. Eventually it became blatant suppression of a free press with egregious effects. In May 1983, *The Angolite* was developing a feature article on a new grievance procedure about to be implemented by the Department of Corrections. Calling the article "ill-timed," the administration cancelled some of the interviews we had scheduled and then quashed the article before it could be finished. Gresham told us it had been "put on hold," a new term for censorship. We were interviewing a Department of Corrections official in our office when he was summoned away. Upon his return, the official said he could not complete the interview.

The grievance article was censored because the DOC was formulating a new grievance procedure that violated federal policy under the Civil Rights for Institutionalized Persons Act. The Treen administration did not want *The Angolite* to point out the flaws in the procedure it was formulating or educate inmates about the CRIPA-approved grievance procedures utilized in other prison systems. The subject was a sensitive issue in the corrections industry in 1983, particularly in Louisiana, where the DOC was under constant scrutiny by U.S. District Judge Frank Polozola.

In the midst of this repression, Rideau and I began experiencing personal conflict as we pursued opposing freedom strategies. My lawyer, a prominent New Orleans defense attorney named Jack Martzell who had once represented Muhammad Ali, met with Rideau's attorney, Camille Gravel. Gravel was the state's leading authority on clemency and Martzell's mentor. Martzell wanted to get a feel for the politics involved in clemency. He walked away from the meeting convinced that my freedom effort should be low-profile while Rideau should continue his high-profile effort to get out of prison.

Rideau embraced the high-profile strategy. Phelps and Gravel believed that the heinous aspects of his crime could be buried with publicity. The story of a downtrodden black intellectual in a southern prison made good copy. Rideau used it to generate more positive publicity than any inmate in Louisiana's penal history. He created anecdote after anecdote to perpetuate that image and used interviews to portray his crime as an "hour of rage" against white people in the South of the 1960s. He could say he was not a heinous murderer who slit his victim's throat while she begged for her life on her knees but rather was a victim of southern racism.

The opposing strategies ultimately spawned a serious rift between us. The extraordinary amount of publicity that Rideau was able to hustle gave him most of the credit for the magazine's success. He never mentioned my name in interviews, claiming that was the way my lawyer wanted it. When I protested that he was taking credit for articles that I wrote, he accused me of being envious of the recognition that he was receiving.

There was some substance to Rideau's charge. I resented the media's tendency to opt for the "black focus."

By choice and design, media attention now was focused exclusively on one editor. What began as a conscious effort to enhance our chances for freedom undermined the partnership that brought *The Angolite* international attention. The magazine might have survived the censorship eating away at it. But it could not survive one editor devouring the other.

31

WHILE *THE ANGOLITE* FOUGHT its battles with the administration, Jodie was engaged in her own skirmishes with the prison. She grew to hate prison officials and the dehumanizing way they treated her. As a prisoner's wife, she had lost the status she had enjoyed as a reporter when she first came to the prison. Administrators were treating her with contempt now. She was a fallen star, just another piece of the human debris deposited on Angola's shore. It was a long time before my wife adjusted to the prison's routines. Jodie ran afoul of the system over and over again for the first few years of our marriage.

The atlas she bought me in 1982 kicked off the first in a series of incidents that ended with her suspension. She found the little paperback at a bookstore not far from the downtown Houston office where she worked as a secretary — her occupation before she went back to school. The store was a refuge where her mind came alive after a morning of clerical work. She would touch the book spines, remembering the days when she had looked forward to the promise of a career — the days before she met me.

Jodie slipped the atlas off the shelf and immediately decided to send it to me. She wanted me to see how close Edinburgh, Scotland, lies to the Arctic Circle and that one of its most ancient thoroughfares is named Sinclair Street. Jodie had already sent me a brief history of Scotland with a picture of the Sinclair tartan and a brief history of the family, one of early Scotland's foremost clans. The Sinclairs could trace their ancestors to Normandy and St. Clair-Sur-Elle, the French version of their name, before they migrated to Scotland in the twelfth century.

The Sinclair earls were favorites of Scotland's kings. The clan dominated affairs in the Caithness region of far northern Scotland, where they built the fortress of Girnigo on a precipitous rock promontory, one mile north of Wick. They lost the castle when the predatory Gordons invaded their territory in the sixteenth century. The brooding ruins of Girnigo, the book said, still stand.

Jodie wanted the little atlas to be a surprise. She knew that I would be pleased with tales of the Sinclairs' exploits, that I would see them as the perfect story of my roots — full of action and the romance of years heavy with significant events. The prison sent the atlas back. The notice sent with it said that it was a breach of security. Jodie was outraged. How could a small paperback with general maps of Europe and nothing other than major landmarks and national boundaries be a breach of security? The security staff was adamant.

Then there was the matter of the pictures. She took them in 1983, the year we began to foolishly dream that I might be released when Edwards returned to power in 1984.

Solemnly, morning cup of coffee beside her, Jodie searched the daily papers for ads with furniture — things needed to set up a home, like a couch and coffee table and some shelves to hold our books. We needed a home, not the kind of furnished apartment she had rented in her reporter days. The sofa she bought was a large, wide, brown velvet mass. It was to make up for seventeen years of nights when my feet hung off the end of prison cots and bunks too short for my six-foot frame. There would be room along its ten-foot length for my feet as well as my head. My arms could lie comfortably by my sides. She organized the room to fulfill a suppressed desire that free men take for granted — home with room enough to stretch out and relax.

Lovingly, she took pictures of the room from every angle. She anticipated the pleasure I would feel at seeing the home that awaited me and mailed the pictures in a special cardboard pouch designed for photographs. On the outside it said, "Photos: Do Not Bend."

The prison returned the photographs. The notice said that the pictures had come in a "package," not an envelope. For security reasons, inmates were not allowed to receive packages unless they came from a retail store with the receipt. Contraband could easily be concealed within their wrapping. Jodie had chosen the envelope because it was made to protect pictures. It was a month before I saw them. They languished in the prison mailroom for three weeks before they were returned to Jodie. She sent them back with two pieces of cardboard cut to size in a standard letter-size envelope so they would not bend, and hoped the weight of their Polaroid backing would not tear through the thin white paper. This time, the mailroom let me have them. This time too, Jodie bucked at the prison's rules. I wrote her a desperate letter, knowing that trouble with the administration was inevitable.

You want to fight. I am a natural born fighter, too. But we have nothing to fight with. Any engagement with authority will be lost. You must get the seeds of rebellion out of your head. You gave up so much — friends, career, and social status — because you believed that right would ultimately prevail in my case. Perhaps most important, you gave up your power to choose, your individual free will, when you became my wife. You often say you are not a prisoner, that you enjoy the rights of a law-abiding citizen. But that is not true, my darling. You are a prisoner of your decision to love a prisoner. The decent man sees you as a reflection of me. You are a traitor to his sense of decency because you chose to love me. I am the decent man's evil and he has the power to do to me what he chooses. The decent man gets upset when you challenge his authority to treat me as he sees fit. You must understand that the decent man initially meant to kill me.

I will never walk out of this prison because it is the right thing. I cannot fight my way up the hill to redemption. I cannot demand a ride on the pulley of fairness. Authority does not reach down to lift me up. It stomps on my hands hoping to loosen my grip. So I sit on the edge of nothingness, torn between falling into oblivion or ripping the system's legs off at the knees. Either way, I would lose you — the only good and decent thing ever in my life. Please believe that we will somehow find a way over the mountain.

But Jodie could not stop fighting the system. Finally, Maggio suspended her for three months. The incident that caused it came without warning one summer morning when, pushed beyond her limits by the exhausting night drive from Houston, her anger boiled over at a guard who baited her at the Front Gate. But it began before she ever reached the prison.

The Angola road was suddenly, inexplicably torn to pieces to make way, we later learned, for a straighter thoroughfare and new asphalt topping. She came upon the shattered pavement unsuspecting. Two weeks before, the road had stretched through the trees and around curves as it always had. There were no signs to warn of impending road work. Suddenly, at sixty-five miles an hour, gravel spurting under her wheels, Jodie desperately tried to control the car as deep potholes threatened her axles and crevasses in the unpaved track grabbed at her wheels. Dust swirled up around her car as it shimmied from side to side. Mud in the potholes from rain several days earlier splattered the windshield and the sides of the car.

Jodie had never seen road construction without warning signs and a well-marked detour. But both sides of the Angola road were a muddied track for seven miles. Jodie crept down the road at fifteen miles an hour as the car bucked and groaned under the strain. The delay would make her late for the first bus down to the Main Prison from the Front Gate despite all her efforts to be on time for its 8:00 A.M. departure. A fulminating anger rose up inside her at the state's contempt for the users of the road — backwoods blacks, prison guards, and inmate families. They would eat dust or plod through mud until the road lay a more symmetrical ribbon through the trees.

At the Front Gate, her nerves already stretched thin, Jodie was forced to listen to a female guard lecture her about a stamp that she had forgotten in her wallet. The guard's tone was patronizing and sarcastic. She was always careful to follow Angola's visitation rules, emptying her wallet of everything but her driver's license before presenting it at the gate. Visitors could buy food from the visiting room's inmate-run concessions during visits or leave money in inmates' accounts. But I never allowed Jodie to put money in my account. My imprisonment brought her enough emotional suffering. I did not want to increase her financial burden any more than necessary.

Stamps weren't the only things that had to be left in the car. Cosmetics had to be left behind as well. They were "heavy-weight" contraband down the Walk. Stud homosexuals would pay exorbitant prices, even resort to extortion, to get these female luxuries for their "wives" — to make them "fine and pretty." I had educated Jodie about the dangers that lipstick, mascara, and perfume posed in the prison community.

Tired and harried, she had overlooked the stamp when she searched her wallet before entering the Front Gate reception area. She smiled and denied any attempt at wrongdoing.

But the guard made the situation personal, jabbing at Jodie again with the same singsong message: I was nothing more than someone to revile. Each time I was maligned, Jodie corrected the guard. Slyly, the guard baited her one more time with the same cutting remark: "They all alike down there."

Jodie went rigid with anger.

"Never speak to me like that again," Jodie said. "My husband isn't like the rest. Don't you ever forget it. Ever." Her cold undertone slashed at the guard's insolence.

Visitors and personnel in the Front Gate's reception room ceased all conversation, openly gaping at Jodie and the guard, as the guard retreated across the room and Jodie went out to wait for the bus. Fighting with herself, knowing better, Jodie returned to the reception room and demanded her stamp. In silence, she took it out to her car. In the official incident report that the guard filed, she charged Jodie with trying to smuggle the stamp into the prison. The guard had succeeded in provoking a confrontation, giving her the right to file the self-serving report to her superiors.

Based on the guard's report, Jodie was banned from the prison for three months. She wasn't asked for her side of the story. The prison sent her notice of the suspension through the mail. Warden Maggio, however, had the decency to call me to his office and personally inform me of the suspension.

"I'm taking Jodie off your list for ninety days," he said. "Warden Lensing investigated the incident report and recommended the suspension. I have to support my staff."

I fought down a rebellious impulse.

"You don't have the whole story, Warden," I said. "You have the guard's version. All I ask is that *you* investigate. Jodie and I will live with the suspension, but you've been lied to."

Maggio did investigate the incident. Finding provocation on the guard's part, he let Jodie visit me for a club banquet before the ninety-day suspension was up. He transferred the guard to tower duty on the graveyard shift — the worst possible assignment. It was Maggio's way of balancing the ledger. Maggio was tough. He adhered to policies that he felt would make the prison safer. But he was scrupulously fair.

When the suspension was over, Jodie came and went in silence. The guards had suckered her with their pseudo-friendliness only to spring a trap on her when she least expected it. I had warned her about their mind games, having seen them do it to inmates a thousand times, but she hadn't believed me. Until they set her up, she chose to think they were friendly.

From then on, she followed my advice. She didn't speak to anyone. Silent compliance was the only way to survive. Self-respect had to live, if at all, quietly within the heart.

32

I N MARCH 1984, Edwin Edwards was sworn in for an unprecedented third term as governor of the State of Louisiana. He buried Dave Treen in a landslide victory, capturing 63 percent of the vote. The Ragin' Cajun inherited a prison system suffering from a lack of effective leadership and management. Dave Treen's tough stance against clemency had left the prison seething with bitterness and resentment. The one smart penal decision that he made during his four years in office — the appointment of Ross Maggio — kept Angola from exploding into a riot.

While Treen was in office, he signed only seventy-four pardons and forty-one commutations. Edwards, on the other hand, had signed 1,227 pardons and 945 commutations between 1972 and 1980. Treen found himself under fire on the editorial pages of the *New Orleans Times-Picayune* and the *Shreveport Journal* for his rigid clemency policy. In response to the editorial in the *Journal*, Treen said in a letter to the editor:

I do not approve of wholesale grants of executive clemency as a means of "buying" good behavior from inmates. This hard-line attitude was criticized in your editorial, but it reflects my view that executive clemency should be used in only the most deserving of cases. I believe the people of Louisiana, especially the victims of crime and their families, agree with my position.

Edwards' return to office was thus a harbinger of hope for the inmates. Despite being politically battered by Treen during the campaign for his clemency policies, Edwards said he would continue to exercise his executive clemency powers in a liberal manner when reelected. He also promised to restore integrity and effective management to the state's floundering penal system. His first cabinet appointment was C. Paul Phelps. Angola inmates embraced the appointment as the sign of a "new beginning."

Optimism grew when Edwards announced the resurrection of The Forgotten Man Committee. Its objective was to identify and release deserving long-term inmates. Lifers would get particular attention. Edwards then appointed a predominantly black pardon board, naming Howard Marsellus, a Baton Rouge politician with close ties to the Legislative Black Caucus, as its chairman. Angola inmates were elated — they had a liberal governor, a progressive corrections secretary, a reform-minded Forgotten Man Committee, and a receptive pardon board. The expectations of every inmate at Angola soared.

These soon floundered as a sea of corruption engulfed the system. In one of his first clemency decisions, Edwards cut the time of a major drug dealer named Mitch Schwartz, a career criminal with ties to the Mafia. Marsellus, accompanied by a couple of Mafia-like goons, personally delivered the "gold seal" to Schwartz at Angola. Ugly rumors began floating around the prison that the "fix" was back; that gold seals were for sale under the new administration.

I first met Marsellus shortly after his appointment to the pardon board. He came to the *Angolite* office to meet its "celebrated editors." Marsellus was an anomaly. A high school principal by profession, he was the epitome of the slick, streetwise con artist. Despite his efforts to be erudite, he could not escape a ghetto mentality. Even a Harvard education would not have displaced the bebop cap he favored.

"Don't bother to get up," he said as he barged through our office door unannounced. He shook hands firmly as Rideau and I rose behind our desks, startled at the audacious intrusion. Three prisoners accompanied him — a Native American inmate and two blacks. He relished the attention they heaped on him.

"I'm afraid you have us at a disadvantage," Rideau said, quickly regaining his composure.

"Howard Marsellus — you should know me. I'm the man who will decide whether you get out or not."

The tag-along inmates laughed.

"Tell him Howard — let him know you got him by the balls," Ashanti said. He was a well-known inmate leader who headed Vets Incarcerated, an organization set up to serve the needs of incarcerated Vietnam veterans.

"Rideau and Sinclair, the salt and pepper combination," Howard said. "You two dudes do some heavy shit — I mean, the fucking *New York Times* listens to what y'all say. I want to be in *The Angolite* — I want to get my message out to not only the dudes in this prison but across the state. I'm about hope, achievement, and all that positive stuff. The Guv gave me the power, and I'm going to use it."

"I hear you," Rideau replied, laughing. "You want to do the interview now?"

"Hell no — we'll do it in my office in Baton Rouge," Marsellus said, removing the bebop cap to scratch a balding head. I noticed that the heels of his scruffy brown suede shoes were worn on the outer edges and they had not been cleaned in a long time. He did not have the appearance of a pardon board chairman. He looked more like a convict in street clothes.

"What can we expect from your board?" Rideau asked.

A sly smile crossed Marsellus' face.

"What do you want?"

"Hell, I want out of prison," Rideau said.

"Let me show you how I operate," Marsellus said. "Take Russo there," pointing to the big American Indian inmate. "He gave me an ice cream in the visiting room a few minutes ago and I'm going to cut his time. He's doing life — I don't know for what, it doesn't matter. What matters is he gave me something and I'm going to give him something."

Silence fell over the room. No one, including Russo, knew if Marsellus was serious.

"What do you want?" Marsellus said, gesturing toward *Angolite* staffer Tommy Mason.

"I want the same forty-year time cut I had under Treen," Mason said.

"You got it," Marsellus casually said, turning to Ashanti and Goldie, a mercenary jailhouse lawyer. "And I'm gonna take care of both of you as well — I have plans for you both. Just remember, take care of me and I take care of you."

"Whatever you say, man," Ashanti replied. "You want the Pope hit, we'll hit the Pope."

Marsellus laughed.

"I like that — you're my kind of people."

"Where do I fit into this scheme?" Rideau asked.

"Your case is going to be a hard one," Marsellus said. "Those white folks in Lake Charles will do everything they can to keep your little black ass in this penitentiary. How much time you got in now?"

"Twenty-three years."

"We can swing a seventy-five-year cut," Marsellus said. "You'll have to do two more for parole . . . give the case time to cool . . ."

"Fuck that," Rideau said. "I want a time cut to time served. I want to walk straight out, free and clear. I don't want to give those people a second chance to oppose me at a parole hearing. I would have to do thirty-five years to discharge at seventy-five. No, I want it all."

"Greedy little sonuvabitch, ain't you," Marsellus said, clearly irritated at the rejection of his proposal. "All right, all right — we'll do a time cut, time served and make it fly."

I had said very little during the meeting. I was studying Marsellus, watching the way he wielded his power over the inmates.

"As for you," Marsellus said, pointing toward me. "You got your issue with that sixty-year time cut those white folks under Treen recommended. They took care of you. It's time to take care of the brothers now."

"The sixty meant nothing — it was never signed," I said. "It was false hope . . . and I wonder if you're not peddling the same thing."

Marsellus stared hard at me. I sensed he was sizing me up.

"I'm real, man — I'm from the streets like most of the dudes in here. A break here and a little luck there are the only reasons I'm not in here with you. I don't peddle false hope — I'm about real hope."

Marsellus left, followed by his three eager converts. I was alarmed. An ugly specter of corruption had followed Edwards throughout his political career. To do positive, meaningful things in the clemency arena, his pardon board had to be free of any appearance of impropriety. Marsellus was shaking the bushes for a bribe.

The pardon board chairman became a fixture at Angola, establishing a network of contacts among inmate power brokers. Within months of his appointment, rumors were prevalent at Angola that a commutation could be bought through Ashanti and Goldie for the right amount of money. The grapevine said Marsellus had a penchant for sex and jewelry. Inmates started sending their sisters and mothers to him with instructions that they do whatever he wanted in exchange for clemency. Other families took blank checks and jewelry to deal with him.

In the midst of the rumors, Rideau established a close personal relationship with Marsellus. He had Marsellus' home phone number and called him often. Marsellus called Rideau at the *Angolite* office, using him to pass information to other inmates about their clemency efforts and occasionally eliciting information from Rideau about inmates. Rideau brokered this special relationship with Marsellus into additional power, creating an impression in the inmate community that he could secure favorable clemency consideration for them from the pardon board chairman. Their unholy relationship became a recurring topic of discussion in the *Angolite* office.

"You better be careful, Wilbert," I warned. "The rumors are spreading about Marsellus being on the take. You're making regular calls to his house. You don't know if his phone is tapped. You should keep a professional distance from Marsellus. Inmates are already saying that if you want a time cut, see Ashanti, Goldie, or Rideau."

"That's prison gossip — and, frankly, it pisses me off," Rideau replied. "When members of the Treen board were at the prison, you didn't hear talk like that. Now that we have a black pardon board chairman, it's called 'corruption.'"

"This has nothing to do with race," I said. "It has to do with kickbacks. I've heard he's selling time cuts for money, sex, jewelry, and God knows what else."

"I have a chance at my first time cut with Howard and I'm going to do everything I can to get out of prison through him," Rideau said. "I don't know if he's on the take and I don't care. You know how business is done in Louisiana."

"But you're putting *The Angolite* in the middle of a potential scandal — Marsellus' name is synonymous with this magazine now. Inmates come to you to pass information to him."

Rideau said nothing. He couldn't. Not only was Marsellus calling him with information about other inmates, but he also called Rideau with information about his own case, revealing the contents of letters opposing his release and giving him advice on how to get around them. Marsellus was blatantly violating the state's confidentiality statute and Rideau was helping him do it.

"Let me tell you something, Billy — I don't give a fuck about appearances of impropriety. I will do whatever it takes to get out of this prison. If the governor wanted a hundred thousand dollars and I could give it to him, I would. I'd buy my way out and never look back."

33

PHELPS INADVERTENTLY CONTRIBUTED to the climate of corruption settling over Angola when he brought back Frank Blackburn as its warden and Blackburn ceded day-to-day operations at the prison to Hilton Butler. Maggio had forced Butler out of Angola in 1981. *The Angolite* questioned Phelps about Butler's appointment as deputy warden. Phelps had once been a staunch opponent of the redneck regime and the likes of Butler.

"Hilton's been reformed," Phelps replied. "He now understands how things must be done. Instead of 'corruption,' we have 'experience.'"

Upon returning to Angola, Butler released Dixie Mafia chieftain Pete Mule from Camp J where Maggio had placed him. Butler then launched an assault on Maggio supporters with Blackburn's blessing. Butler's security system was wide open compared with Maggio's.

"I don't like a tight prison," Butler said. "It keeps the tension too high. I'd rather run a prison through cooperation and accommodation."

Against the backdrop of that penal philosophy, drugs and homosexuality became prevalent once again at Angola. Classification boards released known drug dealers and predatory homosexuals from maximum security. The level of violence increased almost immediately. The lax security attitude sent definite signals to inmate gang leaders that they could control the prison again. With Maggio gone, the beast came lurching to its feet.

As Butler shuffled security personnel around, placing his supporters in key positions, the Dixie Mafia rebuilt its position of power and influence by flooding the prison community with drugs and cash. Several members of the gang established a close relationship with Marsellus, who promptly gave them favorable clemency recommendations.

By the fall of 1984, I had become disillusioned with the Blackburn/Butler administration. Jodie was away in New York at Columbia University, getting her master's degree in journalism, and I was alone, trying to cope with the forces of prison corruption and increasing despair.

Ossie Brown, who had been indicted and acquitted earlier in the year on a corruption charge, was facing Bryan Bush in a tough reelection bid for the district attorney's office in Baton Rouge. Jack Martzell had recently talked to Edwards about my clemency situation. The governor told him that if Ossie got reelected, I would remain in prison for at least six more years (Ossie's term in office). I was sick of politics and corruption. They had controlled my existence for decades.

I expressed my disillusionment to Jodie in a letter shortly after she went to Columbia.

I believe The Forgotten Man Committee is going to be the biggest boondoggle in recent history. It will issue a package of recommendations next year but they will be shredded in the legislature. I don't believe the Edwards administration will get any of the committee's recommendations dealing with long-term inmates through the legislature. And when the legislature shreds The Forgotten Man Committee and spits it out, every inmate in here is going to realize that the door has been slammed shut on him; that he has about as much chance of getting out of this prison as a wasp does of breaking free of the spider's web.

The inherent problem is that the system cannot fulfill its promises — it cannot honor its statutory obligation to rehabilitate inmates. The system has lost its soul. And I don't want to be part of the cruel joke being played on the inmates. As a lot, they don't deserve much but there are some good people in prison.

I'm tired of being used and manipulated. The only thing I have is my professional credibility and my own personal sense of integrity. I've cooperated with the system. I've identified problems and offered solutions; I've spoken out for fairness and equity; and I've supported programs that in reality have little meaning. Like many other prisoners, I've done all the things to make my cage a nice, clean, safe place in which to live. It's analogous to digging your own grave. I'm not going to let my professional credibility be used to shovel bullshit anymore. I'm just going to do my time, and survive.

But a man in my position could not live in a vacuum. While researching an article for *The Angolite*, I uncovered evidence that three thousand dollars from the Inmate Welfare Fund had been siphoned off to purchase a camera/recorder for high-ranking prison officials. A well-placed source told me the camera was being used to make pornographic movies that involved inmates and free people.

As I pursued that story, I also discovered evidence of an embezzlement scheme involving a well-placed prison official and several inmates. Veronica Price, the supervisor in charge of the financial accounts of inmate organizations, was skimming money from club accounts and doctoring the books. I reported the scam to Roger Thomas, the assistant warden in charge of rehabilitation and inmate organizations. The Department of Corrections sent an investigator to Angola to look into my allegation. He reported there was no evidence of wrongdoing. I adamantly insisted that Thomas conduct an independent investigation since his office was in charge of all inmate organizations. He refused, choosing to sweep the matter under the official rug.

I was not on a crusade. I was angry at the system. The Dixie Mafia had regained control of the inmate subculture; Marsellus was dealing in pardons with the help of a cadre of inmate politicians, and Edwards was once again under a cloud of suspicion as a New Orleans federal grand jury investigated him on racketeering charges. (Edwards would spend most of his third term as Louisiana's governor defending himself against the charges in a courtroom in New Orleans. Jack Martzell would successfully defend Edwards' brother Marion during the same trial. Both Edwardses were acquitted.)

Throwing caution to the wind, I stood up before a group of inmate club leaders during a meeting with Blackburn and his assistant wardens and charged: "Warden Blackburn, the head of your inmate accounts, Veronica Price, is embezzling money from the accounts of inmate organizations. The embezzlement scheme is aided by other personnel and several inmate leaders sitting right here in this room. I've made this same charge to Warden Thomas and a DOC investigator — and nothing has been done about it. I call upon you, as warden of this institution, to investigate this serious allegation of corruption."

Blackburn was dumbfounded. As I stood waiting for his response, I returned the hard glares of the inmates involved in the embezzlement scheme, including Goldie and Ashanti. I could not show the slightest fear. As president of the Angola Jaycees, I had made a decision to speak out publicly against the corruption. I could only hope and pray that I would get some support. The dangerous gamble paid off.

"I believe there is some substance in what Sinclair is saying," a black Muslim leader said as he stood up. "Our bank statements reflect we have money but when we try to order something, Ms. Price says we don't have enough funds to cover the order. The money is going somewhere."

"Well, let me see, this is the first I've heard about the problem," Blackburn stammered. "Hilton, check into that for me."

"I will look into it, Warden, but I'm not chasing unsubstantiated allegations," Butler said, looking directly at me.

The decision to speak out against Price put me in an awkward position. Ashanti and Goldie were Rideau loyalists. They were part of a network of black leaders who looked upon him as their godfather.

"You have no real evidence of embezzlement, Billy," Rideau said during an office discussion. "All you have are conflicting bank statements — and that could be the result of sloppy bookkeeping. You're not doing yourself any good pushing this issue so hard — people are beginning to think you're a loose cannon on deck."

"Frankly, I don't give a fuck what this administration thinks about me," I replied. "It's corrupt to the core — and I'm beginning to believe Phelps knows it and is doing nothing about it. There's going to be a major scandal here, and the taint of it is not going to touch me. When you turn your head from corruption, Wilbert, you're corrupt — it's that simple. I'm gonna push the Veronica Price issue to the wall. She's stealing the money and I know it. I will not be intimidated by inmate peer pressure, especially by dudes like Ashanti and Goldie who have a vested interest in protecting the corruption."

Several days later I received a call from Warden Thomas about the Price matter.

"Billy, you should be careful with the allegations you're leveling against Ms. Price," he said. "It appears this is becoming a personal vendetta."

"There's nothing personal about it, Warden," I said. "There has been an official whitewash of an embezzlement scheme involving Ms. Price and several inmates. It's that simple."

"You're running the risk of falling in disfavor with this administration," Thomas interjected. "Maggio is no longer here; you already have the Maggio label with Warden Blackburn. I suggest you exercise a little discretion."

"Are you threatening me, Warden Thomas?" I asked.

"No, no — I'm just advising you not to let your personal allegiance to Ross Maggio get you in trouble."

"Everything with this administration is Phelps versus Maggio. My actions have nothing to do with my feelings about Maggio. This is about a prison official stealing money."

"Just be reasonable, Billy — don't get too far out on the limb."

Two months later a check from an inmate organization bounced at the local bank. The administrative investigation that ensued uncovered a massive embezzlement scheme involving Price and others. The official loss was put at thirteen thousand dollars, but it was closer to thirty thousand dollars. Blackburn and Butler met with all the club presidents to explain that their organizations would be reimbursed.

"Ms. Price's employment has been terminated effective immediately," Blackburn told the inmates. "It is my understanding that she will be charged in St. Francisville with fraud and embezzlement. I have no control over the criminal aspects of the case and will not comment on it further."

The Price affair notwithstanding, the level of corruption at the prison continued to escalate. A high-ranking prison official steered a lucrative cigarette concession to Goldie. It was said that Goldie was paying him several hundred dollars a month in kickbacks. Butler gave Goldie an office in the Education Department that Goldie converted into a den for homosexuals and drug users.

A major scandal at Angola was inevitable.

34

IN FEBRUARY 1985, I became convinced that Marsellus was selling clemency. He came to the prison for a meeting with Rideau, Mason, Ashanti, Goldie, and me in the A-Building. He showed us two letters written from an anonymous prisoner accusing him, Ashanti, and Goldie of wrongdoing. One letter said that Goldie was the prison's "biggest pimp" and that he had paid Marsellus for the thirty-year clemency recommendation he had recently received. The second letter said that Ashanti was Marsellus' "bag man" in a pardons-for-sale operation.

"Copies of these letters were sent to the governor's office and every member of the pardon board, including the board's secretary," Marsellus said angrily. "This is a serious matter. The governor's office sent them to me to investigate."

Edwards' office had assigned the fox to investigate the death of the chickens. Marsellus expressed an urgent need to find out who wrote the letters and "silence him."

"Why don't you turn the letters over to headquarters and ask for an administrative investigation?" I asked. "It's the only way to stop the rumors."

Ignoring the suggestion, Marsellus turned his attention to Ashanti and Goldie with angry demands that they "find out who wrote these fucking letters."

I stood up, excused myself from the meeting, and walked out. What I had heard bordered on criminal conspiracy. I didn't want any part of a plan to find out who had written the letters and "silence him."

"Marsellus is dangerous," I said when Rideau returned to the *Angolite* office. "Marsellus is going to sink the clemency system and our hopes with it. He's dealing in pardons. You know it as well as I do. Word is leaking out everywhere. He can't control the situation much longer. It's going to blow sky high, and I'm not going to be associated with it. You need to be careful, Wilbert," I warned. "You are a journalist. You have a responsibility to the facts. I know Marsellus is important to your freedom effort. Just don't get lost in a potential conflict of interest."

"Do you have any hard facts that Howard is selling pardons?" he countered.

"When a pardon board chairman personally appears before the parole board to argue for the release of his nephew, and when he offers explicit assurances of favorable recommendations prior to hearings, and when he refuses to seek a departmental investigation to clear up serious charges of impropriety," I replied, "I can make a fair assumption that he's on the take."

As the rumors about Marsellus escalated, Colonel Eddie Boeker, the Main Prison's security chief, was relieved of his security responsibilities. A staunch Maggio loyalist, Boeker had been making inquiries about the rumors and the relationship between Goldie and a high-ranking prison official. Hilton Butler immediately named Colonel Robert Bryan, a longtime member of the redneck regime, to replace Boeker.

With Colonel Bryan in charge of the Main Prison, the Dixie Mafia would control the Main Prison. But the move backfired. Over the next two weeks, the Main Prison was rocked with violence that included a major brawl between two black gangs. I enlisted Rideau's help to get an emergency meeting with Blackburn and

Butler which lasted more than an hour; we listed the inmate grievances against Bryan, especially the recent increase in violence.

"Colonel Bryan is a good man who means well," I offered. "But he's set in his ways. He's a product of the 'old school' and there is a new breed of inmates here — namely, black, who perceive Bryan as a 'racist' from the old days."

"Robert Bryan is one of the finest men who ever worked at this prison," Butler exploded. "The man doesn't hate niggers any more than I do."

"This issue really goes beyond Colonel Bryan," I said, choosing my words very carefully. "The level of violence has increased since he took over the Main Prison. It's not his fault — he doesn't have the network of informants Boeker had. The last thing we need is a riot, or any kind of major racial incident. All fingers of blame would point at Colonel Bryan."

Butler glared at me. His hatred was obvious. Blackburn was analyzing the situation.

"What do you think, Rideau?" he asked.

"Billy's right, Warden," Rideau replied. "Colonel Bryan doesn't relate to the young blacks from New Orleans, and they can't relate to him. They know Colonel Boeker. They relate to him."

Blackburn stood up, mashing out a cigar in Rideau's ashtray.

"What you're saying is that Boeker is the key to peace in the Main Prison," he said.

"More or less, that's exactly what we're saying," I said.

Realizing Butler's feathers had been ruffled by the criticism leveled at Bryan, Rideau moved to soothe the situation.

"Look at it this way," he said, looking directly at Butler. "If the prison blows, you have Boeker to hang, not a friend. The Main Prison will be his baby, his responsibility."

"You can bet your ass it will be his baby," Butler said.

The following week, Colonel Boeker was returned to his position.

"You know you've split the blanket with this administration," Boeker later told me. "They now believe you're working on the inside for Maggio."

"*Everything* has been reduced to Maggio versus Phelps," I replied. "You just want to do your job in a professional manner and

I just want to survive and preserve the integrity of *The Angolite*. If Phelps' people think otherwise, I'll just ride the flak."

The Angolite suffered a crippling blow during the spring of 1985 when Peggi Gresham announced her retirement after more than three decades in the prison business. While Gresham cited the illness of her parents as the reason for her abrupt departure, I didn't buy it. Hilton Butler had virtually stripped her of all the power she had accumulated over the years. She had been the most influential official under the preceding Blackburn administration. Butler would brook none of it. He took over her office and moved her "down the hall" in the Administration Building. She became just another highly paid secretary.

Gresham's retirement created a major vacuum in *The Angolite's* operation. We went through several replacements before Roger Thomas, a career social worker, was appointed supervisor of the magazine. Rideau capitalized on Gresham's departure by seizing control of *The Angolite*. He dictated to Thomas how things would be run and what privileges he would enjoy as its editor. Within weeks, Rideau and Thomas had a major clash over control of the magazine. Thomas summoned Rideau to his office. The convict editor quickly established that he was not only more intelligent than Thomas but he had more power. The "supervisor" would never challenge Rideau again.

Rideau also used Thomas' inexperience to enhance his relationship with Marsellus. He began using the *Angolite* telephone to cultivate and maintain political contacts throughout the state. They included a contact in the governor's office. Rideau was receiving extremely good press in 1985. He had clearly established that he was "the editor" of the magazine. The media portrayed him as the reason for its success.

By the fall of 1985, I was ready to make a break. *The Angolite* had not produced a significant piece of journalism that year. While I wrote almost everything that went into it, my heart was not in my work. The magazine was nothing more than a vehicle for Rideau's freedom effort. His only interest in it was his access to the magazine's telephone.

I moved out of the *Angolite* office. I wanted to put as much distance between myself and the Rideau/Marsellus relationship as I could. I cleared out an old office upstairs in the Education Department and moved into it. I continued to do "my job" with the magazine but nothing more.

The move put an end to the Rideau/Sinclair writing team. After several months, I told Rideau that we would never byline another story. He took the decision in stride. He had wanted it for a long time. He had begun calling himself "the nation's most rehabilitated prisoner." He didn't need the "second most rehabilitated prisoner" standing in the wings.

35

THE SPRING OF 1986 found Rideau waiting for a decision on his clemency effort. He had assurances that he would receive a sixty-year recommendation. I was in the *Angolite* office when he negotiated the deal with Marsellus over the telephone. One of Rideau's attorneys called the Department of Corrections to find out how much time Rideau would have to actually serve on sixty years to discharge. Rideau's attorney and Marsellus wanted him to get a sentence that would make him immediately parole eligible. In the event he couldn't get a parole, he would have a sentence he could discharge within a reasonable time.

It violated the Code of Governmental Ethics for Rideau, his attorney, and the pardon board chairman to negotiate a recommendation prior to a clemency hearing. But violating the law was the standard in the Louisiana penal system. Phelps himself had recently been arrested for shoplifting. He was charged with putting a pack of BB's, a pocketknife, and other assorted items in his pocket and then walking out of a Baton Rouge store without paying for them.

Phelps labeled the incident a "mistake," saying he intended to return to the store to pay for the items.

While a city prosecutor with connections to the Edwards administration eventually dropped the charge, Phelps became the butt of jokes throughout Angola. Many believed he had a drug and alcohol problem along with a history of kleptomania. It was evident that he could no longer effectively lead the state's prison system. The shoplifting incident had ruined his professional credibility.

Then Colonel Boeker discovered the locking mechanisms in a Main Prison maximum-security cell block had been tampered with, allowing the inmates to open their cells with a fountain pen. It was time to act, time to let someone higher up know about the serious problems at Angola.

Jodie and I composed a letter detailing the corruption and lax security at the prison. She delivered it to Jack Martzell, urging him to use his contacts inside the Edwards administration to have the situation investigated. We warned that there would be either a major security breach or a scandal if corrective measures were not immediately implemented.

Over the next several months, I became convinced that word had been sent to Phelps and Marsellus that I was a "problem." I had survived in prison by listening to the silent whisperings of my instincts. When Phelps occasionally dropped by the office, he avoided talking to me. I saw Marsellus at two pardon board hearings held at the prison in death penalty cases. He studiously avoided eye contact with me.

I wrote Jodie about the level of official distrust mounting against me.

There are several reasons for the distrust. First, I have never been a Phelps protege the way Wilbert is. Second, there is a belief that I am a Maggio spy, or at least a staunch Maggio loyalist. Third, I believe there are some key people (Marsellus and Phelps) who have been instructed to stay away from me because I conveyed sensitive information to the higher-ups. The power brokers understand that I've seen too much, heard too much, know too much, and they don't know what kind of problem I could pose in the future.

Rideau got his sixty-year clemency recommendation on a three to two vote split along racial lines. Although Edwards had recently been acquitted on racketeering charges by a jury in New Orleans, he needed time to recoup his political losses. Instead of giving Edwards that time, Rideau believed he could pressure the governor into signing his recommendation if he kept up the media attention. So it was that he received news of Edwards' denial in the middle of an *NBC Nightly News* interview. Blackburn walked into the *Angolite* office with the cameras rolling and announced Edwards' decision. Rideau's clemency effort and the governor's action left my clemency recommendation in jeopardy.

"I don't have any confidence I'll succeed," I said to Rideau a few days later. "The politics of my case are enough to keep me locked up the rest of my life. Now Martzell says we must proceed carefully because we need to deal with the 'politics of race' that your clemency effort created."

"Martzell has the influence, if he will only use it, to get you out," Rideau said. "I did not 'create' the politics of race in my case. The system did. I am its product."

As I looked across the room at Rideau, I realized how far apart we had drifted. We no longer really knew each other.

"That may be," I said. "But I told you that if you used that strategy it would place me in an untenable position. As long as the system refuses to let you go, it will never let me go. Black voters put Edwards in office. He won't pay them back by putting the white boy on the street if he won't let the black boy go."

Rideau lit a cigarette. He had started smoking again after the Edwards denial.

"I've never tried to tell you how to conduct your clemency efforts," he said. "Don't try to tell me how to run mine."

I stood up to leave.

"You're right," I replied. "I am going to resign from *The Angolite*. I just have to find the right time to do it."

"Do whatever you feel is in your best interest," Rideau said dryly.

From then on, we no longer maintained even the appearance of friendship.

36

FOLLOWING RIDEAU'S DENIAL, Jack Martzell counseled patience, saying we should wait a few months before trying to approach Governor Edwards about granting clemency in my case.

And so I waited. But a sixth sense told me that I was on the edge of something momentous. I talked to Angola's food manager about a possible job change from *The Angolite* to a clerical position in the kitchen. F. Berlin Hood was a close confidant of Warden Blackburn's. He was also a longtime supporter of my freedom effort and he had often urged me to separate myself from Rideau and *The Angolite*.

My frustration mounted when I learned that Marsellus had pushed a recommendation through the pardon board for Mule. When the daughter of Mule's victim learned about the recommendation, she wrote a letter to the *Times-Picayune*. The New Orleans Metropolitan Crime Commission then blasted the board for its decision, citing Mule's ties to the Dixie Mafia. The Orleans Parish district attorney came out against the recommendation, prompting the board chairman to announce it would be withdrawn and reconsidered.

Curtis Earnest, a prominent Bunkie, Louisiana, banker and his wife, Gladys, two of my most ardent supporters, took my cause to Representative Raymond Laborde. They persuaded Laborde, a close political ally of Edwards, to personally speak to the governor about the possibility of signing my clemency recommendation. Edwards, according to Laborde, said my case was "political" and he could not sign it before the 1987 gubernatorial election. He did say he would entertain a visit from Martzell.

On August 8, 1986, I stumbled on absolute proof of a pardon-for-sale scam at Angola. I went to Hood's office that Friday morning to ask him to call Martzell for me. Hood was on the phone when I arrived. I took a chair next to Chris McAlister's desk.

McAlister, who had been Hood's clerk for several years, was a drug dealer whose massive drug ring operated, by his own admission, under the protection of a ranking official at Angola. The official issued orders prohibiting security personnel from searching Hood's office for contraband.

McAlister was president of the prison's Dale Carnegie Club, a group that had now become an all-white, neo-Nazi inmate organization that served as a front for the Dixie Mafia. Using his influence through the Dixie Mafia and the prison official, McAlister was able to get his cousin, Leonard Pourciau, assigned to the staff of *The Angolite* as its artist/illustrator. Pourciau turned the *Angolite*'s art room into a pot-smoking biker's den under the protection of a ranking prison official.

Sitting in Hood's office that Friday morning, I was approached by McAlister for legal advice. My legal counsel was sought by inmates from all ranks of the prison community, even the rogues. I was offered fees ranging from fifty dollars to three thousand dollars to prepare writs and appeals. I did not charge for my legal services although my clientele of about fifty inmates often pleaded with me to "take something" in payment for the "hope" that my expertise gave them. I turned down every offer.

McAlister had recently received a commutation of his thirty-six-year manslaughter sentence to eighteen years. He was concerned about the status of the commutation.

"Once a governor signs a pardon board recommendation," he whispered, "can they take it back?"

Feet propped up on his massive desk, Hood continued his telephone conversation.

"Who are 'they?'" I asked McAlister.

"You know, the pardon board, or the governor."

"C'mon, Chris, give it all to me — if you want my help, you've got to give me the whole picture."

McAlister was eager to talk, almost as though he wanted to draw me into a web of secrecy.

"Okay, the gold seal that I just got, I bought it through Marsellus. It cost me five thousand dollars. That's how much the gold jewelry I gave him is worth. The bastard loves anything that glitters. He'll sell his soul for gold."

I was careful not to change expression. McAlister had just provided me with proof of pardon-selling. It was dangerous information. But why was he telling me?

"Why do you ask if they can take it back?"

"The sonuvabitch is greedy. The deal went like this. Mr. Hood gave Marsellus the jewelry. He was supposed to get it appraised and give half of it to Judge Roberts. Marsellus works through Roberts."

Judge William "Bill" Roberts was Governor Edwards' executive counsel. He was in charge of clemency matters for the Edwards administration. McAlister paused, waving a hand toward Hood.

"I'm giving it to him, Boss."

He turned back to me.

"Anyway, Marsellus comes to me last week. He tries to shake me down. He says the jewelry isn't worth five thousand dollars, that he's still got to give Roberts his twenty-five hundred. I tell him, 'C'mon, man, don't shuck 'n jive me with that dumb shit.'

"He gets hostile, threatening me. He says he can get my gold seal called back and that he has enough influence to get something done to me in here. It flipped me out. He was trying to extort me! That's against the law, ain't it?"

I burst out laughing. The prison's biggest drug dealer was indignant about a crime being committed against him.

"It ain't funny, man," he said, half smiling. "This guy is serious. He's shaking me down for another twenty-five hundred dollars. What should I do?"

"Don't pay the money," I said. "The gold seal is good. Once the governor signs it, nobody can rescind it. You've beaten the system, again."

"I know, I know," he said with childlike glee. "It's so good. I love this land of opportunity. The man with the fastest buck gets the pie. The hell with that bald-headed bastard."

Hood walked up behind me and put both hands on my shoulders.

"Did you tell him?" Hood asked.

"Everything, boss," McAlister replied. "I laid it all out to him."

"Let's go to my house," Hood said, turning toward the door. "You can call Martzell from there. Besides, I have some more things to tell you about what Chris has been talking about. You may not need Martzell."

It was not unusual for a prison employee living on B-Line to check an inmate out to go to his residence. Inmates often cut grass or performed other odd jobs around the homes of ranking prison officials. I called Martzell from Hood's house asking him if he had gone to see Edwards as the governor had suggested to Representative Laborde. He had not. (Martzell would later meet with Edwards in the library of his New Orleans office to discuss the case and try to persuade the governor to sign the recommendation.)

"Martzell is not going to help you," Hood said after the call. "If your lawyer really wanted you freed, you wouldn't be sitting here talking to me. He's not going to use a political marker to help you. You have to grease the political wheels. That's the way it works in Louisiana — always has and always will. You pay to make the system work. All the journalism awards in the world do not mean anything compared to money in the right hands. If you want a gold seal, you're gonna have to pay for it."

Hood then spelled out exactly how he had worked the deal for McAlister, saying he had worked deals for several other inmates. Half the money, he said, went to Marsellus and the other half went to Judge Roberts. Hood said Roberts was the man on the inside. He had the influence to get a signature from Edwards, as well as access to the governor's signature machine, which he had used to sign gold seals, according to Hood.

"How much?" I asked.

"It depends on the case," Hood replied. "It took five thousand dollars to do Chris. But he's a habitual criminal. In some cases, it's a few thousand; in others, it's a lot more. Yours will be hard for the governor to do because of the opposition and notoriety of the case. We'll have to start at fifteen thousand dollars, but it may go as high as twenty thousand dollars."

"I don't know, Mr. Hood. That's a lot of money with no guarantees."

"I'll protect your money. They know that I know. They won't throw a curve. I'm your guarantee."

"I've got to talk to Jodie. She has the money, so it's something we'll both have to decide."

Hood casually sat down with a Diet Seven-Up.

"I understand. You talk to Jodie. Just keep one thing in mind. Your only way out is to pay for it. That's the political law in Louisiana."

As Hood drove me back to the Main Prison, I felt scared and suspicious. I had been given evidence of a pardons-selling conspiracy involving some of the state's most powerful people. I suspected that information had been given to me for one of two reasons.

Although I posed a threat of exposure because I knew too much about corruption inside the prison and pardon systems — I had already sent information to Martzell about corruption at Angola — buying a commutation would make me "dirty," putting me in a position where I could not squeal on the system. The commutation would make me immediately eligible for parole on the sixty-year sentence. Once released, I wouldn't pose a threat.

Or it could be a reverse sting — Hood in concert with other prison officials was trying to set me up in a criminal bribery attempt. Either way, I would be neutralized as a potential witness. It was clear, though, that by conveying the information about the pardons-for-sale operation to me, Hood and McAlister had placed my life in jeopardy. Some of the inmates who had worked deals with Marsellus would have killed me instantly if they even suspected that I knew about the scam. This was no small-time Veronica Price affair.

I called Jodie the following night, a Saturday, the night for our regular weekend call.

"I have some heavy information," I whispered.

"What is it, Billy?" she said, instantly alert.

I whispered in a sort of code what Hood and McAlister had told me. I could almost hear her considering it. Freedom was a tempting prospect. We talked about it for a few minutes and then backed off.

"We can't do it." The sadness in her voice was profound.

"Hell no!" I said. Anger was back. "Baby, there have been moments over the last twenty-four hours when I've trembled with rage. Why the hell are they doing this to me? I've done everything the system asked of me, and more, and now they tell me I have to be criminal to get out."

"Billy, are you all right?"

"Yes," I lied. I could not tell her how afraid I was. While she had learned much about survival in prison, she still didn't understand how precarious life is on the inside. I knew that death was shadowing me.

"What are we going to do, Billy?"

It was a dangerous dilemma. We certainly couldn't turn to anyone in the prison system. Phelps would later criticize us for not sharing the information with him. But I had warned him about Marsellus in 1985 and he had done nothing. We couldn't go to the DOC or the governor's office. Someone in one of the two offices had tipped Marsellus to the anonymous letters implicating him in the pardons-selling scam.

We knew no one with the state police. In fact, we thought of the state police as an extension of the governor's office. We were also afraid to turn to local offices of the federal government. Barry Seal, the nation's most notorious drug informant, had recently been gunned down in Baton Rouge after both a local federal court and the local FBI had refused to protect him.

Wearily, Jodie said, "Let's sleep on it. We'll decide what to do tomorrow night."

All the following day I kept reliving what Hood and McAlister had told me. "Someone" had sent them to me. I knew too much. The corrupt power brokers were making a move to neutralize me by giving me a "bought" gold seal. It was the only thing that truly made sense. Killing me would raise too many questions. My death would kick off an investigation. So the system decided to co-opt me for a price. That night, Jodie thought of someone we could turn to without fear.

"There is one person in this world we can trust absolutely," Jodie said.

It was her cousin, U.S. congressman Bill Archer. He had a reputation for integrity. Though Jodie was not close to Archer, she placed a call to his Washington, D.C., office the next day, Monday, August 11. Bill Archer said he would speak to a contact in the U.S. Justice Department immediately.

"I'm going to tell him I have a constituent with direct knowledge of pardon-selling in Louisiana. Don't worry, I won't give him your name yet. When the time comes, call me and I'll put him in touch," Archer told her. He made sure that she had his home phone number in Virginia.

The time came quickly. Hood asked to meet Jodie the next time she was through Baton Rouge. She would see him on her way back from a vacation visit with her son in New Orleans. Jodie's call to Archer's Virginia home brought an immediate response from the Justice Department in Washington.

"You can't meet with him on your way back to Texas today," Archer's contact told her. "We don't have a wire down there to put on you. You'll have to stall him. Figure something out."

After she hung up, two FBI agents arrived and attached a recording device to the telephone at her son's house. Jodie called Hood with the tape recorder running.

"Hi, Mr. Hood. Listen, I'm really sorry," she said. "I know I was supposed to meet you a little later this morning in Baton Rouge, but my rotor distributor cap cracked. When that happens you just have to have a Mazda towed in. Those caps go without warning. That car was fine yesterday. I'm not going to be through Baton Rouge until really late. I just really do hate to inconvenience you."

Hood agreed to call her at her home in Texas the next night. One of the agents told Jodie she should get an Academy Award. They left with the tape. The next day two Beaumont, Texas, agents stopped by the TV station in Port Arthur, Texas, where Jodie was now working, to talk to her.

"We'll be by about 9:00 tonight to get everything hooked up for the call," they said.

The agents recorded calls for the next several nights after coaching Jodie each night about entrapment. The burden of the investigation now rested on her shoulders.

"You have to let him tell you," they said. "You can't lead him on or you'll blow the case. If you sound like you're doing that, it's entrapment. Be careful what you say."

Jodie's undercover role placed her under tremendous stress. She was reporting by day for Channel 4, the NBC affiliate in southeast Texas, and staying up past midnight to take Hood's calls with two FBI agents standing by. The conversations were explicit. Jodie was to bring him fifteen thousand dollars in one-hundred-dollar bills in a white envelope.

"Marsellus is greedy," Hood told Jodie. "I want to go out with him in his truck and just starting counting the one-hundred-dollar bills out on the seat. When the stack gets high enough, he'll go for it."

But the FBI blew the investigation. The special agent in Baton Rouge in charge of the operation wanted Jodie to tell Hood that she had a brother who would bring him the money. They planned to send an agent with the cash. Jodie laughed at the idea.

"Mr. Hood isn't stupid. He knows I don't have a brother," she responded.

Then she was told they would wire her up for a meeting with Hood but she would take no money with her. She was to tell Hood that she wanted to go with him to meet Marsellus and that's when she would bring the money.

"Mr. Hood is a coward. That's why Billy and I call him 'the Rabbit.' I'm amazed he's even gone this far. I'm not going to do this. It will blow the investigation. I've worked too hard for you to screw it up now."

And for three days she refused. Finally, she gave in to the pressure.

"Okay," she told the agent on the phone from her newsroom. "I'll do it. And I'll be the most convincing human on the face of this earth when I see Berlin Hood. But mark my words, when I tell him that, you will *never* hear from him again. Just remember that I told you."

The Beaumont agents were sympathetic.

"Hey, we believe you, but they're running the show from Baton Rouge."

Jodie drove to Baton Rouge on a Saturday after the newscast went on the air. The next morning, as instructed, she met the special agent and two other agents in the parking lot of a Burger King in Port Allen just off Interstate 10. One had flown in from Washington with the body wire. He sized her up.

"You are too little for us to put this on you. It will show. So we are going to put it in your purse," the agent said.

"The recording won't be any good," Jodie responded.

"Oh, this one will be okay," she was assured.

"Well, if you activate it now, the tape will run out before we are halfway through breakfast," she said as the agent turned the recorder on and put it in her purse.

"No, it's an extra-long-running tape," was the response. "Now sometime during your breakfast with Mr. Hood, one of us will come in, sit down at another table, and order a cup of coffee. That's just for purposes of identification. Pretend you don't see us. One other thing. Don't go anywhere with him. We won't be able to protect you if you do."

It unnerved me that Jodie would have to wear a wire. The Dixie Mafia was heavily into the pardons-for-sale scam. Its leader, Junior Nix, was part of the hit team that killed "Walking Tall" Sheriff Buford Pusser and his wife. Within three months Nix would put out a contract on a Biloxi judge and his wife, who were later found shot to death, gangland style.

Hood was on time for the August 24, 1986, breakfast meeting that he had arranged with Jodie at the Motel Six in Port Allen, just across the river from Baton Rouge. The agents came and went as planned. When Hood began to discuss the bribe money after the meal, Jodie put her purse on the table and took out her makeup. She wanted to get the recorder closer to the conversation. She opened her purse and reached for her lipstick as she listened to Hood talk about arranging the deal with Marsellus.

"Mr. Hood." She smiled at the grandfatherly figure. "We want to go along but we would feel a little bit better doing it another way . . . what I want to do is go with you to Marsellus . . . when my hooks are in him he can't back out, because not only is there the money, which I think is a good inducement, but there's the implicit knowledge, 'She knows.'"

"Jodie, when two people meet, that's a meeting. When three people meet, that's a witness. I'll let you know."

He smiled, pushed his chair back, and left the restaurant.

Just as Jodie predicted, Hood never called her again. He sent word that she should go to Marsellus on her own. With Hood balking at the three-way meeting, the FBI investigation stalled. Jodie and I were left hanging. I was at Angola without protection. It was only a matter of time before someone learned that I was an informant.

37

On SEPTEMBER 4, 1986, Louisianans were stunned to hear that Howard Marsellus and State Representative Joseph Delpit, a powerful black lawmaker who was Democratic speaker pro tem of the state House of Representatives, were indicted for public bribery and conspiracy in what became known as the pardons-for-sale scandal. The indictments charged that Marsellus and Delpit met with an undercover state police officer named James "Chip" Benjamin and agreed to secure a pardon for a convicted murderer named Juan Serato for one hundred thousand dollars. Marsellus and Delpit believed that Benjamin, who was known to them as Ramon Garcia, was connected to drug dealers from Mexico.

A meeting was set up in early September between Marsellus and Benjamin on the front porch of Marsellus' residence. The meeting was videotaped by the state police from a nearby surveillance van. The investigators were surprised when Delpit showed up. He was known as Edwards' "right-hand man." During the meeting,

Delpit called the governor's mansion to have the license on Benjamin's car checked. He suspected it might be an undercover vehicle.

The state police surveillance tape showed Delpit taking a brown paper bag containing twenty-five thousand dollars as a down payment for Serato's release. But Delpit increased Marsellus' asking price from fifty thousand to one hundred thousand dollars. When Benjamin pressed Delpit for assurances that he could deliver on Serato's release, Delpit wrote on a torn piece of folder, "I am a close friend of the governor. He will be released by Dec. 25."

Following the arrest of the two prominent African American political leaders, the black community rallied behind them. Delpit received support from Governor Edwards and many of his legislative allies. House Speaker Joseph Alario announced he would fight plans to have Delpit removed from his speaker pro tem position in the legislature.

Edwards then found himself the subject of a grand jury inquiry when he announced during a news conference that he had been aware of the state police investigation and had ordered Judge Roberts to warn Marsellus and Delpit that they had better straighten up because they were being scrutinized. Some thought the remarks meant that the governor had attempted to obstruct the investigation. But a grand jury found no evidence of wrongdoing by Edwards.

When the state indictments were handed down, I became convinced that someone had leaked information about the Feds' undercover investigation. Several facts aroused my suspicion. The state police sting began in mid-August, approximately two weeks after the FBI investigation began, and the amount of the bribe was excessive compared with what Marsellus had been charging. He had been doing deals for golf carts, washing machines, sex, and jewelry.

According to Hood, Marsellus had become afraid of a sting. When Benjamin approached him, offering a large amount of money, I believe the pardon board chairman became suspicious. Sensing a setup, he drew Delpit into the negotiations. He knew Edwards' political machine would rally around Delpit, forcing the machine to protect him as well. If the "deal" proved to be straight, Marsellus would be fifty thousand dollars richer.

"Why rig up a counter sting?" Jodie asked when I told her about my suspicions.

"To control the investigation," I replied. "There would be no way they could control it if the Feds got down first. This way, the state will be in charge of the investigation and the direction of the prosecution. Delpit's indictment is an inconvenience. But it will be handled. They can make Marsellus the heavy in the whole thing and save Delpit."

When Delpit said he was conducting his own sting, it lent weight to my theory. He said Edwards had called him to the governor's mansion advising him of the rumors about Marsellus selling pardons. The governor confirmed the story. Edwards said he had summoned Delpit to the conference because he had appointed Marsellus to the pardon board on Delpit's advice. Edwards said he asked the lawmaker to check the rumors out. Delpit said that's when he began investigating the pardon board chairman, and he got his first opportunity to "make a case" against Marsellus when Marsellus told him about the Benjamin offer.

While the political machine worked to confine the scandal to Marsellus, the pardon board chairman cut a deal with state and federal prosecutors to plead guilty in exchange for testifying against Delpit. Marsellus got a five-year sentence in return.

Delpit hired a prominent Baton Rouge attorney named Anthony Mirabella to defend him. Mirabella was a former law partner of District Attorney Bryan Bush. Shortly before Delpit's 1988 trial, Bush took Charles Grey — the prosecutor who ran the investigation — off the case and replaced him with a less experienced prosecutor. State police investigators who worked the case were outraged. They believed it was fixed.

Marsellus testified against Delpit after entering guilty pleas in state and federal courts. In spite of the pardon board chairman's testimony, the jury found Delpit not guilty. His tears on the witness stand and the story that he was conducting his own sting — even though the surveillance caught him taking the money from an undercover agent — were enough for the jury.

As soon as Marsellus was arrested, Hood and McAlister became visibly nervous about being implicated in the scandal.

"What do you think will happen?" Hood asked me shortly after Marsellus and Delpit were arrested.

"The state will pressure Marsellus," I answered. "If they can get Howard to turn over on Delpit, then the pressure will be on Delpit to turn over on the people above him. And there are others up the ladder in this thing."

"What about the people below, people like me?"

Hood was a portrait of fear. I felt genuine sympathy for him. He had come to Angola as a decent family man. But he had succumbed to the inherent criminal nature of the prison environment and it had corrupted him. He developed a craving for power and influence. His ambition was to one day be warden at Angola.

"They will probably get some of the small fish as well," I said, not wanting to spook Hood too much. "Everyone will scramble for the best deal possible. Bust one and he'll give up two. That's the way cops and robbers play the game."

Hood began to distance himself from McAlister. I later learned McAlister had started carrying a .25 automatic. And he started working on a transfer out of Angola. Then the unexpected happened. McAlister's homosexual lover, a kid named Coco, got paranoid. He was serving a twenty-one-year manslaughter sentence and had been led to believe that Hood and McAlister would get him a commutation. With Marsellus arrested, and McAlister pushing for a transfer, Coco was out in the cold. He knew Hood didn't like him. McAlister once slapped the food manager for calling Coco "that little bitch."

Coco decided to "catch out" in late September. But he made a near fatal mistake. He unwittingly confided in a ranking prison official who was in on the drug and sex trade at Angola. Coco revealed everything he knew about the vices and corruption at Angola, including illicit sex, illegal drugs, and the McAlister pardon deal.

I was sitting in Colonel Boeker's office several days later when Coco's name came up.

"What's going on with Coco?" I probed.

"I really don't know," Boeker shrugged. "Whatever it is, it's big. Blackburn put out an order that no one could see or talk to the boy."

A few days later, Coco was transferred from Angola to the Washington Correctional Institute in Bogalusa. That same afternoon, Hood summoned me to a parking area. His truck was loaded down with McAlister's personal belongings. A box of cassette tapes sat on top of the heap. I later learned that the cassettes contained secretly recorded conversations between Hood and McAlister and a ranking prison official about their criminal enterprises. Hood was shaking. He had lost weight. His left eye had developed a nervous twitch.

"You heard about Coco?" he asked.

"Nothing except that he checked out."

"He spilled everything. I mean everything — the punk told about the drugs, the sex, Marsellus — EVERYTHING! Thank God, he spilled it to one of our men on the inside."

"What have you gotten yourself into, Mr. Hood?"

"There's so much you don't know."

"Does Warden Blackburn know?"

"Yes, but he doesn't believe it."

"What's all that?" I asked, pointing to Hood's backseat.

"It's Chris' stuff — we're getting him out of here. He's gone crazy behind that punk, Coco. He thinks I made the kid catch out. I'm afraid of Chris — I've never seen him like this. I've got to get him out of here."

Hood lit another cigarette from the butt of the one he had in his hand.

"We're gonna take care of that kid, too. He's being put in a dorm with the 'right' people. A friend is handling it."

"What are you talking about?" I asked, unable to conceal the surprise in my voice.

Hood smiled. "He'll be taken care of."

He removed a cookie from his pocket and crumbled it in a balled fist.

"Please talk to Chris for me," he rambled on. "That's why I called you out here. Try to get him to cool it until we can get him transferred to Baton Rouge."

I watched Hood get into his car and drive off. For the first time, I realized the magnitude of the criminal enterprise that I had stumbled upon. I construed Hood's remarks to mean that Coco would be seriously hurt, maybe killed, to shut him up. That night, I expressed my concern to Jodie. She passed the information to Ray Lamonica, the U.S. attorney. The state police later confirmed that Coco was in danger.

I became acutely more observant following the Coco incident. Rideau made several unexplained trips to Baton Rouge to see Phelps without me in late September and early October. On one trip, Phelps ordered security personnel not to announce the trip over security radios, violating standard security procedure. Boeker was enraged when he learned that Phelps had given orders to take Rideau to Baton Rouge "off the radio" without his knowledge.

The Rideau trips made me suspicious. I detected a perceptible change in Rideau's attitude toward me. I would walk into the office to find him deeply engrossed in whispered conversations with Tommy Mason, another *Angolite* staffer. They would change the subject quickly as I walked in.

The FBI had cautioned me not to tell anyone about my role in the undercover operation, but I decided to take Colonel Boeker into my confidence. I had to have protection against the official setup that my instincts told me was in the works. I asked Boeker to accompany me to my office where I told him about the role that Jodie and I were playing in the FBI investigation. I swore him to secrecy, knowing that I was placing my life in his hands. By then, it was mid-October.

"What do you want me to do?" he asked.

"If anything goes down, and I only have a hunch that it will," I said, "just fix it so I can call Jodie."

"I'll take care of that," he said, clearly concerned and apprehensive.

"Thanks."

"You really love her, don't you?"

"She's my life, Colonel."

"You know they will probably kill you," Boeker said, standing up.

"For God's sake, please don't ever say that to Jodie."

If they got me, I didn't want my wife to feel responsible.

38

IT WAS A SUNDAY IN MID-NOVEMBER 1986. Jodie and I sat whispering in Angola's main visiting room. She knew I was worried, but I didn't want her to know how much. The federal sting had been shut down for two and a half months. I had no protection from the inmates or the administration if word leaked out about my involvement with the FBI. I was on high alert most of the time, braced for a knife in the back. If I survived, there was another risk. And that's what I chose to tell Jodie.

"I'm looking at lockdown, Jodie," I said, closing my hand over hers. "That's where they put informants to protect them. I could end up in a cell for a long time."

The thought haunted me. I could tell it scared her too. We sat close together in the prison's big visiting room. A crescendo of laughter invaded from a table nearby, interrupting our conversation. I held her hand tighter.

"Billy, the FBI will talk to Hood this week," Jodie said. "Lamonica said it's finally going down."

The news about the FBI's impending move against Hood was a major relief. I hadn't told Jodie that a Dixie Mafia henchman was stalking me. His name was Big Lou. For the last two weeks I noticed that he kept turning up nearby. If I went to the gym to play racquetball, he would appear. He was constantly doing some sort of maintenance work around the Control Center near my office. One morning, I caught him jimmying the lock on my door. He said he was checking it because the doorknob "looked loose." I could tell he was studying my movements.

I would later learn from McAlister that the Dixie Mafia had a hit out on me. He said Laredo was supposed to do the job. Laredo lost four thousand dollars in the pardons-for-sale pipeline. The money came from the last of his father's savings. Laredo had been led to believe that I was responsible for busting Marsellus. McAlister said Laredo and an unidentified inmate were to come in my room, gaining entry on the pretext of needing legal advice, and "slit your throat and mutilate your body as a warning to others not to cooperate" in the pardons-for-sale investigation.

Unaware of the danger that I was in, Jodie turned the conversation to another problem we faced.

"What about Wilbert?" Jodie asked.

"I don't trust him," I replied. "He's too close to Marsellus and Phelps. If I told him, it would be the same as telling them."

I was on thin ice. Hilton Butler and Prentice Butler reinforced that belief when they came to the Main Prison Control Center on Thursday, November 16. Rank didn't spend much time in the main body of the prison. The two wardens ordered all the inmates in the area, including the *Angolite* staff, into the Control Center lobby and locked the gates. Colonel Boeker had no advance warning of the shakedown. The Butlers went directly to my office and began looking around. Boeker asked them what they wanted.

"We're just checking things," they responded. "You can leave now, Colonel. We'll take it from here."

"I'm not going anywhere," Boeker replied. "As long as I am in charge of security at the Main Prison, I will take part in any shakedown."

He stayed to make sure they didn't plant contraband in my room. He watched them rifle through my things and then place a lock on my door before they went downstairs to a major's office.

Meanwhile, Rideau studiously avoided me. He didn't ask me why the Butlers were in my office. He stood on the far side of the lobby with his eyes averted. I sensed he was connected to whatever the Butlers were doing.

Boeker came out of the major's office a few minutes later.

"I don't know what's going on," he whispered. "But it's trouble. Go call your people. Those two are up to something."

The Control Center officer refused to let me leave the lobby. The Butlers had ordered him to keep all inmates locked inside. Boeker issued a direct order to let me go down to the dorm to use the telephone. The officer obeyed Boeker.

I called Jodie and relayed what was going on. She called Lamonica immediately. He sent two FBI agents to Phelps' office. They warned Phelps that I was a federal witness and nothing had better happen to me. Phelps must have called the Butlers. They quickly retreated, but not before they padlocked my office door and posted a note on it saying that I was not allowed inside. I went back to the *Angolite* office where I found Rideau behind his desk drinking a cup of coffee.

"What was that all about?" he asked, trying to be casual.

"I don't know," I replied.

"You don't seem too worried about it."

"I'm not. Why should I be? I haven't done anything wrong."

"It's not what you've done sometimes, but what people think you've done," he said, a heavy tinge of sarcasm in his voice.

I was tired of playing cat and mouse.

"Wilbert," I said. "I'm not worried about Hilton Butler, Prentice Butler, or even Phelps. They have more reason to be worried about me than I do them. I'm a federal witness. I've reported the pardons scam to the FBI."

Rideau was visibly shaken. He virtually collapsed into his chair.

"That's right, Wilbert — I haven't done anything wrong. They have."

I briefly described my role in the federal undercover investigation. Just as I finished, Mason walked through the door. He was shocked to see me in the office. Whatever was supposed to go down, I wasn't supposed to be around by the time he arrived. Rideau blurted out the reason.

"You're a dead man," Mason said.

"They're going to kill you, sooner or later," Rideau added coolly.

I could see him cutting his victim's throat while she begged for her life.

"Why didn't you just take the deal and give them the money?" Rideau said, breaking the silence. "I would have paid the money — that's the way it's done in Louisiana. You know that as well as I do."

We spent the rest of the evening in awkward silence. Rideau left the office several times to make "phone calls." No doubt he was circulating the news among his supporters. I went to the dorm that night at 11:00 as usual. I showered and lay wide awake in my bunk all night. I was concerned about one inmate in particular, a psychotic killer named Henry who had just been released from a maximum-security cell in Camp J. Henry was transferred directly to the Trusty Yard, where he would have easy access to me. I was deeply suspicious. Disciplinary cases didn't become trusties overnight. This particular killer had a long history of violence, including a baseball-bat assault that put him in Camp J. While he was in lockdown at Camp J, Henry managed to make a zip gun and shoot another prisoner.

Though deeply apprehensive, the next morning I went to the *Angolite* office and made a pot of coffee. A lieutenant walked through the door as I poured a cup.

"What's happening?" I asked casually.

"Perhaps you should tell me," he said, sitting in a chair in front of my desk, nonchalantly thumbing through a magazine. He did not look at me directly.

"Nothing's happening, then," I said.

"Let me give you some advice, Sinclair," he said, still thumbing through the pages. "I don't know what you're involved in, and I don't care. But I advise you to keep your mouth shut."

"Are you threatening me, Lieutenant?"

"I'm giving you some advice, Sinclair. You know how the game's played at Angola. You keep your mouth shut — you don't hear, see, or say anything."

He got up and walked to the door and turned to look at me. It was the first time he had met my eyes.

"I hope you know what you're doing," he said before walking out.

I was a marked man. I had been foolish enough to think I could ride out the storm at Angola as I had with the Veronica Price affair. But I was beyond my ability to protect myself. There were too many secrets, too many skeletons in Angola's corrupt world. It would not let me live. Every inmate in the state's prison system would hold me responsible for bringing down Marsellus and the corrupt pardons scam. They would have my blood.

I walked out of the *Angolite* office straight to the dorm telephone. I fought down the urge to run. I watched the hands of every passing inmate. "Always watch the hands," an old con had once told me. The hands, then the eyes. A cat signals an attack with its eyes. A con is no different. I was so close to death I could feel it breathing down my neck.

"Call Lamonica, Jodie," I whispered into the receiver. "I've just been given a warning. Actually, it was a threat."

"Are you going to be okay?" I could hear near panic in her voice.

"Listen to me," I said, trying to maintain an aura of composure. "I'm not in immediate danger. But there is danger now. Let Lamonica know."

Jodie called him immediately. He ordered U.S. marshals to go to the prison and get me.

"Do what you have to do to protect your husband until they got there, Jodie," Lamonica said.

Jodie hung up and dialed Hilton Butler. He took her call immediately. She cut through his greeting with a sharp warning.

"Hilton, let me give you a piece of advice," she said coldly. "My husband is a federal witness. If anything happens to him, your ass is grass and the federal government is the lawn mower." She paused to let the message sink in. "If I were you, I would go down to the *Angolite* office right now and hold his hand until the federal marshals get there."

"Now Jodie, you know I've never meant Billy any harm," he began.

She cut him off again.

"Don't start now."

I went back to the *Angolite* office. Rideau was behind his desk. I told him that federal marshals were on their way to get me. He said very little. Clearly, he already considered me dead.

"You will undoubtedly be asked about my role in the FBI investigation," I told him. "You don't have the whole picture, Wilbert. You only have bits and pieces. This thing is much larger than you know. You should say you have 'no comment,' that you don't know enough about the investigation or my role in it to discuss the matter."

"I'm not getting into it one way or the other," Rideau said.

Two hours later I walked out of the *Angolite* office headed for protective custody. Rideau did not offer to shake my hand and I did not extend mine. There were no parting remarks. I had survived twenty years in one of America's meanest, roughest prisons. It was a major miracle, comparable to surviving a plane crash from thirty thousand feet.

39

THE FEDERAL MARSHALS TOOK ME straight to the East Baton Rouge Parish Prison where I was placed on a maximum-security tier. While it protected me from physical assault, it did not protect me from the jeers of other inmates. Prisoners passing to and from the dining hall shouted threats.

"You ratting bastard, we'll get you. You better not come out of that cell."

At night, they raked metal objects back and forth across the bars of their cells so that I could not hear Jodie when I was allowed to call her. A few days after I left Angola, McAlister was put in the cell next to me. He had made a deal with the state police. He offered them the secret tapes he made of Hood and a ranking prison official at Angola discussing their various criminal activities at the prison. McAlister also agreed to provide the state police with information about the Dixie Mafia and its control of the narcotics trafficking at the prison. He turned over hoping to save himself from a federal charge involving Hood's pardon-selling activities.

I was debriefed by the FBI and Lamonica. I provided them with all the information I had about the pardon scam and corruption at Angola. On November 26, 1986, I also appeared before a federal grand jury. The grand jury expressed concern to Lamonica about my safety. But I was more concerned about Jodie's safety. Shortly before my grand jury testimony, she stopped at a chicken diner in Lake Charles during a trip home from visiting me at the parish prison. Two male patrons recognized her from the extensive pardon-selling media coverage. "Good ole boys" with an ingrained distrust of corrupt government, they warned her: "Little lady, we hope you aren't traveling these Louisiana roads without your buddies."

"My buddies?"

"Yeah, lady, Smith and Wesson."

Their concern was real. The threats of harm were not confined to the guttural curses of inmates.

The day I appeared before the federal grand jury, Governor Edwards' executive counsel, Judge Bill Roberts, announced to the press that he would oppose clemency in my case. I saw Roberts' front-page quote as an attempt to silence inmate witnesses. It was timed to send them a message — they would blow their chances for a pardon or parole under Edwards if they cooperated with the Feds.

Following my testimony before the federal grand jury, I was transferred to the Louisiana State Police Barracks, a minimum-custody facility located in the heart of Baton Rouge. Lamonica placed me there under an agreement with the state police. Phelps and others in the Department of Corrections vigorously opposed the move, although Phelps ultimately signed off on the agreement. Several days after I arrived at the Barracks, I was summoned to the office of the head of the state police.

"I am receiving some heavy political flak in keeping you here," he told me. "I don't know how long I can stave it off. You and Jodie do whatever is necessary to protect yourselves. Talk to Lamonica or the FBI, maybe they can help."

I was safe as long as State Police Investigator Joe Whitmore was involved in debriefing me about the pardon scam and the corruption at Angola. McAlister provided details about his drug business and its connection with the Dixie Mafia. I put the Dixie Mafia's activities in context and provided Whitmore with information about the history of the gang and its activities. In December, Hood was forced to retire. Phelps told the press that the forced retirement involved an "investigation" unrelated to the pardons scam investigation.

In January 1987, Whitmore escorted me to the Baton Rouge district attorney's office. I was introduced to Assistant District Attorney Charles Grey, the prosecutor who had been removed from the pardon scam case. Grey called me before a state grand jury. I gave them the same information that I had provided to the federal grand jury.

Based on the information that McAlister and I provided in early 1987, Whitmore launched an investigation into corruption at Angola. The Butler clique vigorously resisted it. Phelps got it suppressed. Meanwhile, during the first few months of 1987, Phelps was exerting tremendous pressure to have me transferred back into the prison system.

"They want you back in the prison system so they can kill you," Whitmore told me. "They don't have to set you up for a hit — all they have to do is place you with the right people and you will be a dead man. I'm not going to let that happen."

Whitmore proved to be a man of his word. When the order finally came from a new state police commander to transfer me, Whitmore went to his office. He told the colonel that he would obey the order to escort me to prison, but not before he placed a letter in my file, and another in his own file, saying that I would be in grave danger there. The state police commander backed down.

The order for my transfer had already crossed Colonel Boeker's desk at the Hunt Correctional Center just outside Baton Rouge where all inmates are processed into the system. Boeker had been demoted and transferred to Hunt in retaliation for protecting me.

"Oh, my God, they've got him," Boeker later told Jodie of his reaction when he saw the transfer order.

Whitmore saved my life when he stopped the transfer. While the career law enforcement officer was able to block my return to the prison system, nothing could stop Phelps and Rideau from launching a crusade to destroy my journalistic credibility. They charged that I had betrayed journalism's canon of ethics by cooperating with law enforcement authorities. Rideau expressed their "editorial view" in the November–December 1986 edition of *The Angolite:*

> The Sinclair affair caused Corrections Chief C. Paul Phelps to find himself in a rather peculiar position. "Unlike other publishers, I wear more than one hat," he explained. "As publisher of *The Angolite*, I have to regard the integrity of the press and the profession as paramount. Subsequently, I can neither condone nor tolerate staff behavior that compromises it in any form or fashion. What Billy Wayne did certainly compromised not only the integrity of the magazine but also the safety and well-being of the rest of the staff who had nothing to do with his extracurricular activities. And I'm fairly certain that almost any publisher or editor in the country would probably fire him for what he did. However, as secretary of the Louisiana Department of Public Safety and Corrections, I am also a law enforcement official and, as such, obligated to encourage action against crimes and improprieties. If I, as publisher, fired Billy Wayne for betraying the trust of his position then I, as a law enforcement officer, am placed in the position of punishing a person for having assisted law enforcement. It creates a dilemma of sorts.
>
> Fortunately, circumstances permit me the luxury of not having to do anything that would cause my two roles to conflict. This is a situation that takes care of itself, in so much as guaranteeing Billy Wayne's safety now dictates that he cannot return to Angola. Thus, his employment with *The Angolite* was terminated by his transfer from Angola, something that was done by his wife and the federal people. But while I'm spared having to make any decision in my capacity as publisher, there is a need for me to say something about all this for the sake of conveying policy for all concerned.
>
> All journalists, whether in or out of prison, function on trust. Whether Billy Wayne used his journalistic credentials in his undercover activities or not is, as I see it, irrelevant. A journalist, like a priest or a policeman, cannot easily make that kind of separation between what he is and represents professionally and what he does personally, and that's especially

true in the prison world where power, operations, and integrity are too often embodied in personalities. A journalist conducting an undercover investigation to expose improprieties and wrongdoing in his profession is one thing. A journalist, doing this solely for law enforcement purposes is a whole different ball game. As a private citizen, it can be argued that he has a right to do it, and he has — but, still, there's an overlapping effect that you can't so easily escape in your professional life. While I'm not as well versed in the ethics of this as my commercial counterparts, I perceive a problem in this. How the professionals perceive and handle this is their business. But, where it involves the prisoner press, I dictate policy. And it is my thinking that prisoner publications and journalists should not involve themselves, in a collaborative manner, with prison security or law enforcement operations, whether as informants, undercover operatives, or what-have-you. That is not compatible with maintaining the integrity of the publication or their role as journalists. To do so runs the risk of compromising the credibility of the publication as well as possibly placing the safety of the staff in jeopardy, either or all of which should warrant dismissal.

Utilizing his insider influence with longtime friend David Anderson, a *New York Times* editorial writer, Rideau persuaded the *Times* to print an editorial blasting me for compromising *The Angolite's* journalistic freedom by becoming a snitch (spring 1987). The paper rushed to judgment without the facts. Its editorial writer did not contact the state police, the FBI, or the U.S. attorney about my role in the federal investigation. And it ignored my dilemma. Was I to say nothing when I learned of Hood's plan to harm Coco?

In the months following my departure from Angola, Rideau successfully orchestrated articles that were critical of me in the *Columbia Journalism Review* and the *Times-Picayune*. Although Lee Kravitz, the writer of the story in the *CJR*, wrote his article from Rideau's perspective, he made changes once he talked to Jodie and me. Kravitz made a professional effort to achieve journalistic balance.

The *Times-Picayune* story was written with a Rideau perspective. It contained a litany of errors. When Jodie informed *Times-*

Picayune editor Charles Ferguson of the blatant mistakes, he promised they would be corrected in the newspaper's files so that other reporters would not rely on them. I do not know if they were.

In addition to the public campaign to destroy my journalistic credibility, Rideau pursued an insidious smear campaign against me in numerous conversations with reporters. Some relayed his comments to Jodie. Rideau charged that I was "running a scam," that Jodie and I set Hood up. He first made the charges in a conversation with a *Shreveport Journal* reporter on the very day that I was removed from the prison, long before any facts were known about the federal investigation.

His urgent need to smear me was motivated by a burning question that he had to keep reporters from asking. How had a massive pardon-selling network operated at Angola for two years without Rideau's or Phelps' knowledge? Together, they deflected media attention from that obvious question with their charges of unethical behavior. By early 1986, the U.S. attorney's office had reports that linked pardon-selling to *The Angolite*. The state police later established a direct criminal connection between Marsellus and the magazine. *The Angolite*'s illustrator, Leonard Pourciau, who was also McAlister's cousin, had bought a gold seal from Marsellus. Pourciau's aunt was the go-between. Hood brokered the deal.

But Rideau deftly painted a picture of a prison magazine staff with its back against the wall. He told the *New York Times* that my informant role had jeopardized their safety and the magazine's professional credibility. It was a masterful con. The *Times* bought it just as it bought Jack Henry Abbott's con in *The Belly of the Beast*. Abbott's book was no more a definitive look at American prison life than was Rideau's portrait of a staff running scared in the wake of a snitch. But Abbott's book got him out of prison. And Rideau's spin cemented his "in" with the media.

In early 1987, Blackburn stepped down as Angola's warden. Phelps promptly appointed Hilton Butler to replace him. That October, Buddy Roemer was elected governor of Louisiana on a platform of reform. His election was hailed as the "Roemer Revolution." The new governor vowed to remove corruption and politics from the clemency process.

Roemer replaced Phelps with Bruce Lynn, a banker and farmer.

With a new administration in office, Whitmore launched a second investigation into wrongdoing at Angola. This time, Lynn suppressed Whitmore's investigation, as federal court records would later reveal. The new secretary made the decision despite a detailed report from Whitmore containing a laundry list of wrongdoing at the prison.

In July 1988, Roemer's new pardon board recommended a time cut for Juan Serato from forty to ten years. Citing Serato's cooperation with the state police pardon-selling investigation, Roemer signed the board's recommendation several weeks later. The signature freed a convicted murderer who lent his name to the state police sting. Serato had no other involvement.

In October 1988, I had a highly publicized clemency hearing. My release effort was supported by a large number of family members and friends as well as the New Orleans Metropolitan Crime Commission. It was the first time that the crime-fighting group had ever asked the governor to release an inmate. But my clemency effort was opposed by the family and friends of J. C. Bodden and Bryan Bush, the district attorney of East Baton Rouge Parish.

To his credit, Assistant District Attorney Charles Grey wanted to appear before the pardon board to support my clemency application as he had done in every other case involving the cooperating witnesses (including Serato's). But Bush ordered Grey to oppose me.

In the middle of my clemency effort, Governor Roemer denied a pardon board recommendation to cut Rideau's time to fifty-five years. The Rideau denial generated statewide media attention. Newspaper columnists in New Orleans and Baton Rouge criticized Roemer's decision.

In December, the pardon board unanimously recommended that my life sentence be cut to seventy-five years. It was the fourth time in ten years that a pardon board had unanimously recommended relief in my case.

Two months later, Roemer denied me, citing my criminal history and my previous death sentence. He made no mention of my role in reporting corruption in the clemency process. Jodie and I were left dangling. As far as the public record was concerned, I was just a common snitch who had compromised the journalistic integrity of *The Angolite* with a scam story about a bribe attempt.

Meanwhile, Rideau continued his high-profile freedom strategy, making appearances on *Larry King Live* and ABC's *20/20*. He was still calling himself "the nation's most rehabilitated prisoner" in interviews and on the lecture circuit, which included a trip to Washington, D.C., to attend the annual American Society of Newspaper Editors convention. With *The Angolite*'s support, Hilton Butler was named the "nation's best warden" in a national awards contest.

Then, in mid-1989, following a rash of murders, suicides, and escapes at Angola, and upon learning about Whitmore's suppressed investigations, U.S. District Court Judge Frank J. Polozola declared a "state of emergency" at Angola.

In an interview with the *Baton Rouge Morning Advocate*, Rideau said there was no need for a federal investigation, and he accused the federal judge of a hidden "political agenda." Meanwhile, Polozola put Ross Maggio in charge of investigating the prison. Then the federal judge hauled Butler into court, threatening to jail him if he interfered with Maggio.

Using his media contacts and his journalistic credentials, Rideau launched a public relations campaign to shore up Butler's administration. Rideau blamed the prison's problems on "hopelessness" brought on by Governor Roemer's strict clemency policy. It was another attempt to manipulate the public record.

Prompted by the evidence presented in federal court, Roemer ordered the Angola investigation reopened. The state police set up a seventeen-man task force that included Joe Whitmore to conduct one of the most thorough investigations into corruption in Angola's sordid history. It would uncover a homosexual mail scam that made Marsellus' pardon-selling scam look like penny-ante poker.

Later that year, Maggio submitted a report to Judge Polozola that was highly critical of the Butler administration, citing it for lax security and administrative operations that made it "relatively easy" for drugs and other contraband to enter the prison. The report outlined thirteen areas of prison management that were in need of correction. The Maggio report was followed by a preliminary report submitted to Governor Roemer by the state police, one that also cited evidence of criminal wrongdoing at the prison.

"There are some findings that could go to a grand jury fairly quickly," Roemer said after reviewing the report. "If there are allegations of wrongdoing, we have a responsibility to thoroughly check them out. This is a criminal investigation, and we will follow wherever this leads us. If it leads us to the highest levels, that's where we will go.

"We did not go in it to get someone," the governor continued. "We went in to track down the allegations. We did not walk in with conclusions and try to prove them. We walked in with an investigation of a system that needed to be looked at. It had not been thoroughly looked at in years and years."

West Feliciana Parish district attorney Hal Ware then announced he would conduct a grand jury probe of the evidence of wrongdoing at Angola. Simultaneously, Lamonica announced his office would conduct a civil rights investigation into operations at the prison.

Based upon the Maggio report and the state police reports, Bruce Lynn fired Hilton Butler. Lynn gave eight reasons for the firing, including Butler's failure to maintain prison security and the cock-fighting business that Butler operated on prison grounds. Butler's dismissal was upheld by the Civil Service Commission and the Louisiana Supreme Court.

Rideau was strangely quiet during the fast-moving scenario. But he was not inactive. He was methodically submitting material to Random House for an anthology of prison writing. The book gave him credit for securing the state of emergency at Angola and reviving the state police probe, which he had done his best to undermine.

In a matter of weeks, the state grand jury indicted dozens of inmates, prison officials, and free world individuals on hundreds of mail scam and drug-smuggling counts. The homosexual mail scam had raked in as much as $4 million for the Dixie Mafia. Its leaders, Pete Mule and Kirksey McCord Nix, Jr., were charged along with gang members and those with close ties to the gang.

When the state indictments were handed down, Nix was under an intense federal investigation for ordering the contract murders of Biloxi, Mississippi, judge Vincent Sherry and his wife, Margaret. Judge Sherry was the law partner of Biloxi mayor Pete Halat, who was Nix's attorney while Nix was operating the homosexual mail scam. Money earned from the lucrative homosexual mail scams was laundered through the Sherry/Halat law firm, Nix believed. Judge Sherry had skimmed five hundred thousand dollars from the gang's profits.

Nix was furious when he was told about the rip-off of what he called his "pardon board money." According to federal informant and Angola inmate Bobby Joe Fabian, Nix, Halat, and Fabian met at Angola in December 1986, on the heels of the pardons-for-sale investigation. They decided to kill Judge Sherry. Gillich added Margaret Sherry to the hit list because she was leading a community crusade against his strip joints. The Sherrys were killed in their Biloxi home on September 14, 1987, Dixie Mafia style, with a .22 caliber pistol fitted with a silencer. Halat discovered the bodies.

The federal government eventually indicted Nix and Biloxi nightclub owner Mike Gillich, a longtime associate of the Dixie Mafia, on mail fraud and conspiracy charges stemming from the Sherry murders. Although the Feds did not charge Nix and Gillich with the Sherry murders, their investigation and subsequent conspiracy prosecution revealed the depth of the Dixie Mafia's criminal influence. It would be nearly ten years before the federal government solved the Sherry murder case. In 1998 the Feds finally convicted Nix, Halat, and an East Texas carnival worker of the Sherry murders when Gillich, who didn't want to die in a federal prison, decided to "roll over" and testify against Nix and his coconspirators. Gillich's testimony linked the murders to the massive homosexual mail scam that operated at Angola while Hilton Butler, the "nation's best warden," was running the prison in 1987. C. Paul Phelps may have cost the Sherrys their lives. Had he let Joe Whitmore's first investigation into the wrongdoing at Angola continue, the Sherry murder contracts might have been uncovered before they could be carried out.

A grand jury finally indicted Hood on two counts of bribery in connection with my case and Pourciau's. Neither *The Angolite* nor the *New York Times* carried the story, even though *The Angolite* illustrator had corrupted the clemency process and refused to cooperate with the state police probe. He not only kept his ill-gotten commutation, he retained his position on the magazine with Rideau's blessing.

Hood ultimately struck a plea bargain with the district attorney.

As one of his victims, Jodie was consulted about the plea arrangement. Because of Hood's age, she did not ask for prison time. In January 1990, Hood pled guilty to attempted public bribery and was sentenced to five years probation and fined fifteen hundred dollars.

Hood's guilty plea vindicated us for the public record. Jodie and I had not set up the food manager as Rideau led reporters to believe. Our ordeal was finally over. But Rideau was right in one way. It would have been far easier to buy a pardon. I knew it. Everyone knew it. Corruption in Louisiana was the norm. But I had long since broken with the criminal code. And I was determined to never let its ugly ethic touch my wife.

40

NINETEEN NINETY-TWO BEGAN with rare promise for a lifer. My pardon board commutation sat on Governor Buddy Roemer's desk awaiting his signature. He signed it on the ninth day of January, just days before he left office. His signature made me eligible for parole. But it was a qualified victory. The governor toughened it up before he signed it.

The pardon board had recommended that my life sentence be reduced to seventy-five years. But Roemer increased it to ninety years. That put off my discharge date until 2011. If I did not get a parole, it would be nineteen years before I would be a free man. Jodie and I were stunned. We would later learn the DOC sent records to Governor Roemer listing me as a fourth offender. But I was a second offender, not a habitual criminal. I had no way of knowing the error was in the file. Inmates do not have access to their pardon board files. The courts have held that because clemency is an act of mercy, and not a constitutionally protected right, inmates are not entitled to examine their files.

It would take years to get the mistake corrected. And it cost me dearly as my plea for mercy lay before the governor. Still, Jodie and I were more than grateful for Buddy Roemer's mercy. He had signed my recommendation in spite of the mistake. I will go to my grave believing it was deliberately planted in my file years before it ever got to the governor's desk. Still, he had restored my life. For the first time, Jodie and I had a future.

Months before Roemer signed my case he met with a delegation of my supporters to discuss it. State Senator Willie Crain secured the appointment. The governor was warm and informal as he questioned my supporters.

"Where's Donald Ray Kennard in all of this?" he asked, referring to the state representative from Baton Rouge who was leading the fight against me.

"Governor, most of the opposition lives in his district."

"Well then, we know where he's coming from," he said.

Jodie breathed a sigh of relief at Roemer's remark. Kennard was a powerful member of the state legislature. He was also in a peculiar position. He was one of the suppressed witnesses in my case. He and his wife, Ramona, had driven up to the Pak-A-Sak just as I burst through the door with Bodden chasing me. In 1984, both Kennards had signed sworn affidavits describing what they had seen the night Bodden died. In his affidavit Kennard said:

> On December 5, 1965, I was driving down Greenwell Springs Road coming from Central with my wife and child in the car. My wife reminded me that we had no matches for our heater at home and suggested we stop to get some.
>
> I pulled into the Pak-A-Sak grocery located on Greenwell Springs. Just as the front wheels of the car touched the curb, I heard my wife exclaim "Oh." I looked up and saw two men running out of the store. The second man was chasing the first man who was about four to five feet ahead of him. The second man was J. C. Bodden and he was holding a broom over his shoulder as he chased the first man. I remember hearing a gunshot and seeing smoke from the gunshot. But I did (not) see the actual shooting.

Ramona Kennard had been subpoenaed to testify at my trial. She was told that she would not be needed as a witness since she "could not make a positive identification of the man with the gun." The Kennard affidavits stand in stark contrast to what prosecutors told the jury — that I shot Bodden in cold blood inside the store. Years later, Kennard told Jodie that he had to oppose my case because "some friends of J. C. live right down the street."

In 1984, I withdrew the federal lawsuit in which I had planned to use the Kennard affidavits after receiving a phone call from Jack Martzell. He said that Louisiana's lieutenant governor called him to complain about other lawsuits that I had filed *pro se*. One was against a witness who perjured himself at my murder trial. The other was against a state employee who was using his office to oppose my clemency efforts on behalf of the Istrouma/LSU football clique. The lieutenant governor said the suits had the Baton Rouge community so upset that I might never receive clemency. I did not ask Martzell if I should drop the federal suit with the Kennard affidavits. But I did, along with the other suits. It was a terrible legal blunder. The affidavits were my only hope of ever winning a new trial.

Jodie sat directly across the desk from Roemer in the small library at the governor's mansion where he asked the group to gather. Jack Martzell sat nearby. Conversation flowed freely between the governor and those who had come to plead for me — Martzell, members of my family, and other supporters including Rafael Goyeneche, executive director of the New Orleans Metropolitan Crime Commission. The governor addressed each member of the group in turn, asking why he should sign my recommendation. Martzell and Goyeneche made eloquent remarks on my behalf. They were to prove invaluable in securing the governor's signature.

A vicious political dogfight over my commutation broke out during the final week of Roemer's administration when my opposition mounted a last-ditch effort to prevent a signature in my case. Roemer's closest aide told Jodie that fax lines into the governor's office were spitting out messages against me and telephones were ringing constantly with calls urging the governor not to grant me relief.

But Buddy Roemer went his own way in my case, a maverick to the end. Political pressure had always served my opposition well. Letters with misinformation about my criminal record, petitions with headings that overstated it and behind-the-scenes political maneuvering had consistently spelled the end to my freedom efforts.

The boyish forty-seven-year-old Harvard graduate was a tough-on-crime governor. He had approved just fourteen pleas for clemency by June 1989. Only three reduced the sentences of inmates in prison. The others restored citizenship rights to offenders who had finished serving time. By the end of his four years in office, Roemer had issued just seventy-eight commutations and 196 pardons.

Roemer was unpredictable. His quixotic style perplexed enemies and admirers alike. He attended some black tie functions in a business suit. He once read a book in the stands as the New Orleans Saints beat the Los Angeles Rams before seventy thousand fans in the Superdome for a place in the playoffs. He wore frayed jeans and cowboy boots to receive the Japanese consul, after making the foreign dignitary wait two months for an appointment. He was a populist and an eccentric. The *Wall Street Journal* called him a "reformer and a technocrat in a state that has traditionally scorned both."

Governor Roemer's revolution brought good government to Louisiana, a state accustomed to "treating politics like Mardi Gras." Roemer passed strict campaign finance laws, pay raises for teachers, and other good government measures during his four years in office.

But Louisiana cannot tolerate reformers for long. Voters in the state traditionally limit reform governors to one term. In perhaps the strangest gubernatorial contest in U.S. history, Roemer lost his bid in 1991 for a second term against a crook on the one hand and a Nazi sympathizer on the other. The race pitted Roemer against former governor Edwin Edwards, the smooth-talking, twice-indicted Cajun (convicted of extortion by a federal jury in 2000), and David Duke, a former Grand Wizard of the Ku Klux Klan. After Roemer's loss in the state's primary, in which all candidates, regardless of party affiliation, run against each other, bumper stickers appeared urging Louisianans to "Vote for the Crook" in the run-off. Edwards won a fourth term in the election.

Jodie and I celebrated my commutation in quiet exhaustion. She had worked tirelessly for months to pull it off, rallying supporters and writing letters to anyone she could enlist to win my freedom. Though I dared not tell her, I had given up hope. Gus Kinchen, a Baton Rouge minister who had played football at LSU with Billy Cannon, visited the Heisman Trophy winner to plead for forgiveness in my case. "Let him die in prison where he belongs," was the response. Cannon's own conviction on federal counterfeiting charges did not prevent him from passing judgment on me. But Jodie would not give up the fight. As gently as I could, I tried to cushion her against the denial that I knew was coming.

"Please, baby," I begged her. "Don't invest too much hope in this effort. You can beard the lion too many times." She responded with a look that shamed me.

"Don't ever tell me to back off. It's my life too." Tears stood in her eyes. "We will win because it's the right thing and I believe the governor knows it."

She was right. I got the news late one afternoon at the Barracks. "Roemer Grants Clemency to Sinclair, Denies Rideau," the local headline read the next day. But Jodie and I had little time to appreciate the commutation. The inauguration brought back a governor who hated us for exposing the pardons-for-sale scam under his last administration. Edwin Edwards lost no time appointing to positions of influence two men who ended up making our lives miserable.

Edwards named his personal security chief, Paul Fontenot, head of the state police. In 1994, Fontenot turned on me with devastating results. He was a highly unpopular state police superintendent. His four years at the helm of Louisiana's crack state law enforcement agency attracted constant fire from the State Troopers Association. It cited a "200 percent increase in disciplinary action" during Fontenot's tenure. Fontenot instituted a ticket quota and, in a letter to the editor of Baton Rouge's daily newspaper, publicly berated troopers for "spending their workdays eating doughnuts and drinking coffee."

Troopers responded with charges that he was waging personal vendettas against them. Some considered forming a union. In one case, Fontenot demoted a popular captain. When the captain filed a formal appeal to the State Police Commission for reinstatement, Fontenot called members of the commission at home to influence their votes. But the commission ruled for the captain, finding that his demotion was "arbitrary and capricious." When Edwards left office, the Louisiana State Troopers Association mounted a successful campaign to prevent Fontenot's reappointment.

Edwards then picked Richard Stalder to head Louisiana's prison system. Stalder was warden at David Wade Correctional Center in Homer when he was appointed to the top job in corrections. After taking over the department, Stalder permitted the transfer of a number of murderers from Wade to the State Police Barracks. Many earned time cuts and paroles over the ensuing years after being assigned to correction headquarters, where they had daily contact with members of the pardon and parole boards. They included Paul "Tex" Chandler, a double murderer from Caddo Parish; Willie Cummins, a murderer with a prior negligent homicide conviction; James Milsap, convicted of stabbing an elderly nurse to death; and Leon Robertson, another murderer with a prior manslaughter conviction. Stalder would exhibit no mercy toward me.

A few weeks into the new administration, Joe Whitmore paid me a visit to warn me about what I was facing under the new administration.

"These are going to be bad times, Billy," he said, lighting a Winston in the privacy of the Barracks legal aid office.

"A lot of people are hell bent on getting revenge for the pardon-selling scandal," he went on. "My office is now in the trunk of my car. I've been detailed to New Orleans. They will keep me out of the loop. You won't believe this casino gambling business. This administration is going after the money."

"What about me?" I asked. I had grown accustomed to the feeling of safety during the Roemer years at the Barracks.

"You are a target."

Whitmore's blunt assessment awakened old fears.

"They want you back in the prison system," he continued. "You embarrassed Edwards. Don't be surprised if you get hurt."

"Jodie and I are on our own then. That's the lay of the land."

"Pretty much so."

Whitmore had never lied to me.

"I'll be out of pocket but I will try to stay in touch," Whitmore said. "Just be careful. Real careful. A lot of people want to see you fall."

"What about Kennedy? Where does he stand?" Fred Kennedy was a state police captain who served as warden at the Barracks.

"Fred's a good man. He won't hurt you. But he can't go to the wall for you. He'll do as he is told."

Within weeks of Whitmore's visit, I began to feel the heat. Contradictory rulings in the records office of the Department of Corrections were the first signals that the official attitude toward me would be as punitive as possible. Governor Roemer's commutation put my parole at exactly one third of my ninety-year sentence as required by Louisiana law. So I was surprised when a staff member in the records office of the corrections department applied the Old Timer's Law to me, making me immediately eligible for a parole hearing. The law was passed unanimously by the legislature while Roemer was in office. It accelerated the parole eligibility dates of any inmate who was forty-five years or older and had served at least twenty years. But the supervisor of the records office denied me a parole hearing under the Old Timer's Law. He forced me to apply directly to the parole board for a hearing. The board denied my request, deferring to the records office supervisor.

At the same time, in April 1992, the parole board freed three murderers. One was not even eligible for parole. Ron Wikberg was a lifer who had never received a gubernatorial commutation. Yet the board paroled him anyway. Wikberg shot and killed a convenience store clerk in 1968 in Lafayette, Louisiana. The other paroled murderer had served just ten years.

The Wikberg parole had intense victim opposition. But the *New York Times* covered his release in a story that lauded his tenure on *The Angolite*. Wikberg had replaced me as Wilbert Rideau's coeditor. The paroled killer boasted on the *Maury Povich* show that he was the only man in Louisiana history to be paroled when he wasn't eligible because he was still serving a life sentence.

His boast sounded the death knell for a lawsuit filed by twenty-six lifers, including Wilbert Rideau, who argued that they had the same legal right to release. The Louisiana Supreme Court rejected their argument, specifically ruling that state law prohibits the parole of lifers unless the governor has commuted their sentences. By then, Wikberg was dead of lung cancer. But the Louisiana Board of Paroles had helped him cheat the state out of a year behind bars.

Over the next eight years the parole board would release fifty-nine murderers. (Given inconsistencies in parole board records, the count may be as high as eighty-five.) None could match my record of rehabilitation. Nor had they served as much time. Yet I would fight a bitter, uphill battle just to win a hearing. Ultimately, I was forced to file a lawsuit to get it. Once again, I turned to Richard Hand for help. By then, our friendship had endured nearly thirty years of disappointments and setbacks. Yet Richard never flinched or pulled away from me. He held the line every time, fighting hard, always pro bono, to win concessions for me that were routinely granted to other prisoners.

Between May and December 1992, while my suit against the parole board was pending, the board released four more murderers. One had served just twelve years for bludgeoning his wife to death. Lewis Graham stood at the foot of the couple's bed where his wife lay sleeping, raised a sledgehammer over his head, and slammed it into her forehead three times. Prosecutors said he then rolled her over and bludgeoned her on the side of her head. Expert witnesses testified that she survived for twenty minutes despite the blows. Graham then called the police and told them an intruder had killed his wife. In a Baton Rouge newspaper story following Graham's hearing, parole board chairman Ronnie Bonvillian said that the board freed Graham because he "was rehabilitated," and that by law, rehabilitation was the only criterion the parole board could consider in any case. Bonvillian added that he was proud of the decision.

Graham's parole opened the door to the best job I would hold at the Barracks. I replaced Graham as Captain Fred Kennedy's inmate clerk. The position moved me out of Fleet, the garage where state vehicles were serviced and repaired. Kennedy was an easy man to work for. The affable captain was intelligent and fair. But his job made him the target of intense political pressure as legislators and administrators sought to have inmates transferred to the Barracks from Louisiana's prisons against his better judgment. Paul "Tex" Chandler was one of them.

In 1979, Chandler attempted to reconcile with a girlfriend in a Bossier Parish nightclub. But she turned away his advances. Chandler drove home, got a pump shotgun, put it in the trunk of his car, and returned to the nightclub. When the woman spurned him again, he retrieved the shotgun from the trunk of his car. He calmly walked back into the club and opened fire on the woman and several patrons sitting at the table with her. He reloaded and continued shooting until he ran out of bullets. Two people lay dead and two others were critically wounded. One was Chandler's best friend. Chandler escaped the death penalty in a plea bargain. He was not an inmate that Kennedy wanted at the Barracks. Kennedy asked me about the double murderer because I had known him at Angola. He had briefly worked as a part-time sportswriter for *The Angolite*.

"I'm receiving heavy pressure to take this Chandler guy," Kennedy said. "I've got real problems with this man. He killed two people. Actually, he tried to kill four. It was a cold-blooded crime. What do you know about the guy? He's got to have some real head problems."

"I worked with Tex for a year before he was transferred to Wade. He's a skilled carpenter. I heard he developed a lot of 'juice' at Wade because of those skills. We got word at *The Angolite* that he was a heavyweight up there. He's got close family ties, so I don't think he's an escape risk."

"I really don't have a choice here," Kennedy said. He was deeply troubled. "All I need is for this psychotic sonuvabitch to go on another killing spree. He executed two people. And now I've got Corrections pressuring me to assign him here."

The Barracks had less security than any facility in the state. At that point, it was housing forty-five murderers, including three convicted of double murders. Another thirty-five prisoners were doing time for manslaughter, and fifty were convicted of armed robbery. The Barracks was in the heart of Baton Rouge just blocks from Goodwood, a highly affluent neighborhood. Every inmate at the Barracks was allowed to wear free world clothes on Sunday, so there was nothing to distinguish them from the average Baton Rouge resident. But aside from an escape every few years or so when a prisoner would simply walk off the compound, no harm had come to the community.

The greater risk at the Barracks was a scandal with far more potential to smear the reputation of the state police. Corruption was eating away at Fleet. A stick-out program had been converted into a massive rip-off of state parts and inmate labor.

The amount of money flowing through the stick-out program was staggering. It began innocently enough. Inmate mechanics were authorized to work after regular hours on personal vehicles belonging to state police officials. The original purpose of the program was to allow inmates to earn extra money while it saved state workers large repair bills. The inmate mechanic would tell the state worker what parts were needed for the job and the state worker would buy them out of his own pocket at a local parts store. Inmate mechanics were to charge only a nominal fee for their work and it was to be done on their free time.

But the stick-out program soon succumbed to the inevitable forces of corruption so prevalent in Louisiana. State police officers began bringing in cars belonging to family members and friends. As word of the program spread, elected officials and government bureaucrats joined in. Personal vehicles belonging to members of the state legislature, members of the pardon and parole boards, friends of the governor, and law enforcement officials began showing up at Fleet. Inmate mechanics began to work on vehicles on state time. Some officials purchased wrecked cars, had them restored at Fleet, and sold them for a profit. Inmate mechanics were even allowed to bring their family cars in for repairs.

The stick-out program opened the door to a massive rip-off of state parts, supplies, labor, and equipment. Inmate mechanics used official work orders to buy parts that were placed on their own vehicles or those belonging to well-paying "customers." They routinely put used parts on state vehicles to cover it up, including cars driven by state police troopers to patrol the highways.

Some inmate mechanics in the body shop cleared up to a thousand dollars a week in the stick-out program. None paid taxes on their earnings. Two inmates restored personal motorcycles by charging more than twenty thousand dollars in parts to a state police motorcycle that no longer existed. These extremely skilled inmate mechanics enjoyed favors and the protection of highly placed state police officials. They were taken off the compound for shopping sprees and dinner engagements.

I had left Angola after exposing a pardons-for-sale scam only to find myself in the middle of the biggest rip-off I had ever seen. It involved more people than the pardon-selling scam. And it had official protection. As the inmate clerk at Fleet, I was witnessing wholesale corruption. I calculated the odds of surviving another whistle-blowing effort and deemed it out of the question. The best thing for me to do was get to out of Fleet. The Lewis Graham parole gave me the opportunity to go to work for Captain Kennedy.

My own parole effort was going nowhere. Richard Hand had once again flown in from Long Island to represent me in court at his own expense. But the court had ruled that I was not entitled to an Old Timer's parole hearing. The same Department of Corrections lawyers who had failed to oppose Wikberg's illegal parole fought hard to stop mine.

"What's wrong with these people down here?" Richard said after the hearing. "Do they even comprehend the rule of law? This place is worse than a banana republic."

His thoughts mirrored the front page of the *Wall Street Journal* in 1991 when a story described the state as a "foreign country that had inexplicably washed up on the American shore."

I took the denial in stride. The word "denial" was etched into the fabric of my life. I found it in almost every envelope from a court, a pardon board, or a parole board. But Jodie was stunned at the ruling. She could not comprehend a decision that flew in the face of law. Anger born of disillusionment almost overwhelmed her as she prepared for the long drive back to Texas after the hearing. By then, my wife had been doing time for fifteen years.

Inmates do time by rote. They create individual routines within prison-mandated schedules, shoehorning hope into the mix. As long as hope is alive, the schedule is a life preserver. It keeps prisoners shuffling through their days. They can go to bed at night believing that sunrise is worth the wait. If hope dies, the inmate becomes institutionalized. But inmate families have no routines to shield them from the pain of doing time. The years take a heavy toll. When Jodie was asked how she could do so much time, her reply was always the same.

"I don't know," she would say with a pained look in her eyes.

I kept a letter she wrote to me after a visit in 1995. Guilt shredded my heart at her words. I knew there would be no quick relief for her sadness.

> Sometimes when I come to see you, I feel like the car is driving itself. I've been on the road so long, the years blend together. Days turn into weeks and weeks into months and the tires just keep on spinning. I am losing track of time. It could be any year or any season, depending on the music I am listening to. I wonder if I will feel anything at all when I hit a million miles . . .

The loss in state court left me without a clear direction for my release efforts. What would convince a Louisiana judge that the Old Timer's Law applied to me? The solution was a simple but daring idea that Jodie broached one day.

"Let's ask Buddy Roemer for an affidavit. He knows what he meant when he signed your commutation. Senator Tom Casey told me that Governor Roemer didn't mean to deny you any benefit of the law," Jodie said.

Former state senator Tom Casey had been Roemer's executive counsel. The straight shooter from New Orleans had a reputation for honesty and integrity in a legislature where those qualities were in short supply. Jodie's plan to secure an affidavit from Roemer clarifying his intent meant turning to Jack Martzell for help.

Martzell was one of the most able lawyers in the country. He represented me pro bono for a time during the Treen years and into Edwin Edwards' third term. I quit trusting him during a paranoid period after Edwards returned to office. I began to imagine that the lack of progress in my case meant Martzell was working against me. He had real cachet with Edwards. He had defended Edwards' brother Marion in federal court on racketeering charges and won an acquittal. Surely, he could get Edwards to sign my commutation. When he couldn't, I dismissed him, believing that Martzell was serving Edwards' best interest, not mine.

"Billy, how could you fire Jack?" was Jodie's shocked rejoinder. She went to Martzell and apologized.

"Jack, a wild animal will gnaw his own leg off to get out of a trap. Please, take Billy back," she begged. "He was so stupid about this."

Martzell was well aware of the bias and official hostility that fed my paranoia. As he wrote Governor Roemer in arguing for my clemency signature in 1991:

> I am sure there are other pressures, political and personal, being brought to bear on you in this matter. I have felt them myself. There are those who periodically dedicate themselves to keeping Billy Sinclair in jail for the rest of his life. While I do not agree with them, I understand their motivation. Let me suggest to you, however, that this is a matter about which government must be concerned and not just the survivors and friends of the decedent. . . .
>
> I would strongly urge that after almost twenty-five (25) years, this is a matter solely between Billy Wayne Sinclair and the government that holds him in prison. A constitutionally created board has examined his case and now, for the third time, recommended commutation. I realize that your discretion is absolute in these matters, but at some point Billy Wayne Sinclair is entitled to a dispassionate view of *his situation* with respect to the State of Louisiana. I know it will be your purpose and intent to give him that dispassionate look, and I simply wanted to be another voice in urging it.

Jodie pressed me to let her approach Martzell. Aside from my embarrassment at the wrong that I had done him, I felt we would be sending him on a fruitless quest.

"Roemer will never do it," I replied. "The political risks are too great, even for Buddy Roemer."

"He will do it if Jack asks him to," Jodie said without hesitation. She had an unwavering faith in Martzell.

"Why would Jack ask him?"

"Because it's the right thing to do," Jodie answered. "Jack believes in you. And Roemer believes in Jack. Jack will get the affidavit."

Martzell would have no problem approaching Roemer for the affidavit. He had secured the release of Roemer's father from federal prison, where the senior Roemer was doing time after his conviction under the RICO statute for a scheme involving state insurance contracts. Roemer's father, Charles E. Roemer III, was a banker and plantation owner from North Louisiana who had been Governor

Edwin Edwards' commissioner of administration during the Cajun's first term in office. It was the second most powerful position in state government. Martzell was retained to represent the senior Roemer on appeal. Based on Martzell's brief, the court threw out the senior Roemer's conviction.

Jodie's faith in Martzell was justified. He not only secured the affidavit from Roemer, he persuaded the former governor to testify in court if need be. But the affidavit was clear. Roemer had not meant to block a hearing for me under the Old Timer's Law. Riis Suire hand delivered Roemer's sworn affidavit to the parole board. Suire was a classification officer at the Barracks. He handled all inmate relations with the pardon and parole boards.

"This board will never grant Billy Sinclair a parole hearing," was a staff member's immediate response.

By September 1993, the parole board had released nine murderers on parole. One of the parolees had served eighteen years for the execution-style murder of a hitchhiker. He and a confederate — who later bought a pardon from Howard Marsellus for a golf cart — forced the hitchhiker to his knees and blew his brains out with a sawed-off shotgun as the hitchhiker begged for his life.

Chandler and the other Barracks inmates with jobs at corrections headquarters, where the pardon and parole boards were housed, reported the enormous animosity against me by the staff and the boards.

"That staffer hates you," Chandler said. "That woman has to be connected to your victim's family because she knows everything about your case."

Chandler gave me the impression she would do whatever she could to influence board members against me. True to form, Tex had wormed his way into the good graces of staffers and members of the pardon and parole boards in his position at headquarters. It would serve him well when his case came before them. Suire also brought me confirmation of the intense bias and hostility against me on the parole board. Jodie was aghast.

"I guess I never will be anything but a dumb little woman from Houston, Texas, who believes that government agencies ought to follow the law," she said.

I wrote a letter to Senator Willie Crain about the situation.

Crain had set up the meeting with Roemer to discuss my commutation. Perhaps he could find the reason for the animosity against me on the parole board. To my surprise, Crain showed up at the Barracks with the vice chairman of the parole board, C. A. Lowe. Lowe confirmed what I had heard from Chandler and Suire.

Lowe told me, "You could not possibly get three votes for parole right now — no way under the sun.

"Let me suggest this to you," Lowe continued. "Withdraw your request for a hearing. Let things cool down a bit. Wait until October of '95 and reapply for a hearing. I will vote for you and this will give me time to work on getting two other members to vote for you."

"October of '95," I said. "That's after the next governor's election."

"Exactly," Lowe said.

"It's the best deal you can hope for, Billy," Crain said.

In spite of the pardons-for-sale scam, it was still second nature to think in terms of a "deal" in Louisiana.

"Tell them we don't deal," Jodie said. "We didn't buy a pardon and we're not buying this. You deserve a parole, Billy. We shouldn't have to deal to get it."

With the deal rejected, the parole board denied my request for a hearing based on the Roemer affidavit. It issued the denial the same day it paroled a prisoner who had served just fourteen years for murder. Veronica Porteous Scheinuk, a New Orleans lawyer and Jack Martzell's former wife, stepped forward to represent me in the lawsuit that I would now have to file to get a hearing. Jodie and Veronica had been friends since the 1960s.

Veronica used the Roemer affidavit to file suit against the parole board, which triggered an intense backlash. It incensed the parole board and other officials at the Department of Corrections. Riis Suire told me about the criticism he was encountering at DOC headquarters, where many felt that I should be immediately transferred back to prison from the Barracks. The backlash prompted Kennedy to call me into his office.

"I will not tell you how to conduct your legal affairs. But your efforts to get a parole hearing are making a lot of people mad. You need to look at the larger picture. This is not just about right and wrong. I think you should have a parole hearing. You should be released. But that's not my call. My call is to try and protect you. Think about it, Billy. Maybe you should back off."

Kennedy was having serious political problems at the Barracks. A member of the parole board was pressuring him to take yet another double murderer named John Cezere. Cezere was an *Angolite* staffer who had attracted the favorable attention of a powerful corrections department official. As a teenager, Cezere had stolen the family car and run away from home in Florida. He got as far as Louisiana when the car broke down. A couple stopped to help him. Cezere tied them up, forced them to lie down, put bullets in their heads, and stole their car. Legislators, governors, and sheriffs routinely used their insider influence to get murderers transferred to the Barracks. Kennedy was forced to accept them.

Among the inmates under Kennedy's charge were thirteen murderers who were assigned to the governor's mansion. They worked for Louisiana's first family as porters, cooks, and personal servants. Beyond being murderers, they had another quality in common. They were black. It was a requirement for service at the mansion.

"Blacks make the best servants," a state police official told me. "White boys are too defiant. They want to fuck the women and steal the money. We can't send white boys to the mansion."

But there was an upside to the blatant prejudice. The black murderers who worked at the mansion were virtually guaranteed their freedom. It was a tradition in Louisiana for governors to sign the inmate workers' commutations as they left office. It was rare for a governor to leave any mansion worker "unsigned."

Wesley Dyson was one of the few mansion workers that Governor Edwin Edwards ever refused to commute. Dyson was serving a life sentence for killing his wife. He was assigned to the mansion with the help of a Baton Rouge councilwoman. Buddy Roemer "inherited" Dyson when he took office in 1988. Shortly after that, Dyson killed his girlfriend on a three-day furlough. The furloughs compensated mansion workers for long hours of service at the mansion seven days a week.

Governor Roemer ordered an immediate investigation. Although Captain Kennedy had no control over the political decision that had placed Dyson at the Barracks, he rode most of the official heat. Given the number of political transfers to the Barracks, Kennedy was always on the alert for heat. He was determined to head it off for my sake and his.

"I appreciate your position and your concern, Captain Kennedy," I said. "But I didn't ask for this fight. You know what's being done to me and why. There's one standard for everybody else and another one for me. That is the nature of the beast I am fighting. The only way I will ever get a parole hearing under this board is with a court order. I have no choice."

"The Barracks is not a bad place, Billy," Kennedy said. "It's the best place in the system to do time. You can discharge your sentence here. But you can also create a situation where the powers that be will move against you. I won't be able to protect you then. There is just so much I can do. Think about it. Just think how much better it is to do time here than at Angola."

It was a painful moment. Without a parole, I would not discharge until 2011 — another sixteen years down the road. I stood up to leave.

"This is not about doing 'easy time,' Captain Kennedy," I said. "It's about being with my wife. I don't want any part of Angola. But a man who won't fight to be with his wife is a slave. If I'm transferred, it will be because I am Billy Sinclair."

In 1993, the parole board released fifteen murderers. In February of 1994, Buddy Roemer appeared in a Baton Rouge court to testify for me in my suit against the parole board. Under oath, he told the court it was not his intention to deny me a parole hearing under the Old Timer's Law. His appearance was an incredible first. No Louisiana governor had ever taken the stand to clarify a commutation on behalf of an inmate. Testifying in my case did not win the former governor any political points. But Roemer had no trouble stepping up to the plate.

I won the suit. The court ordered the parole board to grant me a hearing. It was set for July 14, 1994. Seven more murderers were released on parole between April and my July hearing. One had served just six years for his crime. My parole hearing was conducted at the Hunt Correctional Center a few miles from Baton Rouge. Members of my victim opposition (that included the football clique) received the red carpet treatment. A prison van picked them up at Hunt's front gate and drove them to the main administration building for the hearing. They waited in a private, secluded area, away from the other crime victims, most of whom were African American.

The black victims were forced to sit in the same room with the inmates they had come to oppose. The board forgot about one of them waiting to testify. The hearing was almost over before the irate victim got an opportunity to speak.

That morning, the Metropolitan Crime Commission had faxed a strong letter of support for me to the parole board. Gus Kinchen sat with us waiting for our hearing. He was clearly uncomfortable. He sensed that the hearing would go against me. He knew my opposition intimately, having played football with former members of the Istrouma team at LSU. And he was right. They were allowed to testify privately before the board. We were not given an opportunity to hear what they said as was required by parole board rules. When we entered the hearing room, my opposition was gone. Department of Corrections attorneys and staffers filled the room. The animosity was palpable.

The vote went against me two to one. When a member of the panel tried to change his vote in favor of parole, after learning that the Metropolitan Crime Commission supported me, he was overruled. But the parole board was forced to acknowledge the merit in my case. In a newspaper article following the hearing, parole board chairman Ronnie Bonvillian said that I had "done a fantastic job" of rehabilitating myself during my twenty-nine years as an inmate. But he said that he had to consider "other factors" in voting against my parole. Bonvillian had not applied "other factors" to Lewis Graham's case. Rehabilitation was the only criterion Bonvillian said that the board could consider when it paroled Graham just twelve years after he savagely bludgeoned his wife to death with a sledgehammer.

The difference in my parole prospects compared with others lay in the fierce determination of my opposition to make me pay as long as possible for the death of J. C. Bodden. Its ability to exert intense political pressure guaranteed that the system would always use a different standard when it judged me. As a high school football buddy of my victim told the Louisiana Radio Network's Jim Engster in February 1999, "Billy Sinclair's problem is that he killed a man with a million friends." In Louisiana, it's *who* you kill that matters — an apt epitaph perhaps for Mrs. Lewis Graham.

The denial was not enough to satisfy those who opposed me. Stunned by the favorable mention of my rehabilitation in the press, they wrote a series of vehement letters against me to the Baton Rouge newspaper. It published four letters in two weeks. Coming on top of the denial, the letters kept my case in the spotlight, making my situation at the Barracks even more dicey. I sensed a definite change in Kennedy's attitude after they appeared.

"Those letters have created a real problem," Suire told me. "They came at the worst possible time. There's a lot of pressure on Kennedy to get rid of you. Be circumspect, Billy. Be circumspect."

Riis Suire was an intelligent, compassionate individual. He was my immediate supervisor. We had often discussed my case, particularly the football angle. Suire was acutely aware of the power that the Istrouma football clique held over my case.

"How am I supposed to be careful, Mr. Suire?" I asked. "I'm about to file another lawsuit against the parole board. There is a U.S. Supreme Court decision based on a Montana parole statute that is identical to the Louisiana parole statute. The Montana law says an inmate has a constitutional right to be free if he satisfies the criteria of the statute. The Supreme Court ruled that Montana had to parole the inmate."

"Another lawsuit at this point would be a mistake," Suire replied. "You are going to have to give up this fight if you expect to stay at the Barracks. I know you are right. I trust your legal judgment. But this is not a constitutional issue. It's a political one. Right now, Billy, you have to think about survival. Your enemies — and believe me, they are substantial — are looking for any excuse to move you."

Joe Whitmore had been right. The political clouds around me were growing dark. The only thing that held a move against me in check was my status as a "protected witness." Roemer's affidavit and his court appearance had embittered my opposition and the power structure in office. I filed my third lawsuit against the parole board anyway. Kennedy soon came to see me.

"Let me first say that I respect your decision to file the lawsuit," he said. "I do understand the legal need to do it. But I can't protect you any longer. When I get the order to transfer you, I will have to follow it. It is nothing personal. You are one of the best inmates I have ever had at the Barracks." He shook my hand and left. An uneasy quiet settled over the office for the next month.

I knew my days at the Barracks were drawing to a close, an awareness that was confirmed when Joe Whitmore came to see me. He was not himself. Confidence had been his hallmark, now he was subdued.

"Always remember one thing, Billy. You did the right thing when you blew the whistle on those bastards. No one else had the balls to come forward. You and Jodie have paid a heavy price for honesty. And I am afraid they will now try to kill you."

Then, out of the blue, Bill Elder, a prominent Louisiana television reporter, called me. Our paths had crossed on occasion through the years. I had met him the first time when I was on death row. He was looking into reports that pardons were again being sold in Louisiana under the Edwards administration. His source was former pardon board chairman Howard Marsellus, who had finished serving time for selling pardons under the last Edwards administration.

"Give me anything you've got, Billy. I will keep it confidential. But if anything's going on, you would be the one to know it."

"There's so much I could tell you," I said, thinking of the Edwards staff member who had a Barracks inmate make furniture in exchange for a pardon. "But my situation is so dangerous right now that I could be transferred just for taking a call from you. Call Jodie. I gave her the information in case something happens to me."

My next court hearing was set for November 30, 1994. Jodie drove in from Texas the day before and headed for the biggest lion in the den. She called Billy Cannon. The football great received her at his office.

"Dr. Cannon, I have always heard that you are the reason why my husband can't come home, that it's primarily your opposition preventing his release. Please, I'm begging you. It's been so many years now. Please don't oppose us anymore."

Cannon looked at her across his empty waiting room.

"I have never asked anybody to keep your husband in jail.

Sometimes when my friends and I are together we talk about it. But I have never called anybody to try and stop his release."

"They just use your name then?"

"I wouldn't know about that."

"Does it make any difference to you that I came to see you instead of believing the rumors that you are behind my husband's opposition?"

"That's the only reason you are still sitting here. Did your husband shoot J. C."

"Yes."

"Then I don't feel sorry for you. You knew what you were getting into."

Cannon was unbending. It was clear that further entreaties would be futile. The next day, I was escorted to the courthouse under armed guard. In the past, Suire had always driven me to court. I felt the tension in the courtroom as I sat with Veronica waiting for the judge to appear. Veronica had subpoenaed several DOC bureaucrats and their records for the hearing. Anyone needed to give testimony was present. As soon as the judge took the bench, the DOC attorney moved for a continuance. Veronica was on her feet immediately objecting.

"We have witnesses present," she said to the judge. "We are ready to go forward."

The magistrate was not impressed.

"Both sides have fifteen days to brief this matter," she replied, abruptly adjourning the hearing.

The drive back to the Barracks was somber. The security guard said nothing, perhaps minding an official cue to keep his mouth shut. I had secured permission to visit with Jodie and Veronica after the hearing. The visit did not go well. Veronica was furious. Jodie was in tears. The judge's abrupt ruling heightened my fears. It was another bad trail sign. I still had not discussed my fears with Jodie and Veronica, but I knew I was close to the end of the road.

I walked Jodie to her car in the parking lot next to the building where I worked. She and Veronica had received permission to leave their cars there before the hearing. I stood by Jodie's car with my arms around her. We had said many goodbyes in that same parking lot during my eight years at the Barracks. I gave her a kiss. She laid her head on my chest and then pulled back from my embrace to pat my stomach.

"When is the baby due?" she teased.

She had fussed about my weight since I had arrived at the Barracks. Free world food had put more than a few pounds on my frame. Out of the corner of her eye she saw a car stop in the driveway and a man get out. Jodie turned back to me and leaned against my chest for a few moments. I knew she was tired. The trip had been a strain and had not resulted in anything that would give us hope. With a final wave, she drove off on her long trip back to Houston. I returned to my office and a number of routine chores. Kennedy walked in as I completed them. His face was tight and drawn. A Barracks lieutenant accompanied him. Kennedy told me to follow him into Suire's office.

"You are being transferred, Billy," Kennedy said. "This is the worst thing I have ever had to do."

"Why?" I asked.

"It's Fontenot," Kennedy replied. "He saw you kiss Jodie in the parking lot and he went ballistic."

"That's not the reason, Captain Kennedy, and you know it."

Tears welled up in Kennedy's eyes.

"I spent two hours in Fontenot's office trying to talk him out of it. He would not relent. There was no reasoning with him."

I dared not show fear.

"Fine," I said. "I'll pack my belongings."

I called Jodie's sister Carol so that someone in the free world would know that I had been "shipped." Suire typed out the official transfer form. "Inappropriate behavior," it said. "Affectionate with wife in public view." My belongings packed, I was handcuffed and put in leg irons for the thirty-minute trip to Hunt. I had lived for eight years on a compound in the heart of Baton Rouge across the street from the free world and I had never violated the trust put in me. The sound of my chains dragging on the floor followed me out the door as I hobbled to the car that would take me back to prison. Before I was eased into the car, Kennedy reached out and shook my hand, pulling me into an embrace. I would never see him or the Barracks again.

I tried to prepare myself for what lay ahead. I was going back to guns and bars and cell blocks full of inmates who had every reason to want me dead. I had ended the easy way out for inmates who could scrape up the money at a time when pardons and paroles were hard to come by. Whitmore's warning flashed in my head. "I am afraid they will now try to kill you."

"Returning Sinclair," the state police officer said as he pulled up to the security booth at the Hunt Correctional Center.

"We've been expecting him," the guard replied.

I stiffened as I heard the prison gate roll shut behind me. My mind clamped shut on anything but survival.

Jodie reached Houston just as I arrived at Hunt. She stopped at her sister's house to deliver the Christmas presents that I had sent them. Her brother-in-law Allen met her at the door.

"Jodie," he said, "Billy's been transferred. He managed to call us before they took him away so you would know."

The news buckled her knees. She fell, scattering the contents of her purse helter skelter across the highly polished brick floor.

"No, no," she cried. "Oh God, no," unable to get any other words out of her throat. Then, sick with fear, too stunned to pray, she went home and uncorked a bottle of wine. She chug-a-lugged most of its contents and spent the night pacing the floor, unable to stop crying. She knew what I was facing. And she had no way to help me.

41

I WAS PLACED IN A MAXIMUM-SECURITY CELL at the Hunt Correctional Center in a dungeon called "the tank." It was a solid concrete enclosure sealed with a steel door. There was a foyer between the cell and the steel door. A caged shower sat in the foyer with a wire-mesh door that was closed and locked with a padlock.

I was given an orange jumpsuit, a toothbrush, a tube of toothpaste, a sheet, and a worn yellow blanket — nothing else. A solid concrete shelf with a mattress covered in plastic was my bed. The roof leaked directly above the bed, flooding the cell when it rained. I endured two violent thunderstorms and a number of rain showers. When water was not pouring in from the roof, the toilet was overflowing. Hours would pass before a mop and bucket would be brought to clean up the mess.

I was held incommunicado. I could not mail letters, use the telephone, or make visits to the canteen. Inmates being held in the same cell block for serious disciplinary infractions enjoyed all those privileges. I was allowed to shower only every three or four days.

Then, I was handcuffed and shackled at the ankles before being put in the shower. The guard would give me a small bar of soap and leave, locking the solid steel door behind him. The water was ice cold. I was forced to wait as long as an hour before a guard returned to give me a towel and put me back in my cell.

Two days after I arrived, I managed to get a guard to give me a piece of paper, an envelope, and a pencil. I drafted a request for an administrative remedy addressed to Richard Stalder (the head of Louisiana's prison system). He did not respond.

Guards frequently referred to me as "the Marsellus snitch." It was obvious the word had been put out on me, giving them license to abuse me. The system was trying to tear down the self-esteem that I had acquired during two decades as an *Angolite* editor and trusty at the Barracks. That became clear two days after the transfer when Eddie Boeker came to see me. Following the pardons-for-sale exposure, Phelps had transferred Boeker from Angola to Hunt as punishment for helping me. During the next eight years, he had risen to the rank of assistant warden at Hunt.

"I need to call the FBI or Corrections Internal Affairs," I said after a brief introductory chat.

Concern registered in Boeker's eyes.

"I will pass the message along to Warden Lensing," he said, backing toward the door. I knew he could not help me this time. The system meant to break me. It had cut me off from all sources of support. I squatted in the corner of my cell, shivering from a cold breeze that blew in through a vent in the ceiling. Big red welts covered my body. I chalked them off to stress. Thirty-five pounds would drop off my body in the next three weeks. I focused all my energy on surviving, calling on the inner resources that had sustained me in my death cell and in the Baton Rouge parish jail where I was tortured by the cold thirty years before.

I knew why I was being held in solitary. It was political retaliation for exposing the pardon-selling scheme and it reflected the level of hatred that I had stirred up on the parole board with my lawsuits. My status at the Barracks had been unassailable as long as Roemer was in office. But Edwin Edwards' reelection opened the door to revenge.

Jodie threw herself into the breach. She rallied family members and supporters. They bombarded the governor's office with faxes and letters protesting my transfer and expressing fear for my safety. The pressure got Veronica in to see me. She was shocked at my haggard appearance. She expressed her outrage to prison administrators. Then she told Jodie about what was being done to me.

The next day, Jodie drove to Baton Rouge, hand delivering a complaint addressed to U.S. District Judge Frank Polozola about the inhumane treatment I was receiving. Louisiana's prison system was still under his control. Jodie did not expect to see Polozola. She left the letter at his office and then held a press conference on the steps of the courthouse to publicize my plight. The story made the top of the news that night. One local television station even confronted Fontenot, questioning the reason for my transfer and the treatment I was receiving at Hunt. Fontenot defended his order to transfer me, saying the scene he witnessed "looked like a soap opera."

"Did he ever break any rules during the eight years he was here?" the reporter asked.

"No," Fontenot said.

On Friday, December 17, the day after the media explosion, the steel door to "the tank" opened. Warden Marty Lensing stepped up to the bars to deliver a curt message.

"You will be out of here Monday," he said. "You are being transferred to the David Wade Correctional Center."

Lensing turned on his heel and left. I didn't know about Jodie's hand-delivered letter or the media blitz. I was still being held incommunicado. But years behind bars told me something extraordinary had happened.

Two days later, I was hustled in chains into a waiting car for the seven-hour drive from Baton Rouge to Wade. The prison is located in the remote piney woods of Claiborne Parish about seven miles south of the Arkansas border. It was named after former corrections secretary David Wade when it opened in 1980. Richard Stalder became warden at Wade in 1988.

Stalder rose to prominence when he secured national recognition for Wade from the American Correctional Association. Wade was the first of Louisiana's prisons to qualify for the ACA's national stamp of approval. Once Stalder became secretary of Louisiana's

Department of Public Safety and Corrections, he secured ACA accreditation for every Louisiana prison. His success earned him the presidency of the ACA.

Jodie scoffed at the ACA accreditation. ACA investigators conducted no surprise inspections. State authorities knew weeks in advance when an ACA visit was coming, giving them plenty of time to disguise violence and corruption. The new paint, clean floors, fire extinguishers, and shiny toilets made Louisiana's prisons look like model institutions. Underneath, the "belly of the beast" was as filthy as ever.

"Good God," Jodie said to the director of the ACA when she called to complain about my treatment at Hunt. "It's like getting the Yard-of-the-Month Award when you've got incest every night behind the front door."

Abuses in Louisiana's prisons have been documented by federal court monitors, the U.S. Justice Department, the news media, prison advocacy groups, and Senator Paul Wellstone of Minnesota. Yet the ACA continues to bestow its highest honor on a backward, lawless prison system rife with political favoritism and brutality.

Kelly Ward was warden of Wade when I arrived a few days before Christmas 1994. We had met on death row in the 1960s. Back then, Ward was a young, longhaired classification officer — one of a group introduced into Angola by Warden Henderson. He was an intellectual at heart. He and I had chatted occasionally about the works of philosophers we had read.

Upon my arrival, I was greeted by a group of his top staffers. It was not a pleasant meeting.

"You must understand," I was told, "your position here is not going to be the same as it was at the Barracks or on *The Angolite.*"

One of them shoved a book of ACA-inspired regulations at me.

"Read them," he commanded. "Our job is to get your mind right."

"I don't need to read them," I said, pushing the book back across the conference table. "I know how to do time."

Another stared at me intently from a wheelchair. I recognized his attitude: Inmates must be told how to think and behave.

"I will be by to see you in a couple of days to discuss whatever mental health concerns you may have," he said.

"No thanks," I responded, anger lacing my words. "I don't have a 'mental health problem.' I have a political problem. I know exactly why I am sitting here."

"Let me give you some advice, Sinclair," the first officer said. "There are some problems in the cell block where you will be housed. Our staff at times must use gas or force to deal with these problems. You shouldn't get involved in these matters. You know what I mean?"

He meant that I was to turn a blind eye and a deaf ear to brutality. But what he revealed was his fear of my legal skills. Ward reflected the same concern when he told Jodie that I was "a warden's worst nightmare."

"As long as you don't gas me or touch me," I said, "I tend to my own business."

With that, I was led away to the disciplinary tier. Housing me on the tier was meant to "get my mind right." After that, my probable destination was N5, the only unit in Louisiana for protection cases.

The noise on the disciplinary tier was staggering. Guttural rambling, shouts, insane conversations, and the rattling of cell doors reverberated up and down the tier. Feces and urine were slung at guards on occasion. Cigarettes were commonly smuggled around the cell block. I met any attempts to attract my attention with silence and a hard stare. Guards told the inmates — most of them young gang-bangers — that I was "some kind of lawyer" who had done thirty years behind bars. They were too young to know or remember anything about Billy Sinclair. When they tried to engage me in conversation, they called me "lawyer" or "old man." The last term pricked me. At age fifty, I didn't think of myself as an old man.

My silence, lack of fear, and the sheer number of years that I had spent behind bars intimidated the young gang-bangers. They quickly left me alone. Ward instructed the guards to give me law books and legal papers. I spent every waking moment scribbling out a strategy for a civil rights lawsuit. I filled legal-size tablets with handwritten notes, legal claims, and arguments.

My civil rights lawsuit preparation was intended for Mary L. Sinderson, a Houston attorney who was a personal friend of Jodie's. Sinderson was a former chief of the civil rights division of the U.S. attorney's office in Houston. She had agreed to put the complaint in proper form and file it in federal court in Baton Rouge pro bono. I focused on her kindness. The legal lifeline she threw me helped me deal with the tier's brutish realities. But the suit would garner the same hostility that greeted the others.

"Your lawsuits reflect defiance," Suire told me while I was still at the Barracks. "They anger and intimidate people in authority. They see you rebelling against them."

Penal administrators demanded obedience to conditions that often violated legitimate inmate rights. Then they charged inmates with "attitude" if they went to court. It was standard operating procedure.

I finally got to see Jodie two days after Christmas. Her letters arrived, sometimes two and three a day, full of love and support. Her tenderness helped me fight off the black depression that had begun stalking me. I was led in chains into the room where she was waiting, intensely beautiful and alive. She stood up as I hobbled toward her, shackled by leg irons, my wrists in handcuffs attached to a chain around my waist. A black box was locked over the short chain between the handcuffs, further restricting my movements. I was ashamed of my appearance. Dressed in an orange prison jumpsuit and plastic prison slides, I had dreaded the moment she would see me in lockdown garb. But she didn't notice. Her eyes were full of unconditional love. We spoke in whispered tones and coded language, mindful that our conversation was probably being monitored. She touched my hands, already swelling from the pressure of the black box, brushed my rumpled hair, and stroked my face. There was concern in every touch and gesture.

"Billy," she whispered as she gently touched my face, "there are a lot of people praying for you. Tell us what to do and we will do it."

"Tell Elder I want to see him," I said.

"I've already talked to Bill," she said. "He has a request in to see you. He will be here in a few days."

"What about the Metropolitan Crime Commission?"

"They're still in our corner. They have expressed concern to the governor's office about your safety."

There was a pause as a guard peered through a window in the conference room door.

"If they hurt you . . ." her voice trailed off.

"They're not going to hurt me. They are going to try and break me. That's what this is all about." I nodded at the chains and the black box.

Nine of my first ten years in prison had been spent in a maximum-security cell under horrific conditions. But the months I spent in maximum security at Hunt and Wade took a serious psychological toll. Weight loss, fitful sleep, and bouts of anxiety gnawed at my soul. I had been stripped of basic human rights and amenities. The noise on the tier reverberated in my brain. My hopes of parole were gone. Governor Roemer's grant of clemency represented relief that I might not live to see.

I was a psychological wreck when Elder visited me late in December 1994. There was so much I wanted to say about what was being done to me. But my words didn't match my thoughts. They tumbled out in a near-incoherent rush. At times, I was on the verge of tears. The interview was a horrible experience. But Elder's report served a valuable purpose. Raphael Goyeneche, the executive director of the New Orleans Metropolitan Crime Commission, expressed strong concern for my personal safety.

"I fear they will put Billy Sinclair in a situation where he will be killed," Goyeneche said on television.

It was a strong indictment of Louisiana's prison system. Goyeneche's voice and those of the others expressing concern for my safety saved my life. They ensured that I would be placed in N5, the only cell block where I would be safe.

N5 was a fifty-two-man, maximum-security protection unit. Phelps established it at Wade in 1980 to house high-profile informants, former law enforcement officers, and prison guards convicted of various offenses from murder to child molesting — prisoners whose lives would be in danger in the prison system. A few years later, juvenile inmates convicted of violent crimes at age fifteen or sixteen were added to the mix. An inmate could only be assigned to N5 if the secretary of the Department of Public Safety and Corrections approved. Richard Stalder approved my assignment there in January 1995.

N5 had an ugly undercurrent of mutual distrust and contempt. Ex-cops in the unit assumed entitlement based on the positions of power and importance they once held. Most vehemently proclaimed their innocence, charging that they were victims of a flawed criminal justice system. They detested being called "dirty cops" and insisted that they had never beaten or framed suspects or prisoners.

Ex-guards assumed the same privilege and status. They hated the ex-cops for lording it over them. But both groups had one thing in common: contempt for snitches. Snitches hated ex-cops and ex-guards in return. All three groups competed for the support of the half-dozen juveniles generally assigned to the unit. But all three were united in their distrust of me. I was the "famous editor" who shut down the pardon-selling network. I had already filed a lawsuit against my transfer from the Barracks and another one challenging Wade's "attitude adjustment program." I caught inmates staring at me with deep suspicion. Guards put the word out that I was a problem. I could feel the target on my back.

After nearly three months in lockdown, I was assigned to a special N5 work crew. Inmates said it had been inactive for two years. But it was revived the day I was released into N5. Crew 20 consisted of twelve inmates. I was the oldest prisoner on the crew. We got the dirtiest work assignments. Crew 20 often did as much work as farm lines with dozens of inmates. Rifle-toting line pushers drove us hard every day. When there was a shortage of line pushers, other work crews could "lay in." But Crew 20 always worked. We were the first crew out the sally port and the last to return.

We cut tall grass with sickles and sling blades, cleared thick underbrush in the surrounding woods, spread and re-spread cow manure, cultivated crops, maintained the sewage pond, and worked in "snake pits" — low-lying areas filled with water moccasins and copperheads — without boots. When there was no field work, Crew 20 was put to work between Wade's double razor-wire fences to "goose pick" grass sprouting in the perimeter. We pulled it out by the roots with bare hands that ached on wet, winter days.

"This is Sinclair work," was a common phrase on Crew 20.

"This is what happens when you piss the Man off," a resentful voice would grumble.

I fought the abuses through the inmate grievance process, the first step in a lawsuit. Then I started a tactic that was new on the line. I pushed myself harder than the line pushers did. It had an electrifying effect on the rest of the crew. Other inmates followed my lead. They enjoyed the line pushers' astonishment. It was a legitimate way to put one over on "the Man."

One day, a line pusher rode toward me. I was drenched in sweat in 100-degree temperatures, fighting off the nausea and headaches that plagued me on the hottest days in the sun. Some inmates were able to "suck it up" and endure the heat. Others dropped over and were hauled off to the hospital. One inmate in the general population, denied treatment after collapsing in the sun, was found dead in his cell the next morning. I kept a tight focus on the next swing of my blade to keep dizziness at bay. The line pusher leaned across his saddle at me.

"Why do you push so hard, Sinclair?"

"It's part of my rehabilitation," I said swinging the blade even harder.

Jodie kept up her efforts to free me on parole. During the summer of 1995, she met with Connie Koury, Governor Edwards' executive counsel. Jodie pressed Koury hard for a new parole hearing, providing her with a score of details documenting the unfairness of my parole hearing in 1994. Jodie's meeting with Koury produced a second hearing before the Bonvillian board in August. This time, it was held at Wade.

We received word that morning that our hearing would be delayed. C. A. Lowe was flying in from Baton Rouge to replace a member of the panel originally assigned to hear my case.

"I'll be denied," I told Jodie. "He's flying in with marching orders to vote against me."

Jodie kept alive a wild hope that the vote would go in my favor. But I knew better. The panel's decision had to be unanimous. Lowe's presence was bad news. Several supporters had reported that he had turned against me after I rejected his proposal when he visited me at the Barracks with State Senator Willie Crain. Other negative signs piled on top of it. While Louisiana law stipulates that parole hearings are to be open to the public, we were not allowed to be present when several members of my opposition and an assistant district attorney spoke against me. Two members of the hearing panel — both former law enforcement officers — voted for me. Lowe voted against me.

"Don't give up, Billy Wayne," Lowe told me after the vote. "Keep up the good work. You'll make it one day."

Jodie didn't hear his remark. She had left the hearing room. The decision devastated her. She was curled up in a posture of grief at a table outside when I told her what Lowe said. She stiffened in outrage at his condescending remark.

"How dare he say that to you? Look at you. You're sunburned black from working in the fields. You weigh forty pounds less than you did at the Barracks. What is the matter with a ghoul like that? 'You'll make it one day,' indeed! What a sick bastard!"

By August 1995, the Bonvillian parole board had released thirty-eight murderers. One had served twenty-seven years; another just four. Four of the parolees worked for Edwards at the governor's mansion. Time served on their murder sentences averaged thirteen years. By then, I had served thirty years.

That same month, the fortunes of Mike Foster, a candidate for governor, began looking decidedly better. The governor's race seemed like a dead heat until former Ku Klux Klan leader David Duke, a perennial Republican candidate himself, threw his support to Foster after Foster secretly paid him one hundred fifty thousand dollars for a mailing list. Foster's standings took a leap in the polls. Foster then announced his switch to the Republican Party. The wealthy plantation owner went on to victory in the October election. In 1999, a Louisiana grand jury began investigating the Foster-Duke relationship. Both men denied suggestions that the one hundred fifty thousand dollars was a payoff.

October was also good to Paul "Tex" Chandler. The double murderer's clemency denial was reversed. During a secret hearing, pardon board member Larry Clark changed his vote against Chandler and agreed that the double murderer's two life sentences should be cut to seventy-five years. Clark, who would be reappointed to the board by the newly elected Foster, defended his decision on the grounds that he was worried about "overcrowding in the prison system."

While crime victims around the state blasted Governor Edwards for his wholesale grant of executive clemency to mansion workers as he left office, Chandler's case sped unnoticed to him for a quick signature. Other murderers received relief as well. A killer who was promised a signature in return for furniture he had made for a state official while he was at the Barracks got a time cut to forty years. Another murderer that Stalder had okayed for a transfer from Wade to the Barracks, Willie Cummings, also got a commutation.

Cummings had killed twice: The DOC orderly had previously been convicted of negligent homicide, only to kill again. Like Chandler, he had served twenty-three years on the life sentence before Edwards commuted his term. Within weeks, the Bonvillian parole board paroled him.

Meanwhile Governor Foster fulfilled his promise to be tough on crime by appointing a majority of victims to the pardon and parole boards. Louisiana's two largest crime victim groups, Citizens and Victims Against Crime, and Crime Fighters, both New Orleans-based organizations, were early supporters of Foster's campaign. The new governor placated the state's victims with the appointments.

The strategy paid off in May and June of 1996 when the parole board released two more murderers. One was a former death row inmate named Jimmie McCauley. In 1969, McCauley went to the home of his victim to collect money. The victim told McCauley to leave. Instead, the killer retrieved a shotgun from some bushes where he had hidden it. McCauley walked back to the victim's house, kicked down the door, and shot him. Then McCauley shot him again, blowing his victim's brains out as he lay dying.

The other murderer, James Milsap, one of the inmates whose transfer to the Barracks Stalder had approved, had kidnapped, robbed, and executed an elderly nurse in North Louisiana in 1968. While Milsap's co-defendant received the death penalty for the vicious nature of the crime, Milsap escaped with a life sentence. Neither parole drew public criticism from the state's crime victim groups or the victim appointees on the pardon and parole boards.

In July 1996, I was assigned to a split shift at Wade with an extra punitive twist. I was given a push mower to use on the yard during the hottest part of the day while other inmates, working just outside the compound, had power mowers. Every night at nine, I was taken to the kitchen to scrub the walls and the floors until 1:00 A.M. I was awakened every morning at five.

A nurse from the prison hospital took my blood pressure every morning and afternoon. By the time I got in from the yard, it was dangerously high. The next morning it had returned to normal and I was sent back out on the yard. The wild swings in my blood pressure and the sleep deprivation began taking their toll. I felt weak and drained most of the time.

My assignment to the split shift came suddenly. I couldn't reach Jodie in Houston to tell her about it. She was in Beaumont during the week, where she had taken a job as an assignment editor in the news department of the ABC affiliate. It was not a job she wanted. But the Houston television station, where for eight years she had been public affairs director with her own show, was sold and downsized in January 1996. Jodie and ten other longtime employees found themselves on the street. She rented the new house that she had bought just six weeks earlier, packed everything we owned, and put it in storage. After four months of unemployment, she settled on the Beaumont job at half her Houston pay. She lived in a cheap southeast Texas motel during the week. I could only call her collect on the weekends at an apartment that she kept in Houston.

"They are trying to kill me," I said when I finally got her on the phone.

I told her about the split shift.

"Why did they start monitoring your blood pressure?" she asked.

"A new prison doctor saw a heart murmur on my chart and wanted to check it out. When she saw how high my blood pressure was, she started monitoring it twice a day."

Jodie immediately wrote Warden Kelly Ward a letter that she mailed by Federal Express to protest my treatment:

> You are not a cruel man so I am sure that you don't know about my husband's new work assignment. But I beg you to alter it immediately. Your medical personnel are so concerned that they are monitoring his blood pressure twice a day. As you know, high blood pressure increases the chances of heat stroke, or worse.

That summer had seen a number of deaths from the heat in North Texas and Louisiana as summer temperatures climbed above

100 degrees day after day. The change came swiftly. A security major approached me on the yard a few days later.

"Do you want a job in the laundry, Sinclair?" he asked. I nodded.

"Report in the morning," was the reply.

That same month, Gilbert Gauthe, a notorious pedophile who had done time at Wade, was arrested in Polk County, Texas, on charges of molesting a three-year-old boy. The arrest came within months of his release from Wade. Gauthe had been a priest in five South Louisiana towns in the 1970s and early '80s where he had molested altar boys, boy scouts, and other children. Some of the abuse occurred in the church rectory. Gauthe had been convicted of thirty-four counts of child molestation. He got a twenty-year prison sentence in 1983 after a special plea bargain. Gauthe got a "good time" release in 1995 after serving nine years in the protection unit at Wade. The serial pedophile was said to have an invincible power behind him — a sitting federal judge. Their families had been friends for generations — sharecroppers with neighboring farms in South Louisiana's Vermilion Parish. As soon as I arrived at Wade, I began to hear rumors from inmates and free personnel about the power, influence, and special privileges that the serial pedophile enjoyed at Wade.

At first, I ignored the stories. The prison grapevine can be wildly inaccurate. But I began to believe them in 1996 after another pedophile priest was assigned to N5. He had been convicted of the aggravated rape of a former altar boy. He had been in the unit only a few weeks when he received several visits from a federal judge, Gauthe, and several members of the Catholic clergy. The judge was said to be none other than Henry Politz, the chief justice of the Fifth Circuit Court of Appeals.

The judge's visits always started the prison grapevine humming with rumors circulated first by inmates and then by guards. Inmates in N5 believed that Gauthe was sexually involved with the teenage prisoners he chose as assistants. They were the same inmates who frequently met with Gauthe and the judge in the privacy of the attorney-client conference rooms. Other prisoners inevitably linked sexual misconduct to the visits. While the inmate talk was graphic, it was unsubstantiated. But the judge's visits fueled the rumors like a wind fanning a brush fire.

By the fall of 1996, reports began to surface at Wade that

Gauthe had been arrested in Texas on another molestation charge. High-ranking officers at the prison dismissed the talk as vicious inmate rumor. Gauthe pleaded no contest to a lesser charge, a nonsexual charge of injury to a child, and received seven years' probation. Texas authorities never received records from Louisiana about Gauthe's previous convictions.

Meanwhile, Jodie was trying to secure permission for my return to the Barracks. She had decided that I would never be paroled. Since all inmate transfers to the Barracks had to be approved by the secretary of the Department of Public Safety and Corrections, she would have to meet with Richard Stalder. But there was bad blood between them. Years of diplomatic efforts on my behalf had worn her down. She was tired of being shuttled back and forth between bureaucrats and elected officials, Stalder among them, who kept passing the ball in my case. She sent him a message through an administrator in his office that infuriated him.

"Tell Richard if we go to war, I am quite aware that I will lose. He is the secretary of the department and I'm just an inmate's wife. But some of his blood will be on the sand before it's over."

At first Stalder refused to see her. She pursued other channels in her effort to get me transferred. She met with Colonel "Rut" Whittington, Fontenot's replacement as head of the state police. She took Whittington a multi-page memorandum revealing the wrongdoing in the stick-out program under Fontenot. The new commander agreed to look into it. At the end of the meeting, she pushed Whittington for a commitment to return me to the Barracks. He told her that Captain Kennedy would "have to ask" for my return. Jodie went straight to Kennedy. He said he "could not ask" but would not say why.

Jodie pressed Stalder again. He finally agreed to a meeting. It took place in the office of the corrections department's top lawyer, William Kline. Stalder refused to sit down.

"I got your threats," he said to Jodie.

"They weren't threats, Richard. I don't threaten. I just present people with the facts so they can make choices about how they want to proceed."

But the secretary was adamant. He would not allow me to go back to the Barracks. Jodie pressed him hard for a reason.

"He's a security risk," Stalder said. "The state police don't want him."

The reply infuriated Jodie.

"That's a bogus reason. Think of something else, Richard. Billy was at the Barracks for eight years without a problem. He was the best inmate on the compound. You know it. I know it. The state police know it. He hasn't had a disciplinary write-up in more than twenty years."

But Stalder was unbending.

"A security risk!" I exclaimed later when Jodie told me what Stalder said. I choked down a boiling rage at his mind-boggling hypocrisy. Stalder had allowed the transfers of a number of killers to the Barracks.

While Jodie was trying to have me returned to the Barracks, Stalder approved the transfer of yet another inmate from Wade to the minimum-security facility, a man who had been convicted in Caddo Parish of a carjacking in a shopping mall. He shot his victim at point-blank range in the upper body and then in the head. She somehow managed to survive the attack and throw herself out of the speeding car. The judge imposed the maximum sentence because the crime was so heinous. But the carjacker ended up at the Barracks anyway.

Meanwhile scandal was enveloping the chairman of the parole board. Ronald Bonvillian resigned after the state inspector general issued reports charging him with breaking the state's open meetings law, repeatedly violating parole board voting procedures, failing to keep proper records, and using his office to help a family friend. Governor Foster replaced him with an accountant named Fred Clark. It would be a year before the board paroled any more murderers.

As the parole board reeled under the negative publicity during the spring of 1997, it granted a new hearing in my case. I was suspicious. The board had used my case more than once to repair its reputation. This time, the hearing would be over a state-wide television hook-up. The panel would sit in Baton Rouge and Jodie and I would respond from Wade. The hook-up was new. Mine was one of the first cases to be heard using the experimental procedure. I sensed a setup. I was a high-profile inmate. My hearing always garnered publicity. A nagging sixth sense told Jodie to go to Baton

Rouge for the hearing. But she didn't want me to face the music alone. If we got denied, she wanted to be there to comfort me.

The Friday before the hearing, Jodie called the parole board to see if any media intended to cover it and was told that none had expressed interest. As soon as Jodie got to Wade on the morning of the hearing, she asked a guard to call Baton Rouge to see if any reporters were present.

The hearing room was crawling with them. The Fox affiliate in New Orleans, the ABC affiliate in Baton Rouge, and the local Baton Rouge paper had reporters on the scene. My opposition was out in force, led by State Representative Donald Ray Kennard. Without Jodie there to remind him of his affidavit, Kennard testified that Bodden's killing was a heinous murder. Reporters had a field day with an emotional story. And the parole board had a high-profile case to show how sensitive it was to victim demands. The assistant district attorney from East Baton Rouge Parish who had been sent to oppose us ridiculed our efforts to expose the pardons-for-sale scam.

"These Sinclairs are smart, clever people," he said. "They knew they couldn't buy a pardon for fifteen thousand dollars so they did the next best thing. They turned in the guy who made the offer so the authorities would love them."

My back went stiff as his words came over the TV monitor. Jodie reached for my hand when she saw tears well up in my eyes. I had risked my life to help the authorities. The assistant D.A. was dead wrong.

In a letter dated August 27, 1990, U.S. Attorney Ray Lamonica had written to parole board investigator Cecil Goudeau:

> Both Mr. and Mrs. Sinclair voluntarily came forward to report criminal activity and both continued to cooperate with this office and the FBI . . . both were advised at the outset that this office could not and would not do any "favors" for them . . . Mr. Sinclair was the only prisoner who voluntarily cooperated with us.

Jodie reached for the microphone and interrupted the proceedings.

331

"Just a minute, Mr. Stassi," she said to the parole board member conducting the hearing. "We never claimed to be responsible for breaking up that entire scheme. You know we always differentiated between the state sting and the federal sting. And you know there was a conviction in this case as a result of our information. The U.S. attorney told us never to let anyone make us ashamed of what we did."

By then, she was shaking.

We lost on a vote of two to one. Ralph Stassi, a former Iberville Parish deputy sheriff, voted for us as he always did. The other two panel members nixed my parole. But the parole board underestimated the journalist in Jodie. She left Wade as soon as my hearing was over, called every newsroom involved and the Associated Press in New Orleans, and faxed them accurate information about my case. The stories that resulted were balanced, mentioning the extent of my rehabilitation and my role in exposing the pardons-for-sale scam.

The state police sent two investigators to ask me about the stick-out program. I detected a witch hunt. I asked to talk to Whitmore. The investigators pressed me for specific information. I gave them details about the handmade furniture that bought a pardon for an inmate who had killed with such force that his victim was nearly decapitated. I told them about several criminal enterprises that inmates conducted at the Barracks, including Chandler's. The investigators showed little interest in the information. They wanted details about rogue state police officials. I clammed up. I was not going to ruin careers to satisfy an internal agency vendetta while others went uninvestigated.

"Send Joe Whitmore," I said. "He's the only one I will talk to."

I never heard from the state police again.

Gauthe was another matter. In April 1997, I wrote an eight-page letter to Bill Elder, one of the state's top reporters, detailing the relationship between Gauthe, Politz, and Richard Stalder. Elder launched an intensive investigation. It took eight months. Sources inside and outside the prison were afraid of retaliation.

Elder's series finally went on the air in November 1997 on WWL-TV, New Orleans' flagship television station. Elder detailed the facts surrounding the charges against Gauthe in Texas, a threatening phone call that Judge Politz made to Shreveport's police chief on Gauthe's behalf, and the legal help that Politz secured for Gauthe in the Texas case.

My interview for Elder's series was the last one that Louisiana authorities ever permitted me to do. As soon as it was over, an administrator who was assigned to be present while I talked to Elder went racing to the warden's office.

As he reached the door, Elder turned and paused.

"Are you going to be all right?" he whispered.

"I made my choice," I said. "I'll live with the consequences."

"They may try to kill you," he mouthed as he went through the door. Warden Ward braced Elder as he left the prison.

"You snookered me," Ward said. "You led me to believe that you wanted to interview Billy Sinclair about his rehabilitation."

"You're mistaken, Warden," Elder said. "We never discussed why I wanted to interview Billy."

"Well, that will be his last interview," Ward said.

Shortly after that, I began to receive whispered warnings from guards that I would be retaliated against for my interview. My cell was thoroughly searched. The guards pored over every sheet of paper they found. It was obvious they were looking for specific documents. During a follow-up search, one guard turned to another.

"This is bullshit," he said. "This man doesn't fuck with anybody." He turned and stepped out of the cell. "You can tell the major if he wants this man set up, he can find somebody else to do it."

I told Jodie to retain Baton Rouge attorney Keith Nordyke. He was the state's best prisoners' rights advocate. Nordyke had a history of successfully battling abuse and retaliation in the state's prison system. He moved quickly to put any retaliatory strike in checkmate. Within a few days he visited me at Wade. The visit was an unmistakable signal that any move against me would result in a civil rights lawsuit that would open the door to the Gauthe story and its potential for stinking up the entire Department of Public Safety and Corrections.

"This visit will put them on notice," Nordyke said. "It's our message that any action they take will be met with a swift legal response."

Nordyke beat off the wolf at the door. But a media firestorm erupted when Elder's series began airing. It quickly became common knowledge in the prison system and throughout the state that I was the source for his stories. In 1998, Evan Moore of the *Houston Chronicle* began pursuing the Gauthe story. Moore recounted his telephone conversation with Ward to Jodie when he called to get an interview with me.

"Warden, I'll be flying over to your area on a story and I'd like to talk to one of your inmates," Moore said.

"We're glad to help you any way we can. Who is the inmate?"

"Billy Sinclair."

"Oh, we never let him do interviews."

Jodie and I were still able to supply Moore with valuable information. I passed Jodie the names of guards who might go on record about Gauthe's activities at Wade. Moore's story resulted in a banner headline in the *Houston Chronicle* on Sunday, November 1, 1998. It read: "U.S. Judge's Help for Pedophile Raises Questions." The subhead said: "Priest Was Given Special Treatment at Every Turn." Moore left my name out of the story at Jodie's request. We hunkered down for another battering anyway.

Moore's story revealed a long relationship between Politz and Gauthe, during which the federal judge secured free attorneys for the serial pedophile in three of the former priest's four criminal cases. Sordid details of Gauthe's obsession with sex emerged in the story. One former guard, who gave Moore permission to use his name, told the reporter that he found pornographic cartoons and pubic hair in a plastic bag during a search of the special room that Gauthe was allowed to use for his daily activities at Wade. The next day the guard's superiors ordered him to "stay out of Gauthe's personal effects."

Gauthe had covered the windows of the special room — one of the few air-conditioned spaces in the prison that inmates could use — with his paintings to prevent the guards from watching him and the teenage prisoners that he chose as his "assistants." Guards told Moore that Gauthe had "sexual trysts" with the inmate teens behind the paintings.

In December 1997, Gauthe faced yet another charge — the rape of a twelve-year-old girl in the early 1980s. It landed the serial pedophile in the Lafayette Parish Correctional Center. But the charge did not stick. Gauthe's original plea agreement protected him from prosecution for crimes that occurred before his conviction. As the controversy swirled around Gauthe, the *Dallas Morning News* reported that the FBI had launched an investigation of Judge Politz's involvement in the pedophile's case.

Then a state senator from Lafayette, Louisiana, announced legislative hearings into the case. At the state capitol, Senator Don Cravins openly charged Richard Stalder with providing preferential treatment for Gauthe. But without subpoena power, Cravins hit rough water. Then his tenure as chairman of the Judiciary Committee was cut short, a move that Cravins chalked up to politics. His legislative investigation shut down.

But scandals continued to plague the corrections department. Prison guards in juvenile and adult prisons were indicted and convicted of brutalizing inmates. Several sheriffs were convicted and hauled off to federal prison for corrupt and illegal activity with the state prisoners housed in their jails. In 1998, two of the state's wardens were convicted of crimes of violence. Former Angola warden C. Murray Henderson, who with his wife coauthored a regionally popular book titled *Angola*, shot her multiple times with a .38 caliber pistol. He sat in an alcoholic stupor for five hours before calling for help. Warden Wayne Summers, head of a state juvenile detention center for boys, was convicted of molesting three teenagers. He would bring them to his office, grease their bodies, and force them to have sex with him under threat of disciplinary action. Henderson and Summers ended up in N5.

Meanwhile, scandal continued to bubble up from parole board hearings. In 1998, a hearing panel paroled Tex Chandler. The double murderer was released despite intense victim opposition after serving just twenty-three years. Citing Chandler's "rehabilitation," parole board chairman Fred Clark told the killer that while he was receiving a tremendous break, "you have earned it."

Indeed, by Louisiana standards, he had. For years, Chandler made birdhouses and repaired furniture for officials, including members of the pardon and parole boards. Chandler used state lumber and supplies he got for free for his handiwork and charged officials nominal fees.

When the press got wind of Chandler's hobbycraft enterprise, members of the parole board expressed dismay and denied any connection between their votes for Chandler's release and his wares. Parole board vice chair Peggy Landry, who paid Chandler three hundred dollars for several birdhouses, told the press: "If I thought it was illegal or dishonest to buy them, I would never have done it." She admitted it "doesn't look good."

Another parole board member who hired Chandler to restore an antique armoire told reporters that her decision to vote for the killer was based on the belief that he was "rehabilitated." She said Chandler only had seven disciplinary reports in twenty-three years behind bars.

But Sandy Krasnoff, the head of Citizens and Victims Against Crime, Louisiana's largest victim watchdog group, didn't buy the arguments. Krasnoff charged that Chandler enhanced his chances for parole through personal relationships that he developed out of his hobbycraft enterprise. The Foster administration quickly announced a ban on the purchase of inmate hobbycraft by members of the pardon and parole boards to "remove any appearance of impropriety." Throughout the media firestorm, the state police remained strangely silent. I had given them ample evidence of Chandler's illegal use of state property, but they did nothing. Yet they had sanctioned my transfer from the Barracks for "hugging and kissing" my wife.

The injustice didn't sit well with Sandy Krasnoff. In an unprecedented move for a crime victims' advocate, he wrote Richard Stalder requesting my return to the Barracks.

> Enclosed please find a copy of a letter to Captain Kennedy. I am familiar with the complete history of this case, including why Billy Sinclair was moved from the State Police Barracks some years ago. I am very familiar with all parties on both sides of the matter in this case, in regards to victims and victims' survivors and advocates for Billy Sinclair. Please advise me as to why Billy Sinclair is not being strongly considered for transfer to the State Police Barracks.

His letter was rebuffed. Then, in January 1999, Jodie convinced the parole board that it had used false and inaccurate information to consider my case. It set a new hearing date for March 8,

1999. At each previous hearing, the parole board called me a third or fourth offender. My state police rap sheet — by law the controlling document — showed that I was a second offender.

Warily, we invested some hope in the March hearing. But it was a stunning payback for suing the parole board and exposing too much about the system. This time we would not get a single vote for parole. My thirty-three years behind bars and twenty-two years without a disciplinary write-up meant nothing to the parole board. It was a wasted exercise until my victim's brother turned to address me. I had written letters of remorse but they brought no reply. The board's vice chair, Peggy Landry, moved to stop him.

"Mr. Bodden, do not speak directly to the prisoner, you must address me," she said.

"No," I begged her. "Please let him talk to me."

I had waited years for personal contact with my victim's relatives. His brother's simple account of J. C.'s last evening hit me like a sledgehammer. He showed me J. C.'s Istrouma High School class ring. He wore it everyday to remind him of J. C. He was not at my hearing to exact revenge. He had come to tell me — no, show me — the pain I had caused him for thirty-three years.

"Mr. Sinclair," he said quietly, "do you know what happened the last night of J. C.'s life? We had a family dinner. He sat down beside me to eat. 'I'll be back,' he said when he got up. He went to the store that night because they didn't have enough help. I never saw him again."

I forced myself to look directly into the eyes of J. C.'s brother. "I'm sorry," I said.

I turned back to face the board, head bowed low. For me, the parole hearing was over. A member of the Istrouma high school football team went on to denounce me loudly. Another flashed a thumbs-up sign and smiled when I was denied.

Peggy Landry addressed me at the end of the hearing: "Mr. Sinclair, you can have another hearing in two years, *if* you can get anyone to give you one."

That summer, in spite of my record of good conduct, two guards put me in a stun belt "on the warden's orders" to go to a court hearing in Baton Rouge. A stun belt delivers fifty thousand volts of electricity. The shock lasts eight seconds. It causes pain that keeps increasing. The belt continues to deliver shocks until it is turned off.

The voltage enters the body through the kidneys. Prisoners fall to the ground, and they frequently defecate and urinate on themselves. The belt's leading U.S. manufacturer does not recommend its use on those with heart conditions: "Fear of activation can elevate blood pressure as much as a shock will." Stun belts have caused fatalities.

Amnesty International calls stun belts instruments of torture. "A stun belt is a weapon worn by its victim," as Amnesty International puts it. The organization has called for a worldwide ban. But prison authorities claim stun belts and other electro-shock devices are a necessity for dangerous prisoners.

When the trip officers came to my cell at five in the morning to make the seven-hour drive to Baton Rouge, I showed them the judge's letter saying my presence was not required in court. They insisted on following their orders.

After they locked me into the belt, they handcuffed me and put me in leg irons. Then they locked a black box over my handcuffs. I could barely step up into the van. Once inside, I could not brace myself on sharp turns in the road. The van had a sudden blowout near Bunkie, Louisiana, a small town several hours from Wade, and nearly sideswiped another van at seventy miles an hour. The guards had no money to fix the flat. When they radioed the prison, they were told no one could be sent to help. We sat in the stifling July heat on the side of the road for several hours. Finally, a local mechanic agreed to fix the tire. By then, the officers had called the Baton Rouge court to announce that I would be late, only to find that I had no court date. I wore the stun belt, the cuffs, the black box, and leg irons for ten hours.

A week before the stun belt was used on me, a spokeswoman for the Louisiana Department of Public Safety and Corrections told the Associated Press in New Orleans that while the stun belt was on the DOC's "approved weapons list," "none of our institutions use it." I have no more explanation for having to wear the stun belt than I do for my last parole board vote.

In December 1999, despite Henry Politz's conflict of interest in my case, he and two other judges on the Fifth Circuit Court of

Appeals denied my lawsuit seeking parole. The panel ignored the U.S. Supreme Court decision on which Richard Hand based my plea. *Allen v. The Montana Board of Pardons* holds that states with parole laws ordering them to release rehabilitated inmates must abide by those laws. Louisiana's law is identical to Montana's. In January, another Fifth Circuit panel upheld Politz's decision.

I have little hope of release before my discharge date in 2011. Parole for me is apparently out of the question.

I was twenty years old when I went to prison. When I discharge, I will be sixty-five. Regrets? I have many. Hard choices? I made plenty. Remorse is not enough. And neither is apology. But I am the author of my own distress. I put myself at the mercy of a violent, corrupt prison system when I took the life of an innocent human being.

How then, should I proceed?

The question reminds me of a childhood photograph. I am sitting in a chair, grinning at the camera. No matter how much my father beat me, my smile always came back.

No matter what the Louisiana prison system does to me, I will continue my fight to be with my wife; I will continue my struggle for personal redemption; and I will continue to speak out against wrongdoing and inequity in the system.

God willing, someday I will make it over the mountain.